THEOLOGY AND LIBERATION SERIES

José Comblin

THE HOLY SPIRIT
and
LIBERATION

Translated from the Portuguese by
Paul Burns

ORBIS BOOKS

Maryknoll, New York 10545

The Catholic Foreign Mission Society of America (Maryknoll) recruits and trains people for overseas missionary service. Through Orbis Books, Maryknoll aims to foster the international dialogue that is essential to mission. The books published, however, reflect the opinions of their authors and are not meant to represent the official position of the society.

First published in this translation in Great Britain in 1989 by Burns & Oates, Wellwood, North Farm Rd., Tunbridge Wells, Kent TN2 3DR, and in the United States of America by Orbis Books, Maryknoll, NY 10545

Published originally in Brazil by Editora Vozes, Petrópolis, RJ, Brazil, under the title *O Espírito Santo e a Libertação*

Original edition © CESEP—São Paulo 1987

English translation © Burns & Oates/Search Press 1989

ORBIS/ISBN 0-88344-368-6
         0-88344-367-8 (pbk.)

Theology and Liberation Series

In the years since its emergence in Latin America, liberation theology has challenged the church to a renewal of faith lived in solidarity with the poor and oppressed. The effects of this theology have spread throughout the world, inspiring in many Christians a deeper life of faith and commitment, but for others arousing fears and concerns.

Its proponents have insisted that liberation theology is not a subtopic of theology but really a new way of doing theology. The Theology and Liberation Series is an effort to test that claim by addressing the full spectrum of Christian faith from the perspective of the poor.

Thus, volumes in the Series are devoted to such topics as God, Christ, the church, revelation, Mary, the sacraments, and so forth. But the Series will also explore topics seldom addressed by traditional theology, though vital to Christian life—aspects of politics, culture, the role of women, the status of ethnic minorities. All these are examined in the light of faith lived in a context of oppression and liberation.

The work of over one hundred theologians, pastoral agents, and social scientists from Latin America, and supported by some one hundred and forty bishops, the Theology and Liberation Series is the most ambitious and creative theological project in the history of the Americas.

Addressed to the universal church, these volumes will be essential reading for all those interested in the challenge of faith in the modern world. They will be especially welcomed by all who are committed to the cause of the poor, by those engaged in the struggle for a new society, by all those seeking to establish a more solid link between faith and politics, prayer and action.

Contents

Abbreviations and Short Forms

AA   *Apostolicam Actuositatem*. Vatican II, Decree on the Apostolate of the Laity. Translations of this and other Vatican II documents in the present work are from Walter Abbott, ed., *The Documents of Vatican II*. Piscataway, N.J., America Press & London-Dublin, Geoffrey Chapman, 1966.

CLAR   Latin American Conference of Religious.

CNBB   National Conference of Brazilian Bishops.

DH   *Dignitatis Humanae*. Vatican II, Declaration on Religious Freedom.

DV   *Dei Verbum*. Vatican II, Dogmatic Constitution on Divine Revelation.

GS   *Gaudium et Spes*. Vatican II, Pastoral Constitution on the Church in the Modern World.

LG   *Lumen Gentium*. Vatican II, Dogmatic Constitution on the Church.

LThK   *Lexicon für Theologie und Kirche*. Second Series, ed. Josef Höfer & J Karl Rahner. Freiburg–Basel–Vienna, Herder, 1958–65.

Medellín   Second General Conference of Latin American Bishops, held in Medellín, Colombia, in 1968. Translations of the final documents (including the sections on "Peace" and "Justice") are in vol. 2 of *The Church in the Present-day Transformation of Latin America*. Washington, D.C.: USCC, 1970.

Nouv. Rev. Th. *Nouvelle Revue Théologique*. Paris.

Puebla	Third General Conference of Latin American Bishops, held in Puebla, Mexico, in 1979. A translation of "The Final Document" can be found in John Eagleson and Philip Scharper, eds., *Puebla and Beyond*. Maryknoll, N.Y.: Orbis, 1979.
PG	*Patrologiae Cursus Completus, Series Graeca*, J. P. Migne, ed., Paris 1, 1857–167, 1866.
PO	*Presbyterorum Ordinis*. Vatican II, Decree on the Ministry and Life of Priests.
SCh	*Sources chrétiennes*. Paris 1, 1941ff.
ST	St Thomas Aquinas, *Summa Theologiae*.
UR	*Unitatis Redintegratio*. Vatican II, Decree on Ecumenism.

Introduction

The experience of God found in the new Christian communities of Latin America can properly be called experience of the Holy Spirit. The aim of this book is to show how this is. Most of the Christians who make up these communities do not know that this is their experience; because of their religious upbringing, the Holy Spirit is still the great unknown for them. The fact is that, virtually from its beginnings, Western theology lost interest in the Holy Spirit, and the traditional liturgy of the West, particularly that of the Roman Missal, also left the Spirit out of account. The lack of interest shown by Christians reflects the lack of interest shown by theology. But now, the new experience Christians are finding in those communities that aspire to the integral liberation of the peoples of the continent of Latin America is precisely an experience of the Holy Spirit.

Once again we are discovering that the way we approach God, according to the Bible and true Christian tradition, is not through discursive reason, or our experience of creation, or through meditating on our inner being, but through a living experience of the Holy Spirit and its gifts. Only a spiritual experience, one of the Holy Spirit active in the community, can lead to the true God—the God of Jesus Christ, not a God of philosophers.

We are also rediscovering that we approach Jesus through experience of the Spirit. Those who read the Gospels from living experience of the Spirit find them speaking really of the true Jesus Christ. Those who read them with their understanding alone, or on the basis of their literary and historical knowledge, cannot approach the real Christ who is alive today. The most they can do is project a Jesus who appeals to them back on to the past. To know God the Father and his Son Jesus Christ who revealed him, we have to start from a spiritual experience, which means an experience provided and guided by the Holy Spirit, a specific and practical experience.

This is because, as Jesus says in the fourth Gospel, "God is spirit" (John 4:24). Jesus is not saying merely that God has no body; this would be too trivial, and besides, spirit does not mean non-corporeal. What Jesus means is that the Father can be found only through a spiritual experience; and we have to understand this in the strongest sense: an experience in the Holy Spirit. Jesus is not trying to give a definition of God; God cannot be defined. He is showing us the place where God can be met.

St Paul, too, says: "This Lord is the Spirit" (2 Cor. 3:17). He does not mean that Jesus and the Holy Spirit are the same person, but that the place where we meet the Lord is the Holy Spirit. Only the Spirit can lead us to Jesus the Christ. Without passing through the experience of the Spirit, in this case the experience of freedom, we cannot possibly know the true Christ.

The Holy Spirit is the great novelty of the post-conciliar period. It is a strange fact that all that is new in this period relates directly to renewal of consciousness of the Spirit in the church. Vatican II opened the gates. By using trinitarian language of God, it broke with a long tradition in the Latin Church, and with the language of Vatican I; whereas Vatican I spoke of "God," Vatican II says "the Father, the Son and the Holy Spirit." The Council did not work out a real doctrine of the Holy Spirit, but by constantly invoking the Spirit, steered Christian understanding toward a renewal of faith in the Spirit. This simple change in expression brought about profound consequences for the faith of the Christian people.

The charismatic renewal movement would not have been possible without Vatican II, and it clearly had—and is still having—repercussions throughout the church. In particular, it has brought about the appearance of a new theological movement: before, there was no pneumatology in the Catholic Church; now it is developing rapidly. The same happening in the Protestant churches, where Pentecostalism arose early in this century. For some time, it did not have much influence on the mainstream churches, which remained rooted in their own traditions, but recently the vitality and missionary zeal of the Pentecostal communities have made their influence widely felt. Implicitly or explicitly, the dynamism of the Pentecostal movement has stimulated and provoked all the churches of the West; they have all been forced to go back to their own traditions of the Holy Spirit and breathe new life into them.

In Latin America the charismatic renewal movement has also developed within the Catholic Church, though without affecting more than a rather narrow sector of society, falling victim to the enormous gulf that separates different social classes there, which means that a movement born in one social class is so marked by it that it cannot make the transition to others. Also, till very recently, Protestant Pentecostalism was looked at askance, looked down on by all levels of society. Only in the last few years has it attracted sympathetic attention from Catholics and Protestants from the "higher" denominations.

Renewal of faith in the Holy Spirit may well provide the best meeting ground for ecumenism. Where the Holy Spirit is concerned, all the Western churches have much to learn from the Eastern churches, which have kept a very deep understanding of the role of the Spirit, in their liturgy and their theology, and in the faith of their people. Catholics and Protestants alike can here learn from the Eastern masters; both also have much to learn from the popular Pentecostal communities, which are much poorer, simpler and more spontaneous than the main historical denominations.

In Latin America, experience of the Holy Spirit often comes about without being named as such. Well, it is one of theology's tasks to give names to realities. Hence this book, whose aim is to bring together actual experiences and the theology of the Holy Spirit.

What is evident is that experience of the Spirit comes about principally in poor communities. There is nothing surprising in the fact that experience of the Spirit regains its value and esteem in the churches precisely when they come to rediscover the meaning of the preferential option for the poor. The return of the churches to the poor goes along with renewal of understanding of the Holy Spirit. Traditional theology held that the spiritual phenomena of the early times had disappeared because they were no longer needed: The strength of the church made them unnecessary for confirming the faith of the people. Was it not rather the opposite; that the (human) strength of the churches closed the doors on the Spirit and its gifts? And is it not to be expected that the church should recover the gifts of the Spirit now that it is ceasing to trust in its economic, political and cultural strength and is becoming once again a poor church of poor people?

Chapter 1 will be devoted to experiences of the Holy Spirit, presenting what is now happening in the light of the Bible and the early church. The following chapters develop the teaching implicit in the experiences described in the first chapter.

The Holy Spirit comes to the church in order to carry out its mission in the world, which is considered in Chapter 2. Theology, on this point, has not devoted much attention to the content of the New Testament. Chapter 3 deals with the Spirit in the church, a field in which theology feels more at home. But this chapter does not set out to provide an ecclesiology, just to suggest some themes to ecclesiology. Chapter 4 deals with the "spiritual life" in a more classic sense: the role played by the Holy Spirit in each individual's ascent toward God in the midst of life in this world.

Chapter 5 situates the Holy Spirit in relation to Jesus Christ. The Eastern churches accuse the Western churches of "christomonism," claiming that they have evolved a theological construct in which Christ has no need of the Spirit, with the progression God-Christ-church. It is true that the great christological treatises place small value on the Holy Spirit; scholastic ones felt no need of the Spirit, and modern ones start from the story of Jesus and also ignore the Spirit. Yet the missions of the second and third Persons of the Trinity need to be shown to complement each other. Finally, Chapter 6 studies the Holy Spirit within the Trinity, trying to steer clear of the great debates with the Eastern churches, while recognizing the important issues at stake in these. The Filioque question is not a matter of theological niceties, but has repercussions on the level of life and faith for ordinary Christians.

I cannot claim to be presenting a complete doctrinal manual on the Holy Spirit in some two hundred pages; rather this book is a series of sketches of the issues that have surfaced in recent years, particularly those that throw most light on the experience of the new Christian communities in Latin America. There has been no space to give chapter and verse in support of my main thesis; besides the bibliography given at the end, I have consulted innumerable works ancient and modern. Interpreting biblical texts relating to the Holy Spirit is a matter of endless research and debate; I have tried to take a sufficiently broad line to avoid controversies that do not affect basic teaching.

This book is based on experiences with Christian communities in different parts of Latin America. These experiences are naturally limited; others would reveal other aspects. I can only hope I have not been unfaithful to what the Spirit is telling the churches today.

I had finished writing this book when Pope John Paul II issued his encyclical *Dominum et Vivificantem* (18 May 1986), and have not been able to incorporate the contributions made by this important document. But with regard to the basic theological arguments of this book, the encyclical does not make any major points that would oblige me to change my view on any issue; it deliberately stops short of theological developments.

Its first part is in fact almost exclusively exegetical; it is a succinct but very well organized presentation of the main biblical texts dealing with the Holy Spirit, especially those from St John. The second part alone is theological, in that it develops a theology of sin based on John 16:8: "And when he [the Paraclete] comes, he will show the world how wrong it was, about sin...." In a way the encyclical could be said to be more about sin than about the Holy Spirit, since this is the subject on which it makes new points and observations. Its third part is a sort of preparation for the Great Jubilee planned for the year 2000.

In both the second and third parts, the Pope repeatedly denounces atheism, particularly in its ideological manifestations such as Marxism. There is a lot of attack on atheism, but not much about "beyond atheism." What is clear is that the church in its present state has not gone beyond atheism; it is rather what has justified and perhaps even brought atheism about. Beyond atheism we can only work for a new era of Christianity and a new face for the church. Otherwise, denouncing materialist atheism will be no more effective than the denunciations of naturalism and liberalism in the last century. The ideas and proposals in this book are put forward in the light of this future beyond atheism; its text must therefore be seen as provisional and always open to improvement in the new age that is to come.

THE HOLY SPIRIT
and
LIBERATION

Chapter I
Experience of the Holy Spirit

Section 1 sets out present-day experience of the Holy Spirit, which has become a major factor in the life of the Christian churches, to an extent totally unforeseeable even twenty-five years ago. No one then would have predicted that the end of the twentieth century would see the Holy Spirit once again in the forefront of Christian concern. Nor could anyone have foreseen that experience of the Spirit would have become the basis for a renewed theology.

Section 2 seeks to show the main aspect of this experience of the Spirit in Latin America and tries to understand that experience in the light of the New Testament. Finally, Section 3 is an attempt to explain what is meant by experience in this context, so as to avoid controversies over interpretation. This experience needs to be situated within the history of Christian theology so as to show that it is not something that falls outside the main body of true tradition, even though it may at first sight appear to do so.

1. THE PLACE OF EXPERIENCE OF THE SPIRIT IN CHRISTIANITY

Christianity itself rests on experience of the Holy Spirit; the New Testament is quite definite on this point. But sufficient attention has often not been paid to what is the clear witness of the Apostles; their witness to the Holy Spirit often fell on badly prepared ground. Of course it was accepted: who would doubt the word of the Apostles? But it was not given the importance accorded to other aspects of their message. Today, however, new experiences of the Spirit are forcing us to look at the old texts with new eyes.

Where do these new eyes come from? For Catholics, from Vatican II and the whole context in which the Council took place. Protestants can see a similar evolution in the World Council of Churches, sometimes moving ahead of the Catholic viewpoints. Reformulation of objectives and methodology has in fact been forced on the theology of all the churches by their experience of the Spirit. At the same time, theologians have become more attentive to the way the faith is lived in Christian communities and less dedicated to purely academic work.

(a) The Place of Experience of the Spirit according to the New Testament

At the origins of Christianity stand two events of equal importance. Christian doctrine teaches that these two events are intimately bound up one with the other, and one cannot be considered more important than the other. The first event is Jesus from his birth to his death and resurrection. The second event is the experience of the Spirit in the early communities.

The "Jesus event" on its own cannot explain the church and Christianity. The life, death and resurrection of Jesus would have had no effect on the history of this world on their own. Without the event of experience of the Spirit, Jesus would have left nothing. It is equally true that experience of the Spirit alone would not have brought Christianity into being; it cannot be separated from the Jesus event. On the contrary: its purpose is to make Jesus enter into human history and produce the fruits of his incarnation.

Western theology, however, has played down the "Pentecost" event and sought to make everything derive from the "Easter" event. A theology mutilated in this way cannot be effective on the plane of action; without experience of the Spirit, Jesus could never have moved men and women of his day as he did, not even those who heard him and followed him. If this was true then, we can take it as being true for all times; the fact of experience of the Spirit has to have existed from the beginning. But theology has not recognized its importance, nor has it been given its due weight in everyday Christian living. Throughout the era of Christendom, the church possessed

powerful human means and arguments for ensuring the
handing-on of the faith; now, however, invoking a christology
is not enough. What can lead our contemporaries to Christ,
except strong, convincing experience? Not words about Christ,
only lived and felt realities, what we call experience of the
Spirit.

(i) Experience of the Spirit according to St Paul. The Pauline
communities underwent real and powerful experiences of the
Spirit. They were founded on such experiences. Christ had a
very definite aspect for them; he was the presence to which
their spiritual experiences referred.

This is why, when Paul sought to base his teaching on firm
ground, to make it convincing and intelligible to his audience,
he appealed to their experience of the Spirit. The Pauline
communities were not built on speeches, words, theoretical
teachings. They started with specific, evident, irrefutable facts.
The communities had experience of the Holy Spirit, and still
have it; this is why they never doubted but remained admirably
faithful. Those who have seen cannot cease believing.

So Paul asks the Galatians: "Was it because you practised the
Law that you received the Spirit?" This is not a reference to an
invisible Spirit, but to a definite experience which they had and
still have. "Are you foolish enough to end in outward
observances what you began in the Spirit?"—again referring to
specific events in the lives of the Galatians. "Does God give
you the Spirit so freely and work miracles among you because
you practise the Law, or because you believed what was
preached to you?" (3:5)—here the Spirit is as visible and
perceptible as the miracles. "Christ redeemed us... so that
through faith we might receive the promised Spirit" (3:13–14)—
the text gets its full meaning only if a very definite gift is
understood. And further on: "The proof that you are sons is
that God has sent the Spirit of his Son into our hearts: the Spirit
that cries 'Abba, Father'" (4:6)—the point is that it is the
presence of the Spirit that cries out, and the Spirit is present
because "you are sons."

In his Letter to the Romans, Paul returns to the theme of
Galatians 4:6, developing its different aspects. "The spirit you

received is not the spirit of slaves . . . It is the spirit of sons and it makes us cry out, 'Abba, Father!' " (8:15). The apostle is not referring to an invisible reality, but to something the Romans had experienced. "Never try to suppress the Spirit" (1 Thess. 5:15) speaks of a reality the Thessalonians could readily perceive and which formed the basis of their faith.

The case of Corinth is absolutely clear; the experience of the Spirit there was so strong that it sometimes came to overlay the tradition that came from Jesus, and Paul found it necessary to reaffirm the link between the Jesus event and the Spirit event.[1] The faith of the Corinthians did not consist only of keeping the memory of a past they had not experienced, but also of their present experience. This experience of the Spirit is not to be confused—as it was by some of those in Corinth—with certain ecstatic phenomena such as the gift of tongues. Still less is it pure emotion or religious sentiment. On the contrary: Paul insists on the secondary, marginal, accessory nature of emotional or sentimental phenomena, as of extraordinary gifts, such as that of tongues. The experience to which Paul's letters refer is tied to a historical undertaking. Far from distancing Christians from actual reality, it plunges them deep into it. It is an experience worked out in action, by which Christians and the whole community build up the church, and, through the church, a new world. The Spirit is known in the concrete activity of building a new world.[2]

This experience does not exclude, but definitely includes the life of suffering and persecutions undergone by the early communities. It is joy in the midst of these tribulations. "Joy" is the word that characterizes the felt presence of the Spirit. Joy is the effect of experience of the Spirit on the senses or emotions.[3]

Whoever its author may have been, the Letter to the Hebrews continues the Pauline approach. Neither its author nor Paul refers to the Spirit as an invisible reality that can be recognized only in faith; they both refer to its presence as a definite starting-point and source of support, since their readers know from experience what it is. On one hand, salvation was "first announced by the Lord himself" (2:3); it is then "guaranteed to us by all who heard him" (2:3). On the other, together with this announcement, God "confirmed their witness with signs and marvels and miracles of all kinds, and by freely giving the gifts of the Holy Spirit" (2:4). These last are as visible and perceptible as the signs and miracles: "As for those people who were once brought into the light, and tasted the gift from heaven, and received a share of the Holy Spirit, and appreciated the good message of God and the powers of the world to come..." (6:4).

(ii) Experience of the Spirit according to St Luke. Luke tried to produce a synthesis between the two great traditions of early Christianity: that of the disciples who collected memories of the Master, and that of the Pauline communities. He understood that the liberation brought by God was worked in two different stages, each marked by the coming of the Holy Spirit: first on Mary to bring about the incarnation and prepare for the birth of Jesus; then on the community of the disciples in Jerusalem to prepare for the birth of the church. Luke brings these two manifestations together through the promises made by Jesus. Jesus promised to send the Spirit after his death and resurrection. But Luke maintains the primacy of the Pauline tradition; the church did not come into being simply through the continuity of the disciples who had known Jesus. The church was not simply a creation springing from their memory of Jesus. This memory was not sufficient. A second coming of the Spirit was needed.

Now this second coming of the Spirit, the one that founded the church and laid the basis for the liberation of the world, was a phenomenon that completely overwhelmed those who experienced it, something so powerful that they could never forget it. Luke describes it as best he can, using his memories of the prophets and other literary reminiscences. But the literary description of the event matters little; what matters is that the experience of Pentecost was so graven on the memories of the communities as to become their unshakeable support in times of trial. And the history of the church shows other similar phenomena, times of fervour and intensity in which the presence of the Spirit could be felt, moments such as those of great religious foundations or great reforms.[4]

The experience of Pentecost was renewed several times: at the time of the first great persecution (Acts 4:23–31), at the institution of the church in Samaria (8:14–17), at the time of the great opening-out of the church to the pagans (10:44–7), at the outset of Paul's mission (13:2). Far from directing understanding inwards on themselves, the experience of the Spirit launches men and women out into the world as though imbued with superhuman energy to tackle superhuman tasks.[5]

The synoptic tradition itself supposes an extraordinary event such as occured at Pentecost, since it lays special stress on the weakness and incredulity of the Apostles, even after the risen Jesus had appeared to them.[6] Therefore, something had to happen to transform those same disciples into intrepid heroes who would face up to all the powers of the world, to the point of accepting martyrdom. The synoptics do not speak much of the Spirit, and some mentions of it may be late additions, but the synoptic tradition postulates an extraordinary coming of the Spirit to effect a radical transformation in the behaviour of the disciples. Luke makes explicit what the disciples knew.

(iii) Experience of the Spirit according to St John. John's writings relate to a community living an essentially spiritual experience, completely freed from Judaism and the Law and living by the Spirit. This way of living is not so much a matter of exceptional experiences, such as described in Acts, or great upheavals, as in Corinth, but of a constant, continuous experience, one prolonged throughout the whole of life. It has often been called mystical experience, and the name fits it well enough, provided we discount the individual, emotive, extraordinary connotations of the word. It is a calm and lasting mysticism. "We know that he lives in us by the Spirit that he has given us" (1 John 3:24); "we can know that we are living in him and he is living in us because he lets us share his Spirit" (4:13). The Spirit is what is clear to the community, the proof that Jesus is staying with it. The Spirit is something that can be perceived; all can see that it is living amongst them.

This experience of the Spirit gives John's community the certainty of having entered on a new life, of having been born again (John 3:5, 6, 8), of being a community that has passed through baptism in the Spirit (1:33). It adores God in the Spirit and in truth (4:23, 24). The community lives by the outpouring of the Spirit promised by Jesus (7:39). According to John too, the church is born of the Spirit, despite the fact that the fourth Gospel makes no allusion to Pentecost. The risen Jesus himself pours out his Spirit, and that is how the church is formed (20:22; perhaps 19:34).

The spiritual experience of the community was so strong that it risked neglecting two fundamental aspects of Christianity: reference to the memory of Jesus of Nazareth and the primacy of practice over contemplation and experience. Hence the reaction found in John's writings. His first Letter insists on confession of Jesus the man: "every spirit which acknowledges that Jesus the Christ has come in the flesh is from God" (4:2; cf 4:1, 3, 6). In the fourth Gospel Jesus insists on the close link between his teaching and his life, on one hand, and everything the Spirit teaches, on the other (14:17, 26; 15:26; 16:13). He does not reject experience of the Spirit, far from it, but makes a point of marking the limits of this experience. Besides this, both the Letter and the Gospel emphasize the primacy of *agapē,* of real and practical love for one's neighbour, which lies at the heart of community as actual, historical institution. The Spirit does not set us apart from the world and its demands. Anything that does is the sign of the presence of a false spirit (1 John 4:11–15; John 13:34–5; 15:12).

The importance of the "experience" aspect of the Spirit would go unremarked if today we were not presented with evidence of similar experiences. When the church was convinced that such phenomena had disappeared, it did not look at these texts in the same way. It has been the lived experience of the new communities that has brought us to re-read these well-known texts, so often repeated down the centuries without revealing the significance we now find in them.

(b) The Re-appearance of Experience of the Spirit Today

Today we are witnessing the upsurge of many and various forms of experience of the Holy Spirit throughout the entire world. They are linked to a deep change in the way Christian people read the Bible, in the way lay people pray, in the vitality of Christian communities. To appreciate the importance and scope of these changes, we can look at what Vatican II said about the changes taking place in our times. Many of these statements by Vatican II show that the way of experience of the Spirit is the only valid response to the challenges of the atheism that sprang from the modern world. What is certain is that this modern world has destroyed the historical expressions of Western Christianity root and branch, and these expressions are beyond hope of restoration.

(i) Renewal of experience of the Spirit. One of the major religious movements of recent years has been the charismatic renewal movement. There is no need to describe it here, since there is a vast literature on the subject.[7] It arose in 1966 and, in its Catholic form at least, was clearly one of the fruits of Vatican II. It has produced a number of debates, as was to be expected. This is not the place to analyze them, merely to point out that the movement is one of the typical signs of the times. New movements are springing up all the time, showing some signs of true experience of the Spirit.

They also, however, appear to be threatened by the dangers that Paul found in Corinth and in other churches. Objections made to them are that they encourage flight from temporal tasks, are seduced by strongly emotional phenomena and devote little attention to social problems. The best representatives of such movements try to keep their communities out of such dangers. They claim that these movements, and the experience of the Spirit they bring, far from leading people away from activity, make them more dynamic and more involved in active love for their neighbour.[8] And of course it is this concern that, according to the Bible, has to be taken as the sign of authenticity.

The Pentecostal churches that flourish on a popular level have been much denigrated, and still are—a reaction that is clearly motivated by their class, rather than religious, character. Yet there are elements of great spiritual value in the Pentecostal experiences of some of these popular churches.[9] They have also been accused of being alienated, removed from the world, conservative, but a more sympathetic examination would show these accusations to be exaggerated and even baseless. What has happened, at least in Latin America, is that they display all the signs of a culture of the poor, and are being rashly judged by people from the Western, modern culture of the ruling classes.[10]

Experience of the Spirit is not something much talked about in the base communities. Yet they all speak of a new experience of God, and what is this if not an experience of the Spirit?[11] Their experiences, like those of other popular movements, have drawn less attention from theologians than those of more culturally developed classes. Yet we can assume that the quality of experience among the poor must be at least equal to that of the rest of us, and—why not?—perhaps better.

So what is the significance of new experiences of the Holy Spirit today? In a way they are a jump backwards over many centuries, back to the early church. Some would see them as a sign that we are entering on a new phase in the history of the church, a process of change as radical and major as any of those that have taken place over the past twenty centuries. Is it feasible to see what is happening today as so important, capable of ushering in such radical change? Let us see what the Council had to say.

(ii) New times according to Vatican II. For the first time in the history of the ecclesiastical magisterium, Vatican II recognized the historicity of the human condition when it pointed to the value and scale of the transformations taking place in humanity at the present time. These, it said, have so changed the conditions in which humanity lives that it is proper to speak of a new era in human history. *Gaudium et Spes* (GS), the Pastoral Constitution on the Church in the Modern World, summarizes the main categories of change in its numbers 5–7.[12] The phenomena it enumerates there confirm that the overall change is on a scale hardly seen since the origin of the human race.

In one of its best-known statements, the Council summed up the process: "The human race has passed from a rather static concept of reality to a more dynamic, evolutionary one" (GS 5). What most concerns us here is that "these new conditions have their impact on religion," which "exacts day by day a more personal and explicit adherence to faith. As a result many persons are achieving a more vivid sense of God" (GS 7). These sections of *Gaudium et Specs* are undoubtedly among the most important texts the Council produced, and point to a religion of experience rather than of static formulas.

There has never, since the origins of Christianity, been such a radical change in the world as the one that is now taking place. For the church, this transformation is more radical than the transition from Israel to the Gentiles, more important than the establishment of the institutional church under Constantine or the Protestant Reformation: the present transformation forces it to a more radical reappraisal of itself and challenges many more aspects of it than have been challenged hitherto.

Only the Spirit can produce the new expressions of the Christian faith needed today. We need criteria for discerning that Spirit, and Vatican II gave us some pointers. We need, for example, to see what in the present-day church owes its existence to an agrarian-based economy; what is static and based on philosophies belonging to a static world—Greek philosophies, for example. Because none of this will survive. Atheism is not a product of bad faith or unbelief; it stems from a radical crisis of all the mental constructs that arose in the Neolithic age, including that of an almighty and unchanging God, creator of the world. Present-day atheists will never return to a church clinging to age-old expressions originating in the context of Neolithic agrarian civilization.

Many church people see this situation as forcing the church to return to its origins, to the time of experience of the Spirit. Equally, only a deep-felt, real experience of actual events will be able to draw our contemporaries, let alone their descendants, back to Christ. Neither the creator God nor the Christ of history will convince them. More than ever we need, with St Paul, to show Christ according to the Spirit, since Christ according to the flesh will neither convince nor appeal.[13]

(iii) Some signs of the times. There is no lack of clear signs pointing to experience of the Spirit. The first of these is the new way the people are reading the Bible.[14] From earliest times,

Christians have practised a "spiritual" exegesis. This was codified by Origen, who channelled it into restrictive patterns. Patristic and medieval exegesis followed the paths marked out by Origen and the Alexandrian school. This spiritual exegesis looked to the Bible for patterns for contemporary Christian living. It laid down the basic rule of all Christian exegesis: the Bible was written for Christians of all times. It is not a matter of reconstructing a teaching for the past, as philologists and historians do. Philologists will never discover the true meaning of the Bible, since they think in terms of the past and not of the present. Well, the Bible speaks today to the men and women of today. Through the Bible, Christ speaks to us today. And the Spirit explains what Jesus means to the people of today.

But Origen saw men and women of his day in terms of their individual spiritual journey,[15] and later exegesis has followed this path. The dialogue of classical philosophy was between individuals, taking no account of history. So classical spiritual exegesis equally discounted history and found no message for humanity as a historical reality.

In modern times, spiritual exegesis entered on a period of decadence. The Bible was replaced first by scholastic theology and then by the magiserium backed up by scholasticism. Melchor Cano laid the ground rules for this theology in the sixteenth century: the only function of the Bible was to provide arguments and justifications for the teaching of scholasticism and the magisterium. St Thomas became, effectively, more important than the Bible.

Nowadays, in many parts of the world, but especially in Latin America, the Christian people are reading the Bible once more in a spirit of spiritual exegesis. But this time the spiritual reading is historical. In reading the Bible they find the guidance of the Spirit and words of Christ addressed to contemporary men and women engaged in liberation struggles.[16] For the people, reading the Bible has become an experience of the Spirit; their reading is often a real process of enlightenment, of discovery of the truth, of seeing the light at the end of the tunnel. The Bible is read in an atmosphere of enthusiasm and joy; it sheds the light of truth on the contemporary world, clarifies the present situation, shows people how they need to act.

Prayer is another sign. For centuries the Christian people were taught to pray through traditional formulations. Praying was reciting prayers, the same old prayers. We shall never know how many came to a freer form of prayer than these formulations, how many practised spontaneous prayer in their work in the fields, while cooking or washing. In any case, the ecclesiastical institution did not encourage this type of prayer, still less when dealing with public prayer in church. There it was the priest alone who led the prayers and he usually just followed the prayer books word for word. Praying meant reciting prayers. Only a few mystics rose above these rules. Free prayer was not encouraged even in religious institutes; even mental prayer was subject to a rigid method, in which mental activity had to be governed by an implacable discipline.

Now, throughout the world, but especially where the base communities flourish, a prayer of joy and freedom is rising up. The Christian people, who seemed dumb and incapable of religious expression, have learned to speak; or rather, the channels that allow them to speak have been opened, and they have shown that they know how to speak to the Father in Christ. Prayer too is becoming a real spiritual experience.[17]

There is also a rebirth of celebration. Till the Council, the Christian people "went to" Mass and the sacraments—went passively. They understood nothing of them, and went because they were under obligation to go. They knew the sacraments were sources of grace and so were very attached to them, but they were not "experiences." They were supernatural gestures, divine gestures that went over their heads. We all know that today the people are abandoning the sacraments. The reforms of Vatican II have gone only half way; the people will never go back to this sort of liturgy, which suits only archaeologists and those who have a classical education—perhaps 1 percent of baptized Christians.

The Christian people are now once more creating a new style of celebration, taking advantage of the gaps left in the liturgy of the sacraments, or the open spaces outside the liturgy. We are only at the beginning of this process, yet some steps have been taken in showing what a celebration is: the dawning consciousness and bodily and collective expression of a community. Far from distancing the members of a community from temporal tasks or moral responsibilities, celebration prepares them for these. It consolidates and strengthens the community, and in this way provides a basis for community action. It gives strength to all the members so that they can carry on their struggle against opposing forces, while feeling the support of the whole community, struggling with the energy of all. Celebration then becomes a worthwhile spiritual experience, as it was in the early days of Christianity.

(c) Toward a Theology of the Spirit

We are witnessing a revolution in theology, parallel with the evolution of Christianity since Vatican II. Latin American liberation theology is not an isolated event. It too is one of the fruits of the Council, and its basic suppositions are those of a much broader movement within the whole church, involving the meaning of theology as well as its methodology.

(i) Critique of Western theologies since the Patristic period. Since the second century, the influence of Roman philosophy, particularly the Stoic philosophy that pervaded the cultural climate of the time, has made Christian thinking tend to start from God the creator, that is, from a rational God. Biblical revelation was not a starting-point, but was referred to in order to respond to questions raised by the religious understanding of the dominant culture. So one started from the God of that culture, then illustrated and enriched that God by referring to the Bible. The statement known as the *Symbol of the Apostles*, which dates from this time, starts from God the creator. So does the Nicene Creed, thereby effecting a tremendous change from the Gospels and the New Testament as a whole. This change was accepted as being very enlightening for the world of the time. Well, what was enlightening then is just what spreads confusion today.

Latin theology increased this distance from the New Testament with its theory of "appropriations," substituting the divine nature for persons in its theological discourse.[18] Eastern theology continued talking in terms of divine persons, but in Latin theology the subject was God; that is, in the Latin understanding the divine nature acted as though it were a single person. God, and not the Trinity, became its starting-point and central point of reference. The main victim of this process was the Holy Spirit, since the person of the Son had a special relationship with creation through the incarnation, but nothing similar was accorded to the Holy Spirit. The mission of the Son was actualized in the incarnation, but the mission of the Spirit was left in a vacuum: the theory of appropriated missions left the Spirit as no more than a literary device to express the actions of the one God. This is the basis for the accusation of "christomonism" still addressed to us by the Eastern churches.

Christomonism derives primarily from the imbalance between the missions of the Son and the Holy Spirit in Western theology; there has always been a christology, but there has never been a parallel pneumatology in the whole scholastic tradition, till recent times. Besides this, christology has virtually ignored the Holy Spirit, which has no part in either the theology of the incarnation, or in the classical theology of redemption. Latin theology, given its fullest expression by St Anslem, explains the redeeming work of Christ without mentioning the Holy Spirit. The traditional theology of salvation has no place for the Holy Spirit.[19]

The ecclesiology that developed in the late Middle Ages and triumphed at Trent followed the lines laid down by Bellarmine, who again left the Holy Spirit out of account. The prevalent pattern was: God–Christ–church. In this pattern, God is revealed by Christ and Christ is made known by the church— meaning by the church hierarchy. The Holy Spirit features only as an aid to the hierarchy in their task of making Christ known. Thus there is christomonism in ecclesiology too. The church is sufficient to establish the link between Christians and Christ.

Ignoring the role of the Holy Spirit led to dangerous dualism in christology, soteriology (the theology of redemption/ salvation) and ecclesiology. In christology it produced a separation between, on the one hand, a Christ defined by the dogmatic theology born of scholasticism—a Christ divorced from the actions of the human life of Jesus, which became superfluous—and, on the other hand, a historical Jesus, studied in philological and historical disciplines as though he were just a man like any other. Between these two disciplines, these two approximations to Jesus, these two theologies, there was no contact: a "Jesuology" on one side and a "mythology" on the other, disconnected, with a void between them. Traditional christology attached no value to the presence of the Spirit in Jesus.

In the same way, the field of soteriology saw a separation develop between a doctrine of justification divorced from history and a secularized theory of liberation, again with a void between them. There was no apparent link between historical action and the invisible process of justification. Hence verticalism and horizontalism, the radical separation of what should be united. This was another result of ignoring the role of the Spirit in the world. Western soteriology finally led to the opposition between a salvation divorced from the world and a liberation of the world divorced from God: the visible outcome of an old theology that has run for fifteen hundred years.

Ignoring the Spirit also produced a similar dissociation in the field of ecclesiology. On one side was the sociological definition of the church along the lines laid down by Bellarmine, which was to lead to secularism. In this, the church is identified with the "institution": it is the institution defined by the Code of Canon Law of the Latin Church. On the other, there was the postulation of a church-as-mystery, a supernatural, invisible reality. An act of faith is needed to bridge the gap between them and believe that the same reality is indicated. There is no apparent continuity between them; they are two juxtaposed realities, each of which could exist on its own, with no need of the other. Only an act of faith in what is invisible can make them one and the same. Again, this separation of mystery and institution into two autonomous realities is a result of ignoring the role of the Holy Spirit.

The whole history of this theology reveals a pattern of radical distinction between matter and spirit, a distinction taken to its extremes by Descartes and his followers. But it came originally from Greek philosophy and underlay the scholastic theology of the Middle Ages. The Holy Spirit is precisely the missing link between body and spirit, between matter and soul.[20]

Yves Congar tells that during the whole of Vatican II the observers from the Eastern churches criticized the absence of pneumatology from the conciliar documents. They taxed *Lumen Gentium, Dei Verbum* and other texts, as well as speeches in the *aula*, with this lack. It is true that the Council's final documents mention the Holy Spirit 258 times, which marks a notable advance on previous Councils of the Western church. But it still did not do justice to the Holy Spirit, and in Catholic teaching there is still no authentic conception of the Holy Spirit which would do justice to the message of the Bible.[21] If the hierarchy of the Catholic Church is still so lacking in faith in the Spirit, what can be said of the people?

(ii) Exclusion of the Spirit in non-theological areas. It was the Jesuit Karl Rahner who pointed out that one of the most likely reasons for the absence of any experience of the Spirit from modern theology was the Jesuit school which effectively imposed its way of thinking on others. In the Jesuit theology of sanctifying grace there is a radical separation between sanctifying grace itself and anything that might be called religious experience. Grace has no aspect of experience. Christians act externally and internally exactly like anyone else; there is no perceptible difference on the level of experience. The difference is purely imperceptible and unconscious. Therefore, anything that might be described as religious experience in their daily lives has to be treated just like any other psychological phenomenon. It would not have any connection with God's grace. Between invisible grace and psychological make-up there would be no communication.[22]

Given these conditions, mystical experiences would have to be absolutely exceptional and in no way related to normal Christian life—almost like miracles. In fact they were treated as such: the hierarchy was always highly mistrustful of mystical experiences, accepting them only in the face of irrefutable evidence. Ordinary Christians, including religious, were kept well away from experiences judged to be exceptional or abnormal. Standard teaching on grace since Trent was a powerful factor in keeping possible experiences of the Spirit well outside the lives of ordinary Christians. Everything in the religious life of the people that could not be brought within the scope of official rationalization was condemned as superstition. Anything that might be connected with psychological feelings or religious sensibility was regarded as dangerous for the clergy.

(iii) The evolution of present-day theology. There has been a turning toward the Holy Spirit in Western theology in recent years. It is noteworthy that Rahner should have broken so clearly with the whole Jesuit school and dominant thinking since Trent.[23] The greatest Protestant theologian of this century, Karl Barth, had a presentiment of this evolution of theology toward the third article of the Creed a few months before his death in 1968. He said that he no longer had the chance to remake this theology of the Holy Spirit, but suspected that all his work lacked the perspective of the Holy Spirit as a basis.[24] The great French Dominican Yves Congar made the Holy Spirit the subject of his later works.[25] He saw this not as complementing earlier theology, but as taking up the whole of theology once more from a more fundamental standpoint. Younger writers give more importance to the Holy Spirit as time passes; the names that come to mind are Jürgen Moltmann and Wolfhart Pannenberg among Protestants, J.B. Metz and Heribert Mühlen among Catholics.[26]

This new turn encourages a re-reading of Hegel and Schleiermacher who, at the outset of the great explosion of the modern world following the French Revolution, were in a way trying to find a new basis for Christian faith in the world. Both saw the incompatibility between the modern age and a religion whose God was imposed from outside and had become the cause of radical alienation. They knew that traditional Western Christian theology led inevitably to atheism. They looked to the Spirit as the starting-point for a re-reading of Christianity.

Such theologies found more acceptance in the Protestant churches than in the Roman Catholic Church, whose response was total rejection of the challenge of modernity. It simply denied the existence of the problem. Particularly from the pontificate of Pius IX onwards, it turned back to a militant reactionary theology which saw humanity accelerating in decadence from St Thomas Aquinas onwards. The condemnation of modernism in the early part of this century marked the high point of the struggle against any sort of reconciliation, based on experience of the Holy Spirit, between Catholicism and the modern world.

For 150 years, Catholic theology under the influence of the hierarchy denied that the modern world existed as a problem. Today it faces theoretical or practical atheism spread throughout the Western world and can only look back on 150 years of failure. Instead of attenuating the most alienating aspects of traditional theology, Catholicism accentuated them by requiring a veritable *"Credo quia absurdum"* which the archaic rationalism of neo-Thomism was powerless to correct.

(iv) The challenge of atheism. Now that the mainstream churches are faced with a massive decline in religious practice, the advance of atheism is impossible to ignore. It is in fact less in the Communist world than in the Western democracies, where its penetration is deeper through spreading in an atmosphere of freedom rather than being imposed by force. Pope John Paul II is constantly voicing his apprehension at this spread of atheism, and calling for a new evangelization. In fact, there is no other course open. There is no longer a place for the traditional strategy, confined to safe-guarding Catholics from contamination by error. Today, defensive strategy is equivalent to suicide.

The problem is: what sort of evangelization? In its traditional form, Christianity is simply unintelligible to modern atheists. Evangelization has to be carried on in a context and in terms that atheists understand, or remain on the level of polite conversation. Theology, dogmas, liturgy and church structures serve only to repel. Only a living experience can command attention and eventually convince: this is now becoming a growing conviction.[27]

In Latin America, the experience of the Christian base communities has undoubtedly succeeded in commanding the attention of atheists, because it is something lived, specific and historical.[28] This is also why many people regret that the authorities of the Catholic Church have not paid more attention to what is happening in Nicaragua. They are so absorbed by the problem of defending the faithful against the threat of atheism that they cannot grasp the idea that the situation in Nicaragua offers ways for evangelizing atheists. They are falling back on the strategies of the nineteenth century, which not only failed to convert either liberals or socialists, but finally discouraged Catholics to such an extent that they behaved like rats leaving a sinking ship.

To conclude this section: we are now witnessing a return to experiences of the Spirit as described in the New Testament. For some time, many movements have been going in this direction. Theology has begun to appreciate the phenomenon and is trying to take stock of it, beginning to recognize the failings of church practice and of Western theology itself. It is increasingly recognizing that the intuitions of Vatican II need to be worked out, and that they must lead to a revolution in church affairs more radical than anything that has happened since the second century. The new era of the church will be under the sign of the Holy Spirit, and the aspect of experience will be valued far more highly in it than it has been since the second century. This is the church context in which the new communities of Latin America, which we shall look at in the next section, are experiencing the Spirit.

2. EXPERIENCING THE SPIRIT IN LATIN AMERICA

The scope of this section is limited to describing how the base communities in Latin America experience the Spirit. I know there are base communities on other continents, but I do not have direct experience of them and so prefer not to comment on them. I know, too, that there are ways of experiencing the Spirit outside the base communities, but I believe that of all experiences of the Spirit today those of the Latin American base communities are the most characteristic and present the most clearly defined features.

I will try to bring out what is really fundamental in these experiences, leaving aside manifestations that St Paul and the other New Testament authors judged to be secondary. The basic manifestations are historical, which means that they fit into a context of action in history. They are not something experienced by the communities outside their actions in history, but within the context of these actions.

Experiences of the Spirit cannot be separated from positive action. They are not a matter of visions of an external being or object, nor are they a matter of being conscious of an "inner person" within the individual psyche. They are all-embracing experiences: the presence of the Spirit is perceived as permeating all aspects of a specific action. This section sets out to show the different aspects of this all-embracing experience. Most members of a community would not know how to say that they are experiencing the Spirit; they do not know what names to give to what they experience. But those who do know the names can confirm the reality of the phenomenon.

The experiences to which I am referring are experiences of an unexpected transformation. People feel themselves taken hold of by new strength that makes them do things they had never thought of doing. Individuals and communities that had been downhearted, lacking in dynamism, resigned to the endless struggle for survival, discover themselves to be protagonists of a history far greater than themselves.

Christians, whether Protestant or Catholic, interpret this faith-experience as a result of divine power. They call its source "God" or "Jesus," their oral tradition not teaching them enough about the Holy Spirit to identify it in such experiences. But when these are compared to the biblical texts, there is no doubt about the identification.

Their experience is one of "conversion" amounting to a sort of total inversion of their lives, something that cannot be reduced to human agencies. It is the advent of a new life corresponding to what the New Testament tells us about new life. It is an all-embracing experience, working on five main areas which include practically all aspects. These are: action, freedom, speech, community and life. Let us look at each in turn.

(a) Experience of Action

The word "action" is not here used in its sociological sense, nor in the sense used by social sciences that study work "objectively." Using a distinction made by John Paul II in his encyclical *Laborem Exercens*, we can distinguish between objective action and subjective action. Action is the full expression of the agents who perform it, the self-projection through which the agents not only become conscious of themselves but actually constitute themselves as agents. Action is the expression through which persons put themselves at risk, define themselves and at the same time master themselves.

Now, since time immemorial the poor of Latin America have not acted, but been acted upon by others. Amerindians locked into the structures of an alien civilization which they did not understand and which rolled over them; descendants of black slaves, equally subjected to another civilization which refused to recognize their right to their own culture; peasants deprived of their land; slum-dwellers; the unemployed and under-employed of the cities, living off the surplus of established society—all have always obeyed the orders of others. All these have always been objects of a history made without them or against them. They have not known what it is to act, to be "subjects" or agents in the sense employed by John Paul II.

Then they have this experience; suddenly they begin to act; they discover that they themselves are capable of action. Before, they had no plans, no projects for the future, only frustrated dreams. They had no confidence in their own judgment, in their capacity to plan and gain practical knowledge of the world. They followed custom or the instructions of their masters. Now they discover that they are acting for themselves, discover that they are capable of setting and seeking goals, of achieving objectives. Before, they gave up before they had started: only the masters, teachers or priests knew what to do. Now they are amazed at their discovery that they themselves are acting in the complete sense of the word.

We are not speaking here of the consciousness of being active, of doing things, that anyone can feel. This is not a matter of self-awareness of engaging in activity. It is a matter of experience undergone by a community of people who feel that something new is coming about in their midst. This experience has the effect of completely reversing their situation, of changing them from mere passivity to activity: it is like the experience of being born. It is the experience of re-birth. This is the experience that has to be attributed to the Spirit.

It is very important to appreciate that a true base community exists only when this experience of new, community action appears. A Christian base community is not the product of its liturgy, its celebrations, its catechesis, its Bible study groups, its discussion groups, but of its community actions in the world around it. Such actions can cover a wide field: they can be a campaign for human rights—the right to life and liberty for all those unjustly detained or accused,[29] the right to land,[30] the right to form workers associations, and so on. They can be mutual, collective efforts of working toward meeting a common need—water, energy, schools, houses, health stations, etc.[31] They can be political representations to the local authorities to make them carry out their duties and provide the public services the poor are deprived of. They can be the work of forming political organizations. They can be the collective struggle to overcome disease, to increase literacy, to improve sanitation, to cultivate common vegetable plots, and a host of other things.

Taken "objectively," each of these activities can perfectly well be explained in normal human terms, and sociology and psychology can give a satisfactory account of them. There is no experience of the Spirit in the objective event (that is, the event taken out of its specific, individual context) of building a school or marching in the streets. The experience of the Spirit has to do with the people who make these events happen. When a little old lady, who has spent her life bent double under the burdens inflicted on her by her situation and all the powers of society, suddenly gets up and goes to the local police station to protest at a sergeant's maltreatment of a peasant, and this because she feels herself a member of a community and this takes away her fear forever, then something has happened that science cannot explain. Something has happened to her and she knows full well that this something is stronger than her. Thousands of similar cases could be quoted.

What is spiritual in such an experience consists first in perceiving a mission. The members of a community feel called on to act. They have never before experienced anything like this. Action becomes a vocation; not any action, but the particular initiative to which the community is called. Then, the poor people who begin to act feel the impact of an unknown strength. This is a human strength, but a human strength that suddenly comes upon people unprepared for it. Then the poor people of the community become conscious of an effectiveness that they have not known before: they manage to plan, to organize and achieve results. If such results were produced by vanguard groups, by trained technicians or by state authorities, there would be nothing extraordinary about them. What is extraordinary is that they are produced by the poor and oppressed. Neither technicians nor revolutionary vanguard groups nor political leaders experience the Holy Spirit: what they achieve is within their natural capabilities. But for the poor to achieve such results is something else. Besides this, technicians, politicians and vanguard groups seek only objective action. The action of the poor is subjective: it is action that transforms them, creating a communion of life between them, the material world and other human beings. Spiritual experience exists in the vital communion between active participants.

(b) Experience of Freedom

For five hundred years the peoples of Latin America have had little experience of freedom. They have had deep experiences of slavery and domination. These are still the basic facts of life for the great majority of them.

They feel that the natural world and material needs hold dominion over them. The privileged minorities can protect themselves against the dangers and sufferings brought by nature. The poor suffer the full impact of any cataclysm, being totally unprotected. In the countryside, the rich may suffer some damage from drought, floods, pests, but they will remain basically intact. They can call on "drought works," "flood services" and the rest.[32] The poor, however, have no defence against adverse forces of nature. In the shantytowns around the cities, floods and drought, heat and cold, pollution and epidemics will all have their greatest impact on the poorest. They have no human freedom in the face of the natural world. They do not dominate creation as God told Adam to do, but are dominated by it.

In their relations with other human beings, this domination

is still more implacable. The exploitation of labour has been denounced in church documents for many years now. As regards Latin America, this domination is articulated in the "Justice" and "Peace" sections of the documents of Medellín and in the Puebla "Final Document."[33] Domination also prevails in relations between the sexes. Machismo is an integral part of the mechanisms of domination in all levels of society.

But now a new experience is making itself felt in the Christian communities that have arisen from this context: that of freedom. This is not something they receive from outside. If freedom were something brought by governments, by revolutionary groups, even by the church, it would not be a true liberation. No one can make anyone else free. The experience of the communities is one of self-liberation. They themselves experience liberation in the act of making themselves free; freedom is won in the struggle for liberation. Christians are freeing themselves—they are caught up in a collective experience of liberation.

This freedom is first experienced in the "praxis of martyrdom in Latin America."[34] Thousands—tens of thousands—of women and men have gone calmly to meet death. They have taken on responsibilities that involved risking their lives at every turn. They have done so with dignity, calm and humility. They have found a way to overcome the traditional fear of death. This situation is much like that of martyrs of the past. The example of the martyrs, far from discouraging others, brings new vocations. The martyrs know themselves to be freer than those who persecute them.

Freedom is also victory over the "desires of the flesh," meaning the promises made by the mighty to the poor, the illusions they create for them so as to keep them in a state of resignation. They are also the bribes with which they try to buy off all emergent leaders. Those whom they cannot silence, they try to buy. Many, of course, consciously or unconsciously, allow themselves to be bought, and bring their followers with them. But in the Christian communities, leaders emerge who cannot be either intimidated or bought. They become free in the face of all tempters—landowners, politicians, teachers. They feel themselves equal and morally superior to all those who impressed them in the past, before whom they used to stand with heads bowed.

Since Hegel and his master-slave dialectic, we know that the slave is the master's accomplice. This happens in Latin America too; the masses are also guilty of domination. They too sin through cowardice, through corruption of their understanding and through fear. Those who become free, become free from sin. They cease collaborating in the social sin. They hold their heads high, feeling their dignity for the first time. This experience of dignity recovered is one of the most visible signs in the communities.

The oppressed of Latin America are also freeing themselves from the law. In Latin America, the law is made by the powerful to be imposed on the weak. The powerful do not obey the laws they themselves make, but they force them on to the shoulders of the weak like a yoke of iron. Liberation begins when the oppressed begin to learn the laws, to demand that they be applied to all equally, and later to demand their reform so that they may be laws of solidarity and not of oppression of the defenceless.

In the Catholic Church, ecclesiastical laws are felt by the poor as laws of domination. They do not understand them, but accept them because they are imposed by the clergy, who are stronger than they are. The traditional view is that the clergy hold the keys of the kingdom of heaven, so those who wish to be saved have to accept all the whims of the clergy—outwardly at least. But with the birth of the communities, Catholics are beginning to free themselves from clerical domination. They are beginning to express their opinions. They are being born to freedom in the church too. As for the popular Pentecostal churches, one of the aspects that gives them greater joy and a greater feeling of freedom and autonomy is the fact of having thrown off the clerical yoke. Many people joined them just because of arguments with priests in which they were treated with disdain or indifference.

This experience of liberation is linked to religious understanding. This is because liberation is not in the first place a political or economic event, but the birth of a new personality. Previously, people had not felt themselves to be responsible beings, capable of exciting by themselves and for themselves; now they have become people capable of acting on their own initiative instead of as a reflex action to the outside world. The passage from one state to another is experience of the power of the Spirit.

(c) Experience of Speech

The poor are speaking out: this is a new reality in Latin America. They themselves are amazed at it. Before, they were treated as ignorant and saw themselves as ignorant too. The ignorance of the poor was a commonplace, in the church and in society. Because of this ignorance, the poor could not speak.

They talked, of course, talked all the time—at home, in the fields, by the rivers where the women washed the clothes. Talked, and talked too much. But only of unimportant things, the minutiae of daily life and events that had been decided by others. In the presence of authority, church or secular, they remained silent. They even made themselves out to be stupid so as to avoid being humiliated. They could not take part in decision-making through using words. Their words were destined to remain unheard.

The miracle began in the communities. There everyone speaks: everyone has something worth saying. How? They all have access to the Bible, and this access means that all can get to know the sources of knowledge. They do not have to depend on others, but can know for themselves. On the basis of their knowledge of the Bible, they can all say something worthwhile. It enables them to make valid comments on matters relating to the organization and work of the community. And it enables them to speak to God in prayer; they no longer recite formulas, as though they could pray only in the words of others, words learned from the priests. They know that their own words are worthy of God because they have learned God's words.[35]

The same miracle spreads out beyond the communities. The poor are beginning to face up to the authorities, demanding their rights, demanding accounts of public spending. They are forming associations and unions to speak out and publicly take the side of the oppressed. They have learned not to worry about their grammatical mistakes, not to be ashamed of the way they speak, to use words they know and to apply them to serious subjects. They no longer accept that speech is the exclusive property of the powerful.

If these speeches were being made by educated people there would be nothing spiritual about them. They would be natural to people with intellectual training, natural to those whose positions of authority have made them at home with words. The spiritual element is that of radical conversion: the dumb speak. The experience of the Spirit is in taking up speech. This is a real taking, a real conquest. Speech springs from the energies hidden in the secret depths of the psyche; it is being brought back to life.

The same experience can be seen at work in the church. The fact that the poor are reading the Bible is having an extraordinary effect. In the Pentecostal churches, personal discovery of the Bible by their members gave them a feeling of absolute superiority. Catholics felt ashamed in front of "believers" because they did not read the Bible, while the "believers" could quote it and find arguments in it to which Catholics had no answer. But in the Catholic communities direct reading of the Bible also transformed personalities. Before, they got everything from the priests; now, lay people can begin to think for themselves.

The effect of conquering speech is that Christians are becoming missionaries. Those who have discovered words feel impelled to make them public.[36] Missionary vocations are spreading in the communities. The experience of speech reaches its highest point when receivers become transmitters. Experience of the Spirit is completed in giving public testimony. When someone who has always been silent begins over the course of a few weeks to proclaim the gospel and found new communities, there can be no doubt: the Spirit is there.

(d) Experience of Community

For practically all Latin Americans, community is a discovery. Of course there have always been elements of life in common, without which life itself is impossible. But society has always been at pains to stifle any manifestation of community spirit among the poor.

To a certain extent, the indigenous communities were protected by the missionaries in the "reductions" of earlier centuries. But the nineteenth and twentieth centuries have seen the completion of the invasion of their territories by the big landowners. The Amerindian tribes have been forced to disperse, to emigrate, deprived of any part in public affairs. The blacks were prevented from forming any communities till the middle of this century, since their very religion was persecuted. Peasants were prevented from coming together in villages as they did in Europe because they had to live where the landowners dictated. The masses who move from the country to the shantytowns and slums of the big cities are the exact reverse of a community. Latin American society is a disintegrated society. The great majority of city-dwellers belong to no sort of association; the only thing that saves them is the remnants of the old family solidarity.

This is why community is a miracle. It is not natural for communities to spring from the midst of a population so alienated by history and geography from any sort of association; it is a miracle from God. The experience of those who come together to form a community is a charismatic, almost ecstatic one, though calmly expressed. The emotional level is high; the members who make up a community are conscious of the radical change it implies in their way of living. The community way of living creates new personalities and enriches them in every way.

The community becomes the centre of their lives; or rather, it creates a social life in which they all take part. It is the source of a higher form of life; those who join a community begin to live life on a higher plane. Community consists in sharing. The fact of sharing goods means that there are more of them. But it is not goods that are shared so much as action. What makes the community is its public action carried out in common.[37]

The name "community" is sometimes given to what is not a community. For example, a parish priest may wish to decentralize his parish. He sets up various house churches, nominates people to various jobs and gathers the faithful round services and other parish activities—catechesis, sacraments, charitable works. He generously bestows the title "community" on these gatherings. Of course they are nothing of the sort. Communities grow from the bottom up. They can be inspired or stimulated by people from outside, but they come into being through the action of their members. These do not meet in churches or chapels, but in places where there is communal work to be done. The leaders or animators or directors of a community get their authority from the community itself and not from someone delegated by the parish priest. If communities were just creations of the clergy or lay pastoral workers, there would be no part for the Spirit, or at least no real experience of the Spirit. This is found only where communities organize and act for themselves and do not come about through the will of others. They are communities in their community action.

Of course celebrations are necessary: they provide a visible sign of the presence of the Spirit, a more obvious manifestation of experience of the Spirit, though not necessarily the deepest. But if celebrations just follow fixed lines laid down by the clergy, they will not be real manifestations of the Spirit. Such communities are made up of Catholics and of Protestants. They are fundamentally the same, though their doctrinal beliefs, services and organization may differ.[38]

(e) Experience of Life

The theme of life is the most far-reaching and also the one that best expresses the experience of the Christian base communities of Latin America. This life comes out of an experience of death, since violence has been the dominant sign in the lives of the people since the Spanish-Portuguese conquest. This violence has not been forgotten, since the conquest of the interior regions of the continent took a long time. Indeed, there are still some Amazonian regions that were never conquered. But we are now coming to the end of the period of conquest, whose history was, and still is, one of violence. The literature of Latin America is full of violence, and death is everywhere in it. Hence the aspiration to life.

The communities are life; life springs from them. Death comes from isolated individuals. The experience of life is one of dedication to the common good, of service. People discover that they live precisely in proportion to the degree to which they allow themselves to become involved in the community and its mission. Life is acting for the good of all, for the advancement of all. This advancement can be seen at first glance. In the communities, the families are more united, the children more carefully brought up, people more neatly dressed. They no longer spend their money on vices; they look better and healthier.[39]

The whole atmosphere is one of people who have discovered an aspiration to a higher life. The communities cultivate not *having* more, but *being* more.[40] Liberation struggles are more about improving human relationships than material conditions. Of course, under present conditions the actual results of this will to live are limited. The communities cannot make up for the deficiencies of the political system; there is no way they can be seen as "the" solution to the problems of Latin America. Without far-reaching political, economic and cultural change there will be no liberation. But here we are looking at just the spiritual dimension, quoting spiritual experiences that are actually taking place. Political, economic and cultural changes will be brought about by human means, based on human reason. They will not transform the people who carry them out; they will not confer the experience of being an active agent of one's own life. In this respect the experience of the politically, culturally and economically most developed nations has been a great disillusionment. It shows that the one-sided development of each of these dimensions does not produce life, but just consumption, excitement and satisfaction of desires, and above all isolation and individualism. This is not an experience of life.

The evolution of the developed nations is a good illustration of the fact that without a deep experience of life capable of unifying, disciplining and limiting the various aspects of development, it can only generate frustration. The best representatives of the developed nations today feel the need for a deep experience to give quality to life and show them how to value quality of life above quantity of goods consumed. They are beginning to find that, with all their deficiencies, historical or new, the poor nations have greater wisdom and know better how to live: their experience of life is a spiritual experience.

(f) Conclusion

Each of the aspects of human experience described above could be explained in purely human terms. Taken out of the context in which it is actually experienced, each could receive a scientific explanation. But scientific investigation concerns itself with just the framework of reality, not with reality as it affects those who live it; it can examine the material supports of life, not life itself. The experience we are describing is an all-embracing one. The descriptions given do not succeed in capturing it in its reality; this can be known only through active participation. Experience of the Spirit *is* not what is written; it is something else, something the words try to suggest. All these words have to be taken together as an approximation of a unique reality; there are not five partial experiences of the Spirit, but one overall experience.

This experience has one single object: God and creation united. It is experience of God in creation and of creation in God. It is experience of God acting on us and on the world at the same time, relating us to the world and the world to us, not in some vague, cosmic contact, but in a specific and limited course of action. There is no separation between the experience of acting and the experience of the Spirit who acts, between experiencing the Spirit and experiencing "me" and "us."

In the same way, there is no separation between action and prayer, practice in the world and celebration of practice. This is so because this is not a matter of technical performance, such as a machine is capable of, but of human activity: a liberating course of action involving the totality of human beings, not divided into sectors, but rather unified in an all-embracing experience. This is what exists in the Christian communities, what can be seen by taking part in them.

There is no separation of individual from community experience. One individual alone could never achieve such experience, yet the community is made up of disparate individuals.

Each community is different and produces different experiences. Their experiences are tentative, beginnings; there is no complete experience of the Spirit, no experience that is enough to satisfy. The experience described is made up of thousands of beginnings of experience. Some commentators have denied that base communities exist, calling them projections made by theorists cut off from reality. It would indeed be impossible to show a perfect community demonstrating everything we have described in a finished, stable, permanent, obvious fashion. All of this exists in unfinished form, ever threatened, always in danger. Nevertheless, what does exist is enough for us to be able to talk of a real experience. The Christian communities of the first century were also imperfect and unfinished. But even so they gave witness of the Spirit.

Religious sociology can produce another sort of reservation,[41] claiming that the really poor people of Latin America do not belong to base communities, with a few exceptions. This claim runs something like this: membership of the communities presupposes a certain level of advancement; true popular religion has found and still finds expression in traditional Catholicism and finds much less expression in the base communities; therefore, this argument concludes, the communities are not representative of the poor, who incline toward traditional Catholicism; rather, the communities have more to do with the clergy, whose roots are in the middle class. Now, there is no denying that there is a great distance between the popular religious mentality of the poor masses and that of the clergy. Clergy and the poor live in worlds separated by several centuries. Yet the communities are forming a sort of bridge between them. If the people are still largely separate from the clergy, this is due to barriers put up by the clergy. The clergy live in the cultural setting of the middle classes; that is where they were educated. Yet even if one agrees that the clergy have played a significant role in the communities, it is still undeniably true that the base communities represent the world of the people. There is still a long way to go in order for the poor to make the communities truly reflect their world, and we can look forward to far richer experiences of the Spirit once the clergy become capable of detaching themselves more from their culture and their attempts to impose this culture on the poor.

3. EXPERIENCE OF THE SPIRIT IN THE HISTORY OF THEOLOGY

From the outset, the Spirit has inspired anxiety in the church: the message of the primacy of the Spirit has produced a feeling of insecurity among faithful and ministers alike. This explains why the dominant theology, which became more or less official doctrine, has tended to play down the role of the Spirit. At the same time, writings that invoked the Spirit against the too human institution of the church were suspect and few of them have come down through history. As always, history favours those who hold authority and power.

It is impossible to deal with the whole history of the theology of experience of the Spirit in a few pages; we can pick out only a few salient features; looking first at the origins of Christianity and then at the intervening centuries that separate us from these origins.

(a) Experience of the Spirit in the Origins of Christianity

(i) The New Testament. To build a people on the basis of an experience of the Spirit is a striking paradox. Indeed, it would seem to be a pure contradiction in terms. How would it be possible to build a church which claimed to be inspired by an invisible Spirit? Yet the authors of the New Testament, the Apostles and those who wrote under their authority, proclaimed the primacy of the Spirit, and of experience of the Spirit, over everything else in life. St Peter saw the authority of the Spirit as paramount; Acts 10:44–8 shows him bowing to a manifestation of the Spirit and agreeing to baptize the first pagans. St Paul warns: "Never try to suppress the Spirit" (1 Thess. 5:19).[42]

Nevertheless, Paul was worried by the direction experiences of the Spirit were taking in Corinth. Chapters 12–14 of 1 Corinthians are a long exposition of the gifts of the Spirit. Paul feels the danger of a serious distortion in Corinth: that the gifts of the Spirit might be taken as ends in themselves, or as the object of a quest for self-advantage and self-aggrandisement. His solution consists in setting graded values on the gifts of the Spirit, putting those that are of service to the community, such as prophecy, highest. The gift of tongues comes lower down. In this way the value of experience is fully recognized, while the gifts are integrated into the community.[43]

The emphasis given by Paul to prophecy is not unique: the other currents of early Christianity all agree—the Jesus movement of the Synoptics in Palestine and Syria,[44] the Johannine community in Syria,[45] and St Luke. By the time of the later New Testament writings, however, prophecy was posing problems. The later writings lay stress on the need for discernment of spirits while still fully accepting the fact of experience of the Spirit. This still produces insecurity in the communities. Disturbing personalities make their appearance in the name of the Spirit. The emphasis now is not on celebrating the charisms brought by the Spirit, but rather on disciplining them through discernment: "It is not every spirit, my dear people, that you can trust; test them, to see if they come from God; there are many false prophets, now, in the world" (1 John 4:1).[46]

(ii) The second century. During the second century the church was still charismatic, still appealed to experience of the Spirit above all else. In general there was no conflict between experience of the Spirit and the institution of the episcopate, since many bishops were also charismatics. Writers of the time make no distinction in their accounts of the church between the service given by bishops and experience of the Spirit.[47] To quote just one, this is what St Irenaeus says on the subject: "It is not possible to count the number of charisms which, throughout the world, the church receives every day from God, in the name of Jesus Christ who was crucified under Pontius Pilate."[48] And: "We know that, in the church, many brethren have prophetic charisms and, by the power of the Holy Spirit, speak all languages, and, for the good of all, reveal the secrets of men and the mysteries of God. The Apostle calls these charisms spiritual: not because they are separate from and

suppress the flesh, but because of the participation of the Spirit and only because of this."[49]

Nevertheless, at the end of the century, the crisis of Montanism arose. It must have been the most decisive event of the century, though unfortunately we know little about its origins and history. It was founded by a prophet from Phrygia called Montanus, and two prophetesses. He announced new prophecies of the Holy Spirit, claiming to be a sort of incarnation of the Spirit.[50] The condemnation of the movement meant that most of the writings of the time dealing with it were suppressed and disappeared. Its most prominent adherent in the West was Tertullian, and it produced a polemic against the institutional church of the day, already based on the episcopate. Tertullian opposed the church of the Spirit to the institutional church, and joined the Montanist movement to free himself from the institution. How much of this was rhetoric and what exactly were the barriers erected between the Catholic Church and the Montanists, we shall probably never know. All the indications are that many people in the church saw the movement as a mortal threat to the unity and order of the church, so the reaction against it must have been very strong. What is certain is that experience of the Spirit became much rarer in the third century. The church stressed the need for institution; the liturgy was formalized, as was the episcopal ministry. Bishops were exalted, using all the priestly symbolism that could be drawn from the Old Testament. In the third century, the church gradually came to take on the features it has retained till the twentieth.

By the fourth century, St John Chrysostom could say that charisms were given to the early church as something exceptional, because of the weakness of the church then. From his time on, there would be no more charisms in the church because the church had no further need of them.[51] In effect, since then, charisms and experience of the Spirit have not been held to be constituent of the church. They are considered exceptional phenomena, like mystical phenomena, individual cases unrelated to the nature of the church or of Christianity.[52]

Would a different response to the Montanist crisis have been possible? Could the church have evolved in a different direction? Without the Montanist crisis, would the church be what it is today?

(b) Later Evolution of Experience of the Spirit

In this section I want to look at three basic developments: the identification of the Spirit with the church, which became progressively closer from the third century onwards; the struggle against the spiritual movement of the Middle Ages, which is probably at the root of modern atheism; and the rejection of all feminine and maternal characteristics of the Spirit, resulting from radical rejection of other religions. These three events determined the general lines on which pneumatology developed in the West.

(i) *The Holy Spirit reduced to the church*. This could have been the result of the Montanist crisis. Or it could have been due to the growth of the church itself, which effectively strengthened the authority of the bishops. Whatever the cause, the link between the Holy Spirit and the church became increasingly close. St Irenaeus summed up the prevailing ethos: "Where the church is, there too is the Spirit of God; where the Spirit of God is, there too is the church and all grace."[53]

The Eastern tradition always kept to a very broad understanding of the church; this understanding saw the church as involving the imperial power of Byzantium or Russia.[54] Within the confines of the empire, everything is the church, and the Spirit is in everything. The world has been transformed by the Spirit. In this way, the world is never out of reach of the action of the Spirit—at least the Christian world already taken on by Christ.[55] In the West, ecclesiology developed along different lines. At least since the struggles between the Gregorian popes and the Holy Roman Empire, the church has been increasingly identified with the hierarchy. The course of this development is well-known. It reached its apogee in the counter-revolutionary Catholicism that dominated the papacies of Pius XI and XII. We had to wait for Vatican II to see the start of a different course.

The action of the Spirit was doubly reduced from the time of the eleventh-century struggles between the papacy and the empire: it became tied to the church-institution that evolved around this period, and it became tied to the concept of power (*potestas*). The theology of the Gregorian popes defined spiritual power over against temporal power. The Spirit was with the church-institution in its struggle against the empire. The Spirit was not on the side of the empire.[56] The Spirit acted in the world, but through the intermediary of the church.

The church was made up of "powers." Though there was debate concerning the number and definition of these powers, it was clearly agreed that the Spirit is present in sacramental power. The sacraments are administered through the power of the Spirit. In the same way, the government of the church is carried on through the power of the Spirit. The Spirit *is* power and confers spiritual powers, understood as embracing at least the powers of order and jurisdiction. The ecclesiology that developed in the fourteenth century tried to define the powers of the church, situating the power of the Spirit within it. The clearest manifestations of the Holy Spirit would be the sacraments, the general councils and the authority of the pope.

The medieval church did not accept this theology without putting up resistance. Not only did imperial theology not accept it; there was resistance too from the movements of the poor, the popular movements, lay movements in general. The most influential formulation of an alternative view is found in the writings of Joachim of Flora (1130–1202). He proclaimed the coming of a third age in the salvation of the world. The first had been the age of the Father in the Old Testament; the second the age of the Son with the coming of Jesus, and this was drawing to a close, to give way to the dawning of the age of the Holy Spirit. The age of the Son still contained many elements of the age of the Father: a religion of fear, of law, of punishments, of priests and temples, and so on. Now the time was at hand for the coming of the age announced by Jesus when he promised the Holy Spirit. This would be a complete renewal of society, a complete change in history.[57]

Such teaching would have been without influence had it not touched the aspirations of many Christians, unconvinced by the

apparatus of power adopted by the Church of Rome in its
struggle against the empire and in order to rule over Christendom. Many saw the birth of the Order of Friars Minor as a sign
of the coming of the age proclaimed by Abbot Joachim, and
the movement of the "Spirituals" that developed within the
Order was based on his ideas.

The church reacted strongly. Abbot Joachim, who had been
a friend to popes, was condemned after his death by the Fourth
Lateran Council (1215), though for reasons not directly
connected with his views on history. He was severely condemned by St Thomas Aquinas; official theology poured scorn on
his views. St Thomas calmly stated that everything that could
be expected of the Holy Spirit had already been given and was
present in the church.[58] Thomist theology favoured the institutional church, regarding it as definitive. It also favoured the
established form of society, Christendom. But it could not be
accepted by the popular movements.

Luther and Calvin did not basically change this doctrine of
the Holy Spirit. Both emphasized the role of the Spirit in
preaching and evangelization. But both tied it closely to the
powers of the church, the power of the word and the power of
the sacraments.[59] Besides fighting against the Church of Rome,
they fought still more assiduously against the popular movements that were springing up in its shadow. Luther dealt with
Thomas Müntzer, the theologian of the popular uprising in
Germany in 1525, in much the same way at St Thomas had dealt
with Abbot Joachim: severely and disdainfully.[60]

The Catholic Church, as it emerged from Trent, and the
established Protestant Confessions evolved in parallel: the Holy
Spirit tied to the institution of the church and with no part to
play in the lay world. This was the time of growing separation
between church and world, paralleling the separation between
spirit and matter. The spiritual is opposed to the temporal, and
what is spiritual is ecclesial.

(ii) The Holy Spirit masculinized. In Hebrew, the word for the
Spirit, *ruah*, is feminine. In Greek, the word *pneuma* is neuter.
This was translated into Latin and the Romance languages as
spiritus, which is masculine.

In the Bible, the role of the Spirit is found in activities more usually associated with maternity and femininity in general: inspiring, helping, supporting, enveloping, bringing to birth. The way the Spirit acts is described in terms of feminine ways of acting.[61] Of course God is sexless, but the words we use to speak of God are words applied to humanity. Human beings are the image of God and provide the analogies that enable us to say something about God. In the Bible, the image of God is the human person, man and woman alike. Consequently, both masculine and feminine forms of behaviour can furnish analogies to express what God is. So the Bible uses both masculine and feminine terms to refer to God. The Spirit represents God's maternal love and so acts like a woman.

In the West, the influence of St Augustine was decisive in eliminating all feminine reference from theology and Christian imagery. Woman, according to him, is not the image of God; only man is. Furthermore, Augustine uses the imagery of man's mental process to explain the Trinity. The Spirit proceeds from the love of God. But this love is love *of* God; not love projected on someone outside, but a love remaining within the interior of the lover. Such love eliminates any reference to human experience of sexual love. Sex in Augustine's philosophy[62] is tied to matter and therefore is of a lower nature.

St Thomas took up Augustine's thought, accepting it as it was and merely trying to express it better. In his theology there is no place for any analogy with maternity or sexual love, even maternal love. From then on, there was no place in the West for femininity in theology of the Spirit, and, therefore, in representations of God. Masculinity is by definition present in the images of the Father and the Son; now the Spirit too is described in masculine terms. So if the Spirit is power, masculinity fits "him" better. The theology of the Holy Spirit could have acted as a counterbalance to the excessive masculinity of a church based on divine power. This did not happen. Instead, the Spirit itself was absorbed by a religious framework that exalted power.[63]

(iii) Sources of atheism. The widespread atheism of the West today is clearly not a product of philosophical or rational

arguments. Reasoning is secondary and used to justify decisions taken at a deeper level. Now various writers are showing that there is a connection between the triumph of atheism and the theology of the Holy Spirit—or rather, the absence of a theology and practice of the Holy Spirit.

The prime source of atheism is the growing intellectualization of Christianity in the modern age. During this period, Christianity has become increasingly concentrated on the clergy and the clergy have become intellectuals. Christianity has become more and more alien to any experience of the Spirit. The education of clergy and religious removes them from any experience of this sort.

It is true that during the last centuries of agrarian civilization the intellectual religion of the clergy did not prevent the country people from practising popular Catholicism. This still persists in the rural areas of Latin America, but it cannot stand up to urban civilization.[64] Everything here points to the worrying fact that in the big cities, the mantle of popular Catholicism will either be taken on by other, more popular denominations, usually Pentecostal in character, or popular religion will eventually succumb to atheism. It would be an illusion to suppose that Latin America will, by some divine and miraculous intervention, be spared from atheism. Popular Catholicism was a religion based on experience. The intellectualism of the priests destroyed the religion of the people, and is the best agent for atheism.

A second source of atheism is the replacement of belief in the triune God by deism. Since the Middle Ages scholastic theology has focussed on "God," a sort of unique being who is the "divine nature." St Thomas deals with God, and scholastic theology largely ignores the Trinity and the Holy Spirit. Of course they were both preserved out of fidelity to tradition, but they are not necessary in the main thrust of scholastic theology, just as they were not necessary to the way the church lived at the time.

Deism has been on the increase in modern times, spreading to the people. Now all that deism can produce is a revolt against its own God. The person of the one God loses his transcendence. He is presented as an all-powerful Lord, unchanging, clearly rational because known from rational argument, known more from reason than from the Bible, more as proof than from faith. This God is complete and absolute master of existence. He demands total obedience. The image of this God is power: the power of the creator, the power of Christ, seen as saviour and king, the power of the church backed by the power of the Spirit, the power of the pope and the hierarchy, the power of the word and the sacraments, the power of canon law. So much theology of power, even stronger in Protestantism than in Catholicism, can serve only to produce a reaction of rejection. Faced with such a God, human beings can do nothing; they are not allowed to be agents, to act spontaneously. They spend their whole lives walled in by obedience. In the eyes of most people today, Christianity is a system of domination over their spirit. It has become something that damages them and is in any case irrelevant. The atheism of today is not just indifference; it is active rebellion. This alone can explain such a widespread phenomenon.

Atheism cannot be fought by reasoning, or by threats, exhortations or constraints. Such a system of spiritual domination was precisely what led to atheism. It cannot be the remedy for it.[65]

CONCLUSION

We are witnessing a resurgence of experience of the Holy Spirit. If this is the case, it is a phenomenon unique in the history of the church since the third century. It is a complete inversion of the course the church in the West has followed since then.

This experience finds different forms of expression. We are here looking at that of the Christian base communities of Latin America, which I have described as a very specific form of experience of God. My thesis is that this is an experience of the Holy Spirit, which is something that cannot in any way be reduced to the charismatic manifestations so highly prized by the Corinthians. Experience of the Spirit comes about within history, in the actions of subjects—agents—of their history. It cannot be separated from acting in the world. It is experience of freedom. This freedom is expressed in speech which is public testimony, effective speech, speech that generates community. Experience of the Spirit is not an individual thing; it is tied to building of community. Such experience of the Spirit is life and resurrection, newness of life. It is felt as new birth.

This renewed experience of the Spirit has now come to the notice of theologians. Not all are convinced, but the best can see that something fundamental is at stake. The great masters of this century have seen the signs, and the impact this will have is something that cannot yet be measured. Reaching an understanding of this phenomenon is not a matter of going back over Catholicism simply as far as Trent, or even as far as Constantine. We need to go back at least as far as the Montanist crisis of the end of the second century.

The challenge of atheism, now so widespread in the modern world, will require far more radical reforms than the first steps timidly taken at Vatican II. We now know that atheism will not spare anything in the old Christendom, will not leave any sheltered isle of it untouched. We will not find a remedy for it by going back to the past, or by restoring old institutions. Compared to the present crisis of the Western church, the Reformation of the sixteenth century was child's play: the reformers left the basis of the Western tradition intact. They changed the surface elements, but failed to reach the heart of the problem.

The new experience of the Spirit is just a step. But if we have read the signs of the times aright, this step is already one into the Christianity of the future.

Chapter II
The Holy Spirit in the World

The Holy Spirit was sent to the people of God. But this people exists for the sake of the world. The Holy Spirit is sent to the whole world to bring about a new creation. The Spirit's action in the church is subordinate to this goal of new creation. For this reason, I propose to deal with the action of the Spirit in the world before moving on (in Chapter 3) to examine the action of the Spirit within the church.

Let us look first at some of the more general passages in the Bible dealing with the new creation; then at the Spirit in history in a general way: how the Spirit penetrates history, guiding it while at the same time subordinated to it. The final section explores the different ways in which the Spirit carries out its single overall action in the world.

1. THE SPIRIT AND THE NEW CREATION

The biblical message on the Spirit in the world can be seen to revolve around six themes: the resurrection, the kingdom of God, the new creation, the new humanity, nations, the maternity of the Spirit. Since the old world is still in being, what do these themes of newness and resurrection mean? How do they impinge on the old world?

(a) The Spirit and Resurrection

It has recently been suggested that the third article of what is known as the Apostles' Creed should be understood as: "I believe in the Holy Spirit in the Catholic Church... for the resurrection of the body."[1] This suggests that the Fathers saw the Holy Spirit as sent to bring about the resurrection of the body.

St Irenaeus was the main exponent of this teaching: "What is the visible fruit of the invisible Spirit, if not to make flesh mature and capable of incorruptibility?"[2] "If our bodily hearts can receive the Spirit now, what is extraordinary about their receiving the life given by the Spirit in the resurrection?"[3] "It will be through the power of the Spirit that believers will rise again when their bodies are once again united with their souls."[4]

The Fathers[5] were basing themselves on New Testament texts: "If the Spirit of him who raised Jesus from the dead is living in you, then he who raised Jesus from the dead will give life to your own mortal bodies through his Spirit living in you" (Rom. 8:11). It was the Spirit who raised Jesus, "who, in the order of the spirit, the spirit of holiness that was in him, was proclaimed Son of God in all his power through his resurrection from the dead" (Rom. 1:4). "It is the same with the resurrection of the dead . . . When it [the thing that is sown] is sown it embodies the soul, when it is raised it embodies the spirit" (1 Cor. 15:42–4). The First Letter of Peter also says of Jesus: "In the body he was put to death, in the spirit he was raised to life" (1 Pet. 3:19).[6]

The gift of the Holy Spirit fulfils the prophecy of Ezekiel about the dry bones that will live (Ezek. 37:1–4). St Paul recalled this prophecy in order to link the Spirit with the resurrection of the body.

(b) The Spirit and the Kingdom of God

The Holy Spirit is the present realization of the kingdom of God. St Gregory of Nyssa adopted the version of the Our Father in Luke, a version found in several ancient manuscripts. Instead of "thy kingdom come," they have: "thy Spirit come upon us and purify us" (Luke 11:2).[7] Luke, in any case, sees the coming of the Holy Spirit as taking the place of the kingdom that is to come (Acts 1:6–8). This is not to deny the ultimate coming of the kingdom; the Spirit in this sense is not the Father's whole and definitive response to expectation of the kingdom, but the pledge, the sign that this kingdom of God is becoming a reality. But the coming of the Spirit is not the whole fulfilment of the promise.[8]

Pauline theology underlies Luke's message; according to St Paul, the Holy Spirit is the proper object of the gospel. His theology has no more than a few allusions to the kingdom of God; in his proclamation of the good news, the place of the kingdom is taken by the Spirit. So in his Letter to the Romans, which is a full explanation of the gospel, chapter 8 deals with the proclamation of the gospel, and it is devoted to the Holy Spirit. Elsewhere in Paul, God "has anointed us, marking us with his seal and giving us his pledge, the Spirit" (2 Cor. 1:22); "Christians are told by the Spirit to look to faith for those rewards that righteousness hopes for" (Gal. 5:5); "And you too have been stamped with the seal of the Holy Spirit of the Promise, the pledge of our inheritance"(Eph. 1:13–14).[9]

In the Gospel according to John, the kingdom is still more muted and the promise is that of the Holy Spirit. John does not exclude a final judgment nor a final fulfilment of the promise, but the Holy Spirit is the centre of his message: what Jesus gives is the Holy Spirit.[10]

In the early communities, there is no doubt that Christians saw the gift of the Spirit as the actual presence of the promises made by God. The centre of their attention was no longer the future, but the present. They lived with the certainty that the Spirit was among them, fulfilling their aspirations.[11] They still suffered the tribulations of this world, but the presence of the Spirit took all cares from them.

The kingdom of God embraces the whole world; it is not confined to the community of the faithful. Consequently, the Spirit who is there as a pledge of the kingdom of God is also a potentially universal gift, embracing the totality of the world. This will be brought out more clearly in the next themes examined.

(c) The Spirit and the New Creation

The medieval hymn to the Holy Spirit sings, "Come, Holy Spirit, and from heaven direct on man the rays of your light."

There has been a shift from the whole of creation to the inner lives of the faithful. The presence of the Holy Spirit in creation has become dimmed. Yet the Bible shows the Spirit at the origin of creation. Divorced from later history, the text of Genesis 1:2, "God's spirit hovered over the water," is unclear. Some modern translations have "the breath of God" or even just "a mighty wind" (*New English Bible*), but both the New Testament and the Fathers saw that what was meant was the Spirit active in creation. God created through the Spirit, and the Spirit was creator. Just as it was at the origin of the old creation, so it is at the beginning of the new creation or renewal of creation.

The Old Testament witnesses elsewhere to the teaching of Genesis.[12] Judith's song of thanksgiving has "You sent your breath and they were put together" (Jth. 16:14); Psalm 104 sings "You give breath, fresh life begins, you keep renewing the world" (Ps. 104:30). St Bonaventure taught that this text referred to the second creation.[13] The Book of Wisdom echoes the same theme: "The spirit of the Lord, indeed, fills the whole world, and that which holds all things together knows every word that is said" (Wisd. 1:7).

Western theology has paid much less attention than Eastern theology to the Spirit in creation; in the Eastern church the theme forms part of the liturgy, and the celebration of Pentecost refers to the transformation of the whole of creation by the Spirit. Pentecost was a new creation: heaven coming down to earth.[14] The rite for the Epiphany celebrates "the great blessing of water." The action of the Spirit on the waters also restores the universe.[15]

(d) The Spirit and the Birth of the New Humanity

Humanity stands at the centre of creation. The renewal of creation by the Spirit includes a regeneration of human beings; that regeneration is the start of a new humanity made in the image of Christ and incorporated in Christ.

Jesus told Nicodemus that it was necessary to be born again, and that this new birth would be the work of the Spirit (John 3:5, 6, 8). In his letters from prison, Paul sets out the central message of the gospel, including Christ and the Spirit in his scheme and insisting on the centrality of humankind. The Pauline message proclaims the coming of a new humanity incorporated in Christ and reconciled in him thanks to the action of the Holy Spirit, who is the creator of this new humanity (cf Eph. 2:15–18; 4:23).

Jesus himself was seen by early tradition as the first-fruits of this new creation and new humanity. The infancy narratives in the Gospels show the beginning of a new creation, a new genesis of humanity. Jesus' entry into the world marked the inauguration of the new humanity by God. To this end, the Spirit was sent to Mary.[16] The Creator Spirit was also present at Jesus' baptism to usher in the messianic era. So it is not surprising that Pentecost has to be understood as a new stage in this new creation of humankind.[17] Vatican II also taught that human beings are "redeemed by Christ and made new creatures in the Holy Spirit" (GS 37d).

The Eastern church faithfully preserves the teaching of the Greek Fathers on men and women as the image of God. They taught that they are this image of God through the breath of the Spirit in creation (cf Gen. 2:7). The Spirit alone was capable of elevating humankind above its natural condition and so making it the image of God. The continual restoration of this image of God in humanity is the work of the Spirit.

(e) The Spirit in the Midst of the Nations

The new creation of a new humanity summons all the nations of the world. Pentecost represents this calling. The nations do not lose their identity: each speaks in its own language; the new humanity does not lose its diversity through being unified in Christ. The Spirit does not oblige the nations all to wear the same clothing.[18]

The calling of the nations was Paul's most characteristic proclamation. His originality lies precisely in this. He carried the principle of the call being to all nations to extreme consequences: even to his break with Judaism, so with his own people, his own religion, his own culture. All the nations become part of Christ with equal rights; if Judaism had historical privileges, these privileges now become obstacles (cf Eph. 2:15–18; Rom. 9–11).

The Book of Revelation shows a community completely adapted to the Pauline message. The Jews are now outside, and feature only as a representative type of the world opposed to Christ. The Lamb that seemed to have been sacrificed had seven horns and seven eyes, "which are the seven Spirits God has sent out all over the world" (Rev. 5:6). The hymn to the Lamb tells that with its blood it "bought men for God of every race, language, people and nation" (5:9; cf 7:9).

The Acts of the Apostles show the road to universality: from Jerusalem to Rome, the centre of the world. "Nations" formed the political, social, economic and cultural reality of the time. The calling of nations included a call to the totality of what made up the social framework of humanity. The message of salvation was not addressed to isolated individuals, but to human collectivities and communities. Individuals are reached through their relationship to the collectivity. The Spirit is sent to the social entities of this world.

Vatican II provided some pointers to the actions of the Spirit in the world. Though not fully worked out, they serve as a starting-point for the task of working out a new doctrine of the Spirit for the third millennium of Christianity. *Gaudium et Spes* speaks of "the Spirit of the Lord, who fills the earth" (11a). This means that the Spirit is present in all human societies as a spur to point them in the direction of accepting liberation.

While Latin theology of the second millennium discerned the Spirit only in the church, Vatican II broadened its horizons and discerned the actions of the Spirit in the world and in temporal activities. "Christ is now at work in the hearts of men through the energy of his Spirit. He arouses not only a desire for the age to come, but, by that very fact, he animates, purifies and strengthens those noble longings too by which the human family strives to make its life more human and to render the whole earth submissive to this goal" (GS 38c). The Council is here giving recognition to the presence of the Spirit not only in movements for social and political change, but also in the economic advances brought about by science, technology and labour, since "man is constantly worked upon by God's Spirit" (GS 41b).

Puebla took up a characteristic phrase from *Gaudium et Spes* (11 and 41) and applied it to the pre-conquest cultures of Latin America: "The Spirit, who filled the whole earth, was also present in all that was good in pre-Colombian cultures. That very Spirit helped them to accept the Gospel." And it goes on to make the following important point: "And today the Spirit continues to arouse yearnings for liberative salvation in our peoples" (no. 201).[19] If the church had said that two hundred years ago, at the dawn of the French Revolution, there might possibly be no problem of atheism today. Unfortunately, at that time the church was saying precisely the opposite.

This last point contains the essence of what we are saying in this section: that the present liberation movements in Latin America are inspired by the Spirit. Creation is not passive, inert, static; it is in movement. Humanity is longing for a liberation, moving toward a new humanity. The Holy Spirit is present and active in this whole process of movement.

(f) The Maternity of the Spirit

We shall return to the question of the femininity of the Holy Spirit in the last chapter, dealing with the Spirit in intra-trinitarian relationships. But the femininity of the Spirit is also significant here in our consideration of the role of the Spirit in the world.

The feminine character of the Holy Spirit was developed by Judeo-Christianity and Syriac Christianity. This fact is of course related to the fact that in Hebrew and Syriac the word for "spirit" is feminine.[20] Several writers compared the Spirit to Eve to complement the comparison of Christ to Adam. As Eve, the Spirit gives life and plays a maternal role.[21] Some would say that the woman in Revelation 11 is the Holy Spirit.[22] The Spirit would thereby be associated with the church. The maternity of the Spirit, however, extends beyond the church; as the new Eve, it embraces the whole of humanity.

If the Holy Spirit is the maternal being who embraces the

whole of humanity, giving it life and leading it toward its liberation, then we should accept that this role was conferred, though confusedly, in the religions that worshipped a universal mother goddess. The difference in Christianity is that God is not sexed: none of the divine Persons has a sex, neither the Father, nor the Son, nor the Holy Spirit. But in their action in humanity and the world, each Person is manifested under names borrowed from the sexes: the names of Father and Son are sexed. An old Christian tradition held that the Spirit too proceeded in a manner that required "sexed" names: those of mother and woman. In the Greek and Latin traditions, however, this idea fell into disuse, largely because the word for "spirit" is neuter in Greek and masculine in Latin, but also because of the *machismo* prevailing in Greco-Roman culture.

Maternal divinities provided a prefiguration, though confused and erroneous, of the Holy Spirit. In Latin America the most obvious example is the "Pachamamma" of the peoples of the high plains of what are now Peru and Bolivia, who made up the former Inca empire.[23] Instead of purely and simply rejecting this cult, so important to the religion and culture of the indigenous peoples, we could see it as a providential preparation for experience of the Holy Spirit. The missionaries did not do so, partly because they were committed to the total eradication of Amerindian religions, partly because they themselves were ignorant of the theological tradition of the Holy Spirit as a maternal figure.[24] Nor did Puebla go as far, but we trust that the next regional conference of Latin American bishops, to be held at Santo Domingo in 1992, will manage to deal positively with the religious traditions of the Amerindians.

In Catholic tradition, both Western and Eastern, the cult of the Virgin Mary took the place of the cult of the Holy Spirit. The maternity of God took visible form in Mary, but Mary is still a creature. Her spiritual motherhood is not enough; it does not reach into the very being of God. She is never other than below God, even in the exaggerations of popular devotion. Mary compensated for the lack of a theology of the Holy Spirit that would express the motherhood of God, but this was not enough.[25] She could not prevent the imbalance of having an exclusively masculine image of God, which gave Christianity—

and Islam—the historical shape of a religion of domination, authority and order, with no compensating feminine features.

2. THE SPIRIT IN HISTORY

Speaking of development in the social and economic orders, Vatican II said that "God's Spirit, who with a marvellous providence directs the unfolding of time and renews the face of the earth, is not absent from this development" (GS 26e). The same Spirit who guides history also helps us to interpret it: "With the help of the Holy Spirit, it is the task of the entire People of God... to hear, distinguish, and interpret the many voices of our age" (GS 44d).

It is worth looking into the way the Holy Spirit guides history. Theology has paid little attention to history, the place in which the action of the Spirit is carried out. Despite this, Christians have always tried to make sense of it and to discern the directions in which the Holy Spirit wants the church and the world to move. What was lacking was the theology behind this endeavour; theology tended to favour the Greek notion that history is not a proper object of study since there is nothing rational about it. The scholastics could not understand history, and St Thomas wrote his whole summa of theology with scarcely a mention of the history of his time.[26]

There is no space here for an exhaustive study of such a new subject. Let us concentrate on just four aspects: the meaning of poverty in the history of the Spirit, the question of the spiritual messianism represented by Joachim of Flora and his disciples, the dialectical route suggested by St Paul in his discussion of Jews and pagans, and finally the theme of reform as return to sources and its relevance to world history.

(a) The Spirit and the Poor

Poverty has always been a challenge to the church, and voluntary poverty has always been there as a response to this challenge. The call to poverty goes back to the origins of the Old Testament; it extends from the condition of slaves of the children of Israel in Egypt, from the poverty they suffered in the desert, from the formulation of the prophetic ideology of a return to the desert as the place where poverty and fidelity were indissolubly linked. The later Old Testament prophets developed the themes of the poor of Yahweh,[27] the rest of the poor, the poor hidden from Yahweh.

From the beginning, Jesus' disciples sought to draw conclusions from his poverty—a double poverty, of birth and free choice. They pondered Jesus' sayings on riches and the need to be poor to be saved. St Paul witnesses to the oldest and truly universal Christian tradition: you cannot serve two masters. There are two rival and incompatible powers in the world: the power of the flesh and the power of the Spirit. Christians must trust solely in the power of the Spirit and renounce the power of the flesh. God chose the weakest in whom to make God's power, the power of the Spirit, show forth.[28]

This message, so clear in the Bible, is first and foremost a call to the church. It is also the revelation of how God acts in history. God acts in this way in the church because God acts in this way in history; there is not one law for the church and another for history. And the Spirit works in history by means of poverty.

The problem of poverty in history arose at a high point of Western civilization, and the way it was posed then has left lessons valid today, as well as questions still unanswered today. Reflection on the Spirit and poverty in history could take the "spiritual" movement of the poor from the twelfth to fourteenth centuries as a precedent for the movement of the poor in present-day Latin America. To pursue this would go beyond the limits of this book, but any young theologians looking for doctoral theses could do worse....

The question of the Spirit acting through the poor was posed by several movements in the twelfth century, of which the most important was the Waldensian.[29] The Waldenses were condemned as heretics for denying the institutional structure of the church, but this condemnation was really a cover for suppressing the movement because of its virtually revolutionary potential. In the Middle Ages, movements of spiritual poverty, invoking the inspiration of the Spirit and attributing the call to the poor to the Spirit, always went closely in hand with popular political movements. When the poor came together and proclaimed themselves directed by the Holy Spirit, they were challenging the social order, based as it was on the privileges of the nobility with the emperor at their head, and those of the clergy with the pope at their head: poor lay people had to work and obey!

The movement that posed the greatest challenge—to the empire as well as to the pope and the clergy—was the Franciscan Order.[30] St Francis was for his followers both a poor man par excellence and a man of the Spirit.[31] He ushered in a new type of human being and a new model of human society. On his own, St Francis would not have constituted a political force, but his message was taken up by thousands of disciples who, deliberately or otherwise, made it into a force that shook the whole structure of society.

For the Franciscan "Spirituals" the Holy Spirit was visibly at work in Christendom, working through the poor. Hence their struggle for the authenticity of Franciscan poverty, and hence Rome's intransigence in mitigating and finally condemning the Spirituals' interpretation of Franciscan poverty.[32] Spiritual poverty[33] threatened not only the church but the whole of society. The pope saw that it contained the threat of a break between a spiritual church and a bodily church, the church as it existed.[34] The new spiritual church would define the whole structure of society differently; it would not accept that the world should be governed by a power that called itself "spiritual." It would emancipate the world from the tutelage of priestly power; it would mean a revolution—three hundred years before that of the Saints in England.[35]

The political consequences of the Spiritual movement became apparent in the fourteenth century. Historians have shown the clear influence of the movement on the uprising led by Cola di Rienzo in Rome, which deposed the pope from his temporal power and set up a republic—which in practice was a dictatorship of the people.[36] His uprising was helped by the fact that the popes had taken refuge in Avignon, but he was eventually deposed by a coalition of the powers he had challenged.

At that time, messianic ideas pervaded all movements

concerned with poverty, the Spirit and history. There is a latent messianism running through the whole course of Christianity. The ideas of Joachim of Flora on the age of the Spirit fermented and inspired all movements to poverty. This messianism prevented, or at least hindered, political thinking, and this lack of political thinking hindered, at the time, a clear understanding of what the poor could achieve in history, and so of what the Holy Spirit can achieve through the poor.

Political thinking was virtually impossible at that time. Politics was dominated by political monotheism, which involved power being seen as sacred, that of the emperor and kings as much as that of the pope. A theology of the Holy Spirit was developed in opposition to this theology of empire, but the problem was a political one, not a theological one. Theological controversy led nowhere at the time, though it did gradually help to inform the development of true political thinking. But this did not make its appearance till the seventeenth century, first in England and then in New England and France. It was not till then that the people—lay people, the unprivileged—began to understand that they had a political purpose of their own.

When this concept of the political power of the people made its appearance, theology had forgotten both history and the Holy Spirit. It made no connection between the democratic revolutions and the advent of the Spirit in history through the poor. The question had been posed virtually complete in the twelfth century, but is still waiting for an answer.

The Holy Spirit acts through the poor in history. When the poor succeed in becoming agents in history, then the Spirit of God is at work. Contrary to the view prevailing in the age of political monotheism,[37] the Holy Spirit does not act in history through the emperor alone, or through the elite classes. Both are subject to criteria of discernment; they can produce effects that benefit the people, but not necessarily through being permanently in power. In the same way the temporal power of the popes may have been beneficial to the people in some ways, such as in their struggle against the absolute power of the emperor and against attempts to copy a Byzantine political structure in the West. But the attribution of political power to the popes, let alone the sort of imperial power enjoyed by a line of popes culminating in Boniface VII, does not in itself indicate a direction taken by the Spirit. On the contrary, the poor have a special privilege in the political direction of the world: in this sense the achievement of so-called "democracy" can have spiritual value. But this does not mean that the poor on their own have an exclusive vocation to politics. This would be falling into a sort of messianism, distracting from the historical "necessity" to make the Spirit the sole guide of history.

(b) The Spirit and Political Messianism

Christianity took shape in a messianic environment, filled with apocalyptic as well as political hopes. It arose in circles formed by apocalyptic writings,[38] in which people expected the coming of the kingdom of God and the age of the Holy Spirit. The New Testament is full of references to such expectations. Messianism has never been completely absent from the history of Christianity; all ages have produced religious movements which renewed the hopes of the first decades. Today such hopes are more alive than ever, with a plethora of religious groups announcing the end of the world, the coming of the Messiah, the coming of the kingdom of God. Some of these movements see the end of the world as the entry into the messianic kingdom; others proclaim an earthly kingdom. Here, "messianic" means those movements that proclaim the marvellous coming of God's kingdom on earth through supernatural means, through the power of the Spirit rather than by natural forces.

The New Testament makes a clear distinction between the coming of the Spirit and the fulness of the kingdom of God. All its writings put forward basically the same teaching on the subject. Neither Luke nor John says that the Spirit cancels or takes the place of the last coming of the Messiah. The Holy Spirit is given for this period of trial and persecution before the final coming of the kingdom. Paul had to combat those enthusiasts who thought that all was now consummated with the gifts they had received from the Spirit. We are, he says, in the age of the Spirit, but this age still contains all the trials provided by history. The Holy Spirit does not suppress history and all its requirements. In the age of the Spirit we still know alienation, material needs, domination by some over others. We must not think that the Spirit is going to do away with all this, not till the final coming of Christ and the kingdom of God. "From the beginning till now the entire creation, as we know, has been groaning in one great act of giving birth; and not only creation, but all of us who possess the first-fruits of the Spirit, we too groan inwardly as we wait for our bodies to be set free" (Rom. 8:22–3).

We possess only the "first-fruits of the Spirit," and in the time of these first-fruits history marches on. Sociologists and historians can tell us that the same old forces are still at work; they cannot discern the presence of the Spirit with any certainty. Sure discernment and perception of the workings of the Spirit are possible only to those who experience participation in the Spirit.

The tension between present experience and future hope, so characteristic of St Paul,[39] began to slacken with the conversion of Constantine and the creation of an imperial theology. Byzantine, Russian and Eastern theology were deeply influenced by this imperial theology. The East developed a vision of the world transfigured and glorified by the Spirit. Faith in the resurrection and the primacy of the Spirit produced a concept of redemption already fulfilled.[40] This led to the disinclination of Christians to take part in social and political action. If the world has already been spiritualized, what matters is to live contemplating the presence of the Spirit in it. Some would explain the virulence of contemporary Russian atheism as a reaction against this purely contemplative stance of Eastern Christianity.

In the West, the Romano-Germanic empire also had its imperial theology and imperial theologians,[41] but their views did not prevail. What prevailed was a perception of the non-presence of the Spirit, which left a wide-open space for the rise of messianic movements proclaiming the imminent arrival of the age of the Spirit. This is why Joachim of Flora's messianic ideas were so influential in the movements to poverty. In official Catholic teaching, the Holy Spirit had already been sent to the church and was wholly in the church. There was nothing further to hope for other than the grace of the Spirit poured out in the sacraments through the channels of the ecclesiastical institution. The movements of poverty were not content with such limitations, but did not know how to express their hopes coherently. They came to believe that the history in which they were living would be supplanted by another history. A different history would begin under the guidance of the Holy Spirit, operating on a very different plane from that on which history had been operating till then. Messianic illusions carried many movements over the threshold of historical realism.

The question was this: is it right to hope for the coming of a new era in history that would be the resolution of existing conflicts, the final overcoming of all alienation, all domination, all necessity? Is it right to hope for the coming of an age of freedom exempt from all necessity in this world? The answer is that nothing in the sources of Christianity allows us to entertain such hopes.

Despite this, such hopes never completely disappeared from Western Christianity after the Middle Ages and gave rise to innumerable revolutionary movements.[42] Hegel's theology included the proclamation of an age of reconciliation in which all antitheses would be resolved. Marxism inherited this temporal messianism from Hegel, and also proclaims the end of dialectic.[43] What Christianity questions in this is not the dialectic of history but the end of dialectic.[44] The problem is not the class struggle but the end of the class struggle.[45]

The Spirit was given in history and will be active in history till the end of history. There will be no reign of the Spirit outside history or beyond the history of this world. Because of this, the Spirit will always be in tension and conflict within history. The conflict between human beings and nature, between freedom and necessity, between opposing groups of people, will go on and begin anew with each new generation. The Spirit will promote constant renewal of the struggle. There is no stable state beyond struggle on this earth.

(c) The Dialectic of History

St Paul put forward a dialectic law for the history of salvation, the dialectic of Jews and pagans. It could be argued that all the dialectics of modern history follow directly or indirectly from St Paul. His argument is, in any case, illuminating for understanding the history of our own times.[46] It could be applied to the history of the church, but Paul saw it as having universal application, since his theology treats Jews and pagans as categories of universal history, not confined to the church.

His dialectic brings two expressions together in opposition: Jews and pagans. The pagans live in sin, the Jews under the Law; the pagans have no law and the Jews have a Law; the pagans reject the Jews and the Jews reject the pagans; and so forth.[47] Till the coming of Jesus and the Holy Spirit, Jews and pagans lived in opposition to one another; now, through the Holy Spirit, Jesus has brought about a reconciliation between Jews and pagans. The Jews have not made concessions to the pagans, nor the pagans to the Jews, but both categories have been subsumed into a third expression, the new humanity. In this new humanity, Jews and pagans are reconciled in unity.

This doctrine of reconciliation, put forward in Ephesians and Colossians,[48] seems to be teaching that reconciliation has already been achieved. In fact, Paul is not saying that everything is complete; he is talking of a movement in which humanity is taking part. Romans 9–11 shows that the Jews will be with us to the end of time; there will always be Jews opposing pagans. The church and the people of God will be incomplete and in process of reconciliation till the end of time. Reconciliation is a lasting challenge.

The dialectic of pagans and Jews has wider implications than the antagonism between two sociologically defined peoples, because "Jew" and "pagan" are used as universal categories. Origen was the first to apply the same dialectic within the Christian world: in a society that calls itself Christian, there are still Jews and still pagans, and the antagonism between them is still there, since Christians carry both the Jew and the pagan within themselves.[49] Origen applied the dialectic to the inner lives of Christians. Today, theologians show that the same dialectic can be applied to categories of contemporary Christianity, and to antagonistic tendencies in the world outside Christianity.[50] So the Spirit who brings reconciliation between Jews and pagans still has much work to do in this world.

Societies exist in a state of tension, between the structural rigidity of Judaism and the relaxation and permissiveness of paganism. They fail to achieve a stable balance between the two. A period in which one is dominant is succeeded by one in which the other predominates. Balance requires continual and immense effort. History oscillates, though with high points at which balance seems to have been achieved. But this balance is always threatened, either by forces external to a society or by inner conflicts, and the struggle for reconciliation in the Spirit is a permanent process.

(d) The Spirit and Reform

The theme of reform dates from Christian society of the Middle Ages. For centuries the people cried and pleaded for a reform of Christian society. In the sixteenth century religious leaders appeared who became known as Reformers. Many broke away from the Roman Church and founded what became known as Reformed churches. Yet the Council of Trent was conceived as a Council for the reform of the church and its decrees were designed to "reform" the Catholic Church; reform is not exclusive to Protestantism.

Historically, the term "Reformation" is applied above all to the events of the sixteenth century. But this is not an exclusive application: the Protestant Reformers themselves declared that the church was permanently in need of reform: *Ecclesia reformata semper reformanda*. Today, various Protestant theologians have pointed to the need for a "new Reformation."[51]

It is the role of the Holy Spirit to promote reform in the church. Vatican II declared: "By the power of the gospel, he makes the church grow, perpetually renews her" (LG 4b); that, strengthened by God's grace, the church, "moved by the Holy Spirit,...may never cease to renew herself" (LG 9h). The objectives of this reform are a return to the gospel on one hand, and a willingness to learn from the experience of history on the other: "The church also realizes that in working out her relationship with the world she always has great need of the ripening which comes with the experience of the centuries" (GS 43k). "Christ summons the church, as she goes her pilgrim way, to that continual reformation of which she always has need" (UR 6b).

This vision of continual reformation counterbalances the impression of constant progress given by triumphalist modern ecclesiology. This held that each new step in history taken by the church was a step forward. It respresented the institutional church as an ever more perfect structure. Each new canon law, each new doctrinal concept, each new moral precept, each new liturgical innovation, had to be a new step forward. History had to be an ever upwards march. The concept of reform, however, recognizes that there has been corruption, decadence, falling-away. A reformation supposes that many now superfluous or harmful historical accretions will be abandoned. The history of Christianity is not an unbroken straight line, but more like a spiral. It is always in need of re-simplifying, going back to its origins, ridding itself of the excessive superstructure it has acquired through history.

The idea of reform is not applicable to the church alone. In countries such as Mexico or Guatemala, the term "reform" has come to mean revolution. Revolutions too contain an element of return to what is seen as a better past; the modern idea of irreversible progress has to be abandoned. It is in fact a myth promulgated by the ruling elites of this world. Today we are becoming progressively more convinced that the simpler civili-zations of the past, and the present, contain elements that need to be reconsidered and recaptured. Reformation in the Spirit extends to the whole of society.

To sum up: the Spirit acts in history. Its action cannot be perceived by an ordinary observer looking in on its actions from outside, nor by historians. We can know its action in history to a certain extent from its action in the church.

With regard to the establishing of a new world within the old world, we should realize that this new world cannot easily be described in categories belonging to the old one. Nevertheless, Paul's dialectic of Jews and pagans and movements of reform and messianism are useful pointers to interpreting the world as a movement of the whole of humanity with its nations and its civilizations.

3. THE ACTION OF THE SPIRIT IN THE WORLD

The action of the Holy Spirit on humanity and through the new humanity is at once simple and complex. It can be avoided through five key concepts, those applied to the base communities in chapter 1, concepts that everyone knows but which are neglected by the social sciences, which do not know how to deal with them. The Holy Spirit produces freedom, speech, action, community and life. Of course the realities suggested by these words existed in some form before Christianity. The Spirit has in fact been active in all peoples since the dawn of humanity. But these realities are nevertheless the proper fruits of the Spirit, and they are not so common in the life of the world. They represent five aspects of the human calling, since what the Spirit produces is also what men and women are called on to produce. There is no separation between what the Spirit does and what human beings do, despite the fact that far from everything that they do proceeds from the Spirit—very much to the contrary.

(a) The Spirit and Freedom

Vatican II reintroduced the subject of the Holy Spirit; it was also the Council that dared to tackle the question of freedom, ignored for two hundred years, or ever since the Middle Ages. The Council, however, failed to unite Spirit and freedom through its lack of a true theology of the Spirit and a true theology of freedom. Both subjects were new to the Council Fathers and they were unprepared to treat them systematically.

As Vatican II said: "Never before today has man been so keenly aware of freedom" (GS 4d). Is this awareness one of the fruits of the Spirit, or a sign of the distance that separates the desires of contemporary society from the world as it is? And do Christians and non-Christians attach the same meaning to the word "freedom"? The freedom experienced in Christian communities today forces our attention on the good news of freedom as preached by St Paul, though this news is not exclusive to him; the whole New Testament proclaims the coming of a new age for humanity. Paul, however, gives expression to consciousness of the coming of a freedom that is

something radically new in both its conception and its realization.

How far does the consciousness of freedom experienced by
the Christian communities in their liberation struggles coincide
with Christian memory of the past and biblical roots? In what
does it differ from these? Those who take part in these struggles
are the ones to judge, but we can suggest material to reflect on.

There is still, especially in the Roman Catholic Church, an
inadequate perception of what Christian freedom means.
Vatican II took a few steps towards this—steps that were
enough to frighten the minority who were in control in Rome
at the time, and their successors, but not enough to respond to
the longings in the world after two thousand years of Christianity. Nor is the recent Vatican *Instruction on Christian Freedom
and Liberation* an adequate response, though it does represent
an advance on earlier pronouncements.[52]

By Christian freedom we do not of course mean people's
freedom to do exactly as they please, a commonly held notion.
Nor can Christian freedom be reduced to the idea of free will
as used in traditional moral theology. This concept of free will
expresses the conviction that individuals are responsible morally and juridically for their actions. It has been much attacked
by modern social sciences, but despite their criticisms still holds
as an expression of human responsibility. But it has little to do
with the biblical concept of freedom, which is not very
interested in this approach.

A first and basic meaning of Christian freedom is that found
in the illustrations put forward in Pauline theology.[53] Freedom
is the capacity to act on the level of the new humanity, to act
in a fully human way, overcoming the resistance that comes to
humanity through sin. It is a freedom from sin, from death and
the fear of death, from the devil, from the flesh and the desires
of the flesh. All these keep humanity in a many-sided slavery,
a slavery rooted in human beings themselves. Basic freedom is
what sets human beings free from what they find in themselves.
Hence the deep consciousness of freedom experienced by
Christians in even the worst external conditions, especially in
situations that call for martyrdom: in prison, under persecution,

surrounded by the adversities and obstacles placed in their way by nature and their fellow human beings. The Apostle Paul was himself a living example of this Christian freedom.

"Where the Spirit of the Lord is, there is freedom" (2 Cor. 3:17). This freedom applies also and indeed above all to the religious sphere and our relationship with God. The Old Law was a religious system built on fear of the Lord, on constraint, on observance. It was not a spontaneous movement toward God. Life under it was an imposed life. But the new life is a life that wells up from within human beings themselves; its source is internal to them, not external. The Spirit guides the new humanity from within, replacing obedience with spontaneity. As St Augustine put it: *Ama et fac quod vis.*[54] The spontaneity of sons and daughters conquers the submission of slaves: "The spirit you have received is not the spirit of slaves bringing fear into your lives again; it is the spirit of sons, and it makes us cry out, 'Abba, Father!'" (Rom. 8:15); "We are the children, not of the slave-girl, but of the free-born wife" (Gal. 4:31).

This freedom is a gift of the Spirit, the effect of the Spirit's presence in men and women. But as a gift of the Spirit it is also a human work, since the property of the Spirit is not to act of itself but to tell creatures what to do, or to work through what they do. This is why the gift of freedom is also a calling; the gift of the Spirit is the call to be able and obliged to win freedom: "You were called... to freedom" (Gal. 5:13). Such freedom places Christians above any system of obligations and constraints, above any system based on fear and punishment. In particular, it places them above the Judaic system of law, and free from it: "When Christ freed us, he meant us to remain free. Stand firm, therefore, and do not submit again to the yoke of slavery" (Gal. 5:1).

If this principle were taken to its most radical expression, no system of laws and obligations, no system of repression and of course no system based on domination and poverty could stand. Such freedom would be the reign of spontaneity and abundance, the realization of the dreams behind modern revolutions. Freedom, however, exists in the form of a calling, not yet in the form of complete realization. As long as it remains a call, incomplete, it will have to co-exist with the reign of necessity and with social systems based on constraint and domination. The newness of Christians consists in that, being free, they nevertheless accept other necessary systems out of solidarity with an imperfect world, though they themselves are not motivated by these systems. They act out of freedom and not out of constraint.[55] The world, therefore, can move in the direction of the reign of freedom only to the extent that men and women of the Spirit steer it in this direction.

Pauline freedom is not opposed to community in any way. On the contrary, freedom is expressed through adherence to the community. Being free does not mean acting on one's own, for oneself or on one's own account. Being free means collaborating in a community. Since new men and women act in community, they form a unity in Christ: "Be careful, or this liberty will prove an opening for self-indulgence. Serve one another, rather, in works of love" (Gal. 5:13).

There is a second form of freedom associated with the Spirit which underlies all that the Bible has to say on the Spirit and freedom.[56] It also underlies Vatican II's Declaration on Religious Freedom. This invokes the dignity of the human person, the example of Christ and the freedom of the act of faith as reasons for religious freedom, without linking these to the Holy Spirit, who is their ultimate foundation. The Spirit is the power that acts through appeal, through attraction, not through constraint: through maternal, not paternal authority. God acts among human beings as a mother; the direction of the whole of human history demonstrates the motherhood of the Spirit. We are free to sin. Without this freedom, there would be no freedom of the spirit. Of all the Council documents, the Declaration on Religious Freedom is the one that will have the most lasting effects on pastoral work and indeed on the future of humanity. It was the most discussed and the one that met with most resistance. It forces the churches of the West to make a radical change in the way they have behaved for fifteen hundred years, when they neither respected freedom nor believed in it. The Roman Catholic Church in particular has preached precisely the reverse.

In the East, the churches have remained far more faithful to the gospel. They have always understood morality as a call to a change of life, they have had a flexible and even vague canon law, and they have not systematically sought the help of the secular arm to make their baptized comply with their legal and moral code. They have let their people sin.[57] Does this mean Eastern Christians have sinned more than Western ones?

In the West, the churches in general and the Roman Church in particular have promoted three systems for dominating people's consciences so as to deprive them effectively of the freedom to sin: an inflexible moral code with severe punishments and sanctions, a canon law that allows no room for sinners, and permanent recourse to the civil power to compel all the baptized and even all the inhabitants of countries where the majority are nominally Christian to comply rigidly with moral and canonical laws.[58] The effects make up half the history of the Western world. For centuries sin was forced into clandestinity. Has this produced any less of it?

The banner of freedom has been raised against the church since the Middle Ages. During this time the church has come to stand as a symbol of the forces opposed to freedom. For hundreds of years the banner was carried only by the educated few; now, in the twentieth century, the mass of the people have taken it up. The banner of liberation was raised in the Third World twenty years ago. Will this banner too be raised *against* the church? The cards are not yet down, but there is a danger that the church will approach the liberation of the Third World in the same way as it treated the freedom of the Western world.

We need discernment in judging the freedom movements of the modern world. The church has so far condemned them in the name of the moral and social order. Its theology does not recognize freedom to sin: St Augustine did not accept it, St Thomas rejected it, and with their theology dominating in official circles, the church failed to see what was happening.[59] Of course modern freedom movements have their bad aspects that cannot be reconciled with the message of the Spirit. But each aspect has to be judged for what it is and approached with sympathy. Modern freedoms have, for example, produced the world-wide phenomenon of individualism.[60] Individualism means capitalism in economics, nationalism in politics, individual autonomy in culture, science and art, competition as the universal law of living together, self-affirmation. Commentators on the twentieth century have already said enough about the evils that derive from modern individualism, which tends to produce a sterile affirmation of the rights of the individual, rejecting all solidarity and all continuity, and exhausting itself in a vain quest for isolated human value. In this struggle between isolated individuals, the strong crush the weak.

Yet, on the other hand, the same movement has produced the emancipation of dominated peoples, the struggle for class liberation, for the liberation of nations, of women, of oppressed races, struggles for human rights and for democracy. The Holy Spirit has not been recognized as being at work in this last series of actions. Can it really have been absent from all that? If the Spirit guides history, as Vatican II said it does, must it not have been active in modern times and their liberation struggles?

It is difficult to separate the good from the bad. Theoretically easy, but history refuses to conform to theoretical schemes. Traditional theologians seem to fear sin more than they fear God. They think they have to save the world, and succeed only in building up such a wave of resentment and rage against the church as has never been seen before. A paternalistic church has forgotten the motherhood of the Holy Spirit.

(b) The Spirit and Speech

Human beings speak. They were created in this way so as to give names to things and tell these to others. In the beginning human beings received a power of speech that now has to do with the Spirit. Yet not all speech comes from the Spirit; not all words indicate the Spirit. The coming of the Spirit brings new words which proceed directly from it.

The most basic of these is the cry that rises up from the oppressed poor. This cry has a long history in the Old Testament, and it sounded out once again from Jesus on the cross. Jesus identified himself with all the oppressed and on the cross gave vent to the same cry, which is at once one of fear of death and one of faith and confidence in the final triumph of life.[61] With Jesus' resurrection, the cry of the oppressed became a shout of triumph, and confidence overcame fear. St Paul shows the Spirit behind the cry of the poor of the world who make up the new people of God, the new humanity.

The cry was taken up and elaborated on by the prophets. All the prophets did was to give expression to the voice of the poor in the midst of the corruption of an Israel being false to its calling by relying on riches and the power of the mighty.[62] For purely circumstantial reasons, the voice of the prophets was not attributed to the Spirit before the Exile. Later, however, the obvious was acknowledged. Like the cry of the poor, the voice of the prophets comes from the Holy Spirit.[63] After Jesus' resurrection, once the cry and clamour of the poor had become a shout of victory, the people began to proclaim this victory. The cry became good news, proclamation, witness. The poor not only spoke, but challenged the world with their shout of victory. This is the gospel.

In human history, the gospel (preaching, proclamation, witness) means the words of the poor reaching the world. In all cultures, civilizations and nations, those who speak are the educated, the elite, the wise, the officials, the priests, the initiated; not the poor. But this time, with the gospel, the Spirit makes the words of the poor resound through the world. We need to get rid of the presumption of the formalism and formulations in which the vocabulary relating to the word of God and the gospel has been wrapped up for centuries. Such words end by covering over hateful things. The poor are now enabling us to rediscover the newness these words originally possessed.

The poor speak in public, and say different things. They speak not to confirm or consolidate the established system, nor to justify or explain it. They speak to announce something new, speaking out before tribunals and authorities. Such was and is the miracle of the Holy Spirit. St Luke describes the poor speaking like this symbolically in his account of Pentecost: all these uncultured persons spoke all the languages of the world.[64] Later the Twelve were to appear before the Sanhedrin, and they spoke out openly, bodly: "They were astonished at the assurance shown by Peter and John, considering they were uneducated laymen" (Acts 4:13).

In Pauline theology also the power of the Spirit is prominently shown in speech. The weaker and less eloquent the speaker, the stronger the word of the gospel. It is a poor word because it comes from the poor, but it is a word that can count on the power of the Spirit, because what it says is new and it revolutionizes those who hear it: "In my speeches and the sermons that I gave, there were none of the arguments that belong to philosophy; only a demonstration of the power of the Spirit" (1 Cor. 2:4).[65] In John's theology too, the Spirit produces speech.[66] Jesus is the Word: he gives witness, lives the word of the Father. This word reaches us through the Spirit; without the mediation of the Spirit the Word would say nothing.

It is a fact that during the first centuries the gospel was handed on by the poor. There was no special missionary body, no planned mission, no worked-out missionary teaching. The poor spoke to their friends and acquaintances. The pagan philosopher Celsus was scandalized: what could a religion preached by slaves, servant girls, ignorant, unlettered foreigners be worth? Origen's reply was to show the power of the Spirit: this was God's sign that the poor were victorious; they were peacefully conquering the world through their illiterate speech.[67]

The words of the poor speaking in the Spirit are effective. They created Christianity as a socio-historical and cultural event. They not only saved millions of people, but to some extent changed the face of the world, even if this change is still incipient and incomplete. A more learned theology can only accompany the historic action of their word through history, or its action on the level of eternal life, insofar as this is perceptible by us. We need only think of the power of the witness given by the martyrs. The Gospels associate the Spirit particularly with the witness of martyrdom, where the greatest weakness goes with the greatest strength.[68]

How far does the presence of the Spirit in words spoken in this world reach? How far does the gospel extend? When science or art succeeds in restoring health, improving the human condition, giving the humiliated back their dignity, and so on, is there nothing of the Spirit in them? The church watched the growth of science, or rather ignored it, as though it had nothing to do with its message. It heard the political messages of peoples in search of their liberation as though such discourses had nothing to do with the Spirit.

Gaudium et Spes says: "Whoever labours to penetrate the secrets of reality with a humble and steady mind, is, even unawares, being led by the hand of God" (GS 36c).

(c) The Spirit and Action

From the beginning, the Spirit has manifested itself as capacity for action, as a force producing actions. So it was the Spirit who raised up the judges who were the liberators of Israel, who raised up the kings Saul and David.[69] The Spirit's actions later became more specific, working through the prophets. In the Old Testament and even the earliest parts of the New, the Spirit does not yet appear as a person: it is a power, an energy.

The Spirit will be upon the servant of Yahweh: "I, Yahweh, have called you to serve the cause of right... I have appointed you as covenant of the people and light of the nations, to open the eyes of the blind, to free captives from prison, and those who live in darkness from the dungeon" (Isa. 42:6–7). Applied to Jesus at his baptism, the prophecy means that the work of the Spirit is to re-fashion the people of God. The Spirit raises up what was fallen, saves what was lost and rebuilds the people of God. The anointing of baptism consists in receiving the energy of the Spirit in order to carry out the work of justice entrusted to the servant of Yahweh.[70] Luke applies the prophecy of Isaiah 61:1–2 to Jesus:

The Spirit of the Lord has been given to me,
for he has anointed me.
He has sent me to bring good news to the poor,
to proclaim liberty to captives
and to the blind new sight,
to set the downtrodden free,
and to proclaim the Lord's year of favour! (Luke 4:18–19)

Jesus' anointing passed on to his disciples. They too were given the energy to work, since they saw Jesus' life as a work, a labour: "God has anointed him with the Holy Spirit and with power, and because God was with him, Jesus went about doing good and curing all who had fallen into the hands of the devil" (Acts 10:38). St Paul saw the danger in experiences of the Spirit being taken as purely for personal benefit, and the need to emphasize that the Spirit is a force for building. So the gifts of the Spirit that should be most highly prized are those that benefit the community: "The one with the gift of tongues talks for his own benefit, but the man who prophesies does so for the benefit of the community" (1 Cor. 14:4); "Since you aspire to spiritual gifts, concentrate on those which will grow to benefit the community" (1 Cor. 14:12).

Paul's own apostolic life was an extraordinary indication of the energy of the Holy Spirit.[71] What he achieved was to open up a way, bringing to pass what Jesus said: "Whoever believes in me will perform the same works as I do myself, he will perform even greater works" (John 14:12). This work of the Spirit is different from the way the world works. It is carried on without the resources employed by civilizations in building their great works; without the political power to mobilize masses of people like that wielded by the Pharaoh of old or modern Pharaohs; without the economic power to carry out huge public works; without the ideological power to move people through self-interest or collective enthusiasm. The Spirit's work is work of the poor, carried out by poor people, just as Paul carried out his mission without resources, without prestige, without power.

The works of the Spirit have no material grandeur: it does not produce the pyramids of Egypt or the towers of Babylon, but human realities, free people and free communities living in free association. The Spirit produces complete human beings.

Such works of the Spirit can be seen in the labours of missionaries and evangelizers. The whole vast continent of South America was evangelized by a few thousand missionaries, virtually without material means, filled with the energy of faith, that is with the energy of the Spirit. Unfortunately, since the church in Latin America is in a state of almost exclusive dependence on the Western church, Puebla was unable to produce a doctrine of the Holy Spirit. Otherwise it would have praised the labours of the missionaries as an example of the fantastic energies of the Spirit.

The Spirit does not act in the church or through the church alone. While the world produces works of self-aggrandisement that have nothing to do with the power of the Spirit, it also contains forces working to build up humanity and restore it: everything that works for salvation and liberation in the world is also inspired by the Holy Spirit. As Vatican II said: "The Holy Spirit... gives life to the People of God and... impel[s] all men to love God the Father as well as the world and mankind in him" (AA 29c).

(d) The Spirit and Community

The next chapter deals with the relationship between the Holy Spirit and the people of God or the church. But the action of the Spirit tends to form communities and peoples before the church and outside the boundaries of the church. The formation of communities is the proper work of the Spirit, the effect of freedom and of liberating speech.

The Spirit works to bring all people together: it comes down on all so as to involve all in a great charismatic community. This movement precedes the church and prepares the way for it. The phenomenon of Pentecost expresses this in two ways: first, by fulfilling the prophecy of Joel announcing the coming of the Spirit on all sons and daughters;[72] second, because the promise is extended to all nations through the intermediary of languages.[73] After this, Pentecost was renewed for the Samaritans and then for the pagans. According to St Luke, the expansion of the Spirit proclaims the onward march of the churches. Paul too saw the Spirit seeking out all nations so as to integrate them in the unity of Christ. This is the movement that gives rise to the great church (Eph. 2:11–22; 4:2–4).

The Spirit brings *agapē* and *agapē* is the force that generates communities and peoples. Our translation of *agapē* by the word "love" is deceptive, since love is more of a personal state than a community force. *Agapē* is the cohesion that binds members of a group together, active solidarity. It is the same as "service." Paul regards *agapē* as the greatest fruit of the Spirit, the greatest

gift to which we must aspire (1 Cor. 12:31–13:13). The fruits of
the Spirit are the same thing as *agapē* (Gal. 5:22–5); *agapē* is
what builds the community.

Communities are brought into being by people and mission.
Missionaries go out to meet people so as to offer them the
wellspring of life, which is communion in Christ through the
Spirit. Since the fourth or fifth century though, the type of
mission that has come from the Christian countries has taken
on the aspect of conquest, which it has still not lost. Even
Vatican II's Decree on the Church's Missionary Activity carries
overtones of conquest. Conquest may be effective in human
terms, but it does not proceed from the Spirit. The mission
envisaged in the Gospels and in St Paul was quite different, not
a matter of conquering, but of opening the gates of life. This is
the mission that is the work of the Spirit.[74] This generates a
communion of peoples in an overall community embracing the
whole of humanity. Mission precedes church and defines
Christian action before any ecclesial commitment.

Human beings made new in Christ live as missionaries, as
people sent to other, different people, open to other, different
people. They live not what they themselves are, but what others
are. This was how St Paul lived, not with his own life, a life
turned in on himself: "I live now not with my own life but with
the life of Christ who lives in me" (Gal. 2:20); "Life to me, of
course, is Christ" (Phil. 1:21). This means that Paul is caught
up into Christ's work, and this work is mission. Paul lived his
life entirely as a missionary, which means not one who comes
to conquer, but one who lives in others. *Agapē* produced the
same way of living in the following period when communities
had already been formed. Before community comes life as
service to community, life as projection or gift of oneself to
humanity. This is more important than the church itself because
it is what produces the church.

Modern Western civilization has destroyed, or is in the final
stages of destroying, all traditional forms of community. These
survive only in isolated groups, such as some indigenous tribes
in Latin America, or in fragmentary attempts to recapture
traditional ways of living, such as certain types of commune.
Does this mean that this destruction of old forms of community

living has been nothing but an assault on the Holy Spirit? Not necessarily: many communities were also obstacles to real emancipation of human beings, of their intelligence, rights and individual development. The conflict between individual rights and community rights underlies the great political problems of today. But one cannot condemn everything in the modern movement for individual emancipation from oppressive situations in family, clan, tribe, neighbourhood, religion, race, language or culture.

The old community life is now disappearing from those parts of the Third World that have been colonized by Western culture. In the West today, people live not for others but for themselves. Their most prized value is egoism. Mission has become incomprehensible, and disinterested solidarity is seen as madness. Under such conditions, the task of the Spirit is to rebuild community life. This means re-making community people, persons who live for others and not just for themselves. Such action by the Spirit would be a reversal of the dominant trend in modern civilization.

Many Christians have been deeply contaminated by the sacred value of egoism, the sole god of contemporary culture. So the actions of the Spirit can often be produced by less modernized non-Christians. Experience shows that the new communities are springing up among the poor; in rich circles they are virtually unthinkable, and they are difficult enough in middle-class circles.

(e) The Spirit and Life

Everything the Spirit brings about in this world converges on the one end, which is life—ever more life and an eternal life. Freedom brings life, speech brings life, action brings life, community brings life. All these mean more life and form the actual content of life.

In the first place, the Spirit brings bodily life, since the Spirit is in the body and produces bodily life. This is its first aim. Christianity absolutely rejects any separation into two worlds, that of the body and that of the spirit, characteristic of civilizations based on slavery and the division between so-called manual labour and intellectual work. The Spirit is the source of eternal life in the resurrection of the body. It is given now to the body as a pledge of resurrection: "If the Spirit of him who raised Jesus from the dead is living in you, then he who raised Jesus from the dead will give life to your own mortal bodies through his Spirit living in you" (Rom. 8:11).

This eternal life has already been given to us; we are now living the beginning of this resurrection. Life is lived at various levels of intensity: bodily life is a personal and not a purely animal life; the person is in his or her body, is the living body. Then this personal life is given a fresh impulse by the Spirit; the body produces effects through the Spirit which it could not produce without the Spirit. It is dynamized, charged with energy. Life becomes more worthy of the name of life.

This dynamized life, overflowing with energy, is called "faith." Scholastic theology destroyed this concept of faith and managed to devalue the word itself, making faith a purely intellectual act, which is little less than absurd. In the New Testament, faith is the spring of life that gives strength to the body itself, since people have faith with their bodies. It might be a suffering body, but through faith it lives and produces abundant fruit; without faith a person takes no risks, repeats the same gestures, goes through life but has no future, and, through lack of a future, wastes the present.[75]

True life is coming to knowledge of the reality of God, and understanding of God's plans and designs. The Spirit carries our understanding to these heights: "These are the very things that God has revealed to us through the Spirit, for the Spirit reaches the depths of everything, even the depths of God... [which] can only be known by the Spirit of God. Now instead of the spirit of the world, we have received the Spirit that comes from God" (1 Cor. 2:10–12). This life is the same thing as the joy that is its constant fruit: "The kingdom of God... means righteousness and peace and joy brought by the Holy Spirit" (Rom. 14:17). "It was with the joy of the Holy Spirit that you took to the gospel" (1 Thess. 1:6).

Rightly did the Creed of Constantinople confess: "I believe in the Holy Spirit, the Lord and Giver of life..." And Vatican II ended part 1 of *Gaudium et Spes* with this vision of the Spirit:

"Enlivened and united in his Spirit, we journey toward the consummation of human history, one which fully accords with the counsels of God's love: 'To re-establish all things in Christ, both those in the heavens and those on the earth' (Eph. 1:10)" (GS 45c).

CONCLUSION

The Holy Spirit is sent to the entire universe and since creation has been transforming it, carrying it toward the final resurrection. It is now a pledge of that resurrection. It has already introduced the leaven of the kingdom of God into the world. It is already ushering in a new creation, and human efforts to improve the world are not made without the impulse of the Spirit.

The same Spirit renews humanity: its action is equivalent to a new birth of new human beings making up a new humanity. This new humanity must move all nations, each in accordance with its diversity. The Spirit unites without imposing uniformity.

The word for "Spirit" is feminine in Hebrew, neuter in Greek, masculine in Latin and the languages derived from Latin. We should bear in mind the feminine character of the operations of the Spirit. Its actions can be compared to those of a mother, thereby counterbalancing the masculinizing and paternalist impression left on our minds by the words "Father" and "Son."

The Holy Spirit works in history, guiding it and changing it, though its actions may be hidden. The Spirit works through the poor and in the poor, who do not possess the instruments of power that are ready in the hands of the rich. Nevertheless the poor are effective in history. We cannot say that the Holy Spirit gave its all in the founding of the church; it can still produce, in history, the first steps to the liberation of the poor. It will not, in history, bring in the kingdom of the Messiah: there will not be a complete break between all the previous history of humankind and a new age which will be the pure kingdom of the Spirit. But humanity will be able to progress beyond the structures it has built up till now. Human struggles for liberation, in the past as well as at the present time, are not divorced from the Holy Spirit.

The Spirit struggles in history against two extreme poles already identified in the Bible: pagan and Jew, sin and the law that represses sin. Not all ages of Christianity are equal: far from it; each period has its own distinct marks. The Holy Spirit subjects itself to the same history that it changes without imposing constraints on it. History is not a continuous progress. The ideology of modern times, one of permanent progress, infected the churches themselves, which saw it as a justification of all their structures: each church was the most perfect possible because it was the product of history. Not so: the time for reform is at hand.

The more specific works of the Spirit in history are to bring freedom and give speech to the poor. With this gift of speech, the poor begin to act in the world. These same poor carry the hopes of new communities. In a society that has destroyed traditional forms of community, the Spirit encourages new forms of community, based not on oppression but on free participation. Through all these channels the Spirit brings life and leads history to life on this earth and in the land of the resurrected. All that the Spirit has done and is doing in the church is being done for the sake of this transformation of the world, through the liberation of the poor and the oppressed.

Chapter III
The Holy Spirit in the Church

The Holy Spirit was not sent to an already formed church; it was the sending of the Spirit that formed the church. The church exists because the Holy Spirit was sent to form it; the gift of the Spirit is the basis of its existence. So the church is neither before nor outside the Holy Spirit. There was first a sending of the Spirit to the whole of creation, to call it into being. The church arose and exists as part of this general mission.

This statement is important; it shows that the action of the Spirit is not determined by the action of the church. It is not for the church to tell where the Spirit blows. The reverse is the case: the church must follow—and exists only in following— where the Spirit blows. The Spirit makes the church its instrument and means of acting in the world—one of its instruments and means, though a special one.

This chapter examines what the Spirit does in the church and with the church. The first section looks at the general concepts evolved by tradition to define the relationship between the Spirit and the church. The second looks for signs of the Spirit in the traditional marks of the church. The third sees how the Spirit acts in the ministry of the church, and the fourth sees the Spirit at work in the ministerial offices in the church.

1. THE RELATIONSHIP BETWEEN THE SPIRIT AND THE CHURCH

Christians of the East accuse those of the West, Catholic and Protestant, of not recognizing the role of the Spirit in the church. Indeed, in both its theology and its practice, the church in the West seems to have regarded the Spirit as something added on to an existing reality. For Protestants, the church is formed by the word of God; the word pre-dates the church. The Spirit intervenes to communicate or accept this word; it helps, but does not bring into being. For Catholics, brought up in the theology of Robert Bellarmine, which dominated theory and practice till Vatican II and still holds sway in practice today, the church is an organization founded by Jesus, directed by the hierarchy, who guarantee faithful execution of the functions defined by Jesus thanks to the powers received from him. The Holy Spirit comes in to authenticate, sanctify, sacralize, lend strength and authority to what the church does. Both, in practice, act as though the Holy Spirit did not exist. Having decided on and carried out a course of action, they then attribute what they have decided and done to the Holy Spirit, thereby conferring an authorization that sanctifies and sacralizes their basically human actions. In this way, the Holy Spirit is not really in the church; it is above it as a sort of seal of approval, not the author from whom the church and all its works proceed. Many times in the history of the West, as Eastern writers have pointed out, the actions of the church have not seemed very different from those of political powers or cultural authorities: its law is the same; its rules are the same; its theology tries to assimilate them as far as possible, defining the church as a parallel institution to the state, though acting on a higher plane.

Let us look first at the traditional formulas used to express the connection between Spirit and church. We shall then try to see how the Spirit modifies the human behaviour of the church, what is properly the fruit of the Spirit in the church. Finally, we shall show that the Spirit is community or communion, that the Spirit exists in community and creates communion.

(a) Traditional Formulas Used of Spirit and Church

(i) In the New Testament. At first sight, the Bible does not contain much to clarify the relationship between Spirit and church. Nevertheless, it is important to remember that all the New Testament writings are dealing with the church. They are

not concerned with what happens between individuals and God, but with what happens between God and the community, God and the peoples of God, just as the Old Testament was.

So the promises of the Spirit in St John were made to the church. When he says "you" he means the church. So the Holy Spirit is "sent" to the church (15:26; 16:7); it "comes" to the church (15:26; 16:7,8,13); it will be "given" by the Father (14:16); it will lead the church to the "complete truth" (16:13). The gift of the Spirit after the resurrection is not confined to the Twelve (20:22).

The Letters of St Paul provide a framework which defines the concept of church. The church is never divorced from the particular, local, actual community; it will never be a purely heavenly or abstract entity. Thinking "church" means thinking immediately and primarily of the actual community, and the actual community is inspired, brought together and guided by the Spirit: "In the one Spirit we were all baptized, Jews as well as Greeks, slaves as well as citizens, and one Spirit was given to us all to drink" (1 Cor. 12:13). The gifts of the Spirit serve to build up the church: "Since you aspire to spiritual gifts, concentrate on those which will grow to benefit the community" (1 Cor. 14:12). The community at Corinth is a letter of recommendation for the Apostle Paul who founded it: "A letter... written not with ink but with the Spirit of the living God" (2 Cor. 3:3); it was the Spirit who made the community, and it is clear that the action of the Spirit can be seen in the church there. Paul's "we" is the church, the community.

Paul also conceives of the church as the universal people of God, spread throughout the entire world, reuniting Greeks and Jews. This reconciliation of enemies, Greeks and Jews, in the body of Christ, is brought about by the Spirit. Here the church is in the Spirit (cf Eph. 2:18–22; 4:3–4).

In Luke's theology, the Spirit comes first. The Spirit makes the Apostles, and through them, makes communities; in each community is the church. The same people of God is in the communities and in the missionary movement that brings them together in a dynamic unity.

This creative presence of the Spirit has to be understood in its most complete sense. It is not a stamp of approval put from outside on a human process: the communities are really born from their experience of the Spirit. They are not just communities of mere pupils learning the doctrine taught by the Apostles, nor are they new recruits receiving the signs of initiation into the church-organization. The members of the communities experience a new reality for themselves. The word on its own does not produce a Christian community, nor does mere belonging to an ecclesiastical organization. It is not a matter of recruiting new members by purely human means and then attributing the results to the invisible Holy Spirit. A community does not exist simply through passive adherence to a pre-existing church; a community is produced through people having an experience of the Spirit together. This experience is one of active assimilation of the word and entry as active members into the church organization. The New Testament shows that the church does not derive directly from Christ, certainly not from his activity during his mortal life; the Gospels show the disciples passive at the end of it. The church was born only when the passive became active, and this happened only after the coming of the Spirit. It was not even the risen Jesus appearing to the disciples who gave the church its origin; it was the Holy Spirit as a reality experienced and lived by the disciples.

(ii) In the Fathers of the Church. The union of church and Holy Spirit is a constant theme in the tradition of the Fathers, though their teaching on the subject is somewhat vague. The best known text is St Irenaeus: "Where the church is, there too is the Spirit of God; and where the Spirit of God is, there is the church and all grace. He is the Spirit and the truth."[1] St Irenaeus was replying to the Montanists, who wanted only a prophetic church distinct from the organizational church already firmly based on the bishops and the bishop of Rome. Irenaeus is not denying or minimizing the Spirit, but he does set the Spirit in the church. This he could do with credibility because there were still charisms of the Spirit in the church. The Spirit for him is still a concrete reality; it is a gift made to the church. His disciple Hippolytus of Rome likewise sees the Spirit as a gift made to the church.

The Fathers typically link the Spirit with baptism and the eucharist. These two spiritual signs, generators of church, are witnesses to the gift of the Spirit made to the church. Baptism and eucharist are celebrations of church and not simply favours bestowed on individuals. They show the presence of the Spirit in the church.

Till the fourth century, the Spirit was a gift received in the church and dwelling in it. After the fourth century, the Holy Spirit became something less definite and more personal. Experience of the Spirit was replaced by trintarian speculation.[2] For St Cyril, the Spirit was "guardian and sanctifier of the church,"[3] "sanctifier, helper and teacher of the church."[4] The Spirit had become a person guiding the church, in place of a gift living in it. Both sets of attributes were applied in subsequent centuries: the Spirit was gift—received, accepted, living in the church; the Spirit also guided, directed, enlightened the church.

The Eastern church remained more faithful to the Fathers' concept of the Spirit, because it kept a broader and more definite concept of church. In the East, the church exists above all in liturgical celebration, and this has always been a truly spiritual experience, in which the Spirit is not only evoked but in a sense perceived. Eastern liturgy is an anticipatory presence of the kingdom of God: in it the Spirit gives access to the risen Christ, and through him to the Father. In the East, the church was seen more as a means to salvation than as the reality of salvation. In the Catholic Church, on the other hand, the liturgy hardly evoked the Spirit, and the faithful were not able to recognize the Spirit in its liturgy. They received the sacraments as means necessary to salvation, means instituted by Jesus and administered by the hierarchy;[5] spiritual experience was something added on.

(iii) In official documents. The early credal statements united faith in the Holy Spirit with faith in the church: "I believe in the Holy Spirit in the Catholic Church," bringing the two realities together.[6] Later, the church was separated from the Spirit and became another article in the Creed.

The Councils of the Western church invoked the Holy Spirit,

but as a means of supporting and confirming the decisions they had taken. There was no real doctrine of the Spirit in the church. Vatican II introduced a radically new process in the Western church, but even it did not attempt, let alone achieve, a complete doctrine on the relationship between church and Spirit. The inability of the Council fathers to do this reflected the general state of the Catholic Church, which still has a long way to go before it gives the Holy Spirit due recognition.

Vatican II at least marked an important change which will probably be the first step in a new direction. Number 4 of *Lumen Gentium* has collected together a number of biblical texts on the church and the Spirit, though without examining them systematically.[7] Number 4 of *Ad Gentes* likewise presents texts dealing with Pentecost and the sending of the Spirit. The Council fathers held back from attributing too much to the day of Pentecost, and therefore restricted the role of the Holy Spirit to its manifestation on that day, in accordance with the rather conservative traditional exegesis.

(iv) As "soul of the church." The history of theology shows numerous attempts at defining the church. Since the sixteenth century, the definition provided by Robert Bellarmine has prevailed in the Catholic Church: this starts from the sociological construct, making the church the society of those who have been baptized, who believe and submit to the authority of the hierarchy. In the nineteenth century there was a period in which the definition of the church as the mystical body of Christ tended to prevail. This was the burden of the project that Vatican I was prevented from discussing, but it still inspired Pius XII's encyclical *Mystici Corporis*. Vatican II drew back and refused to make the mystical body a definition, treating it instead as a figurative description of the church. If the mystical body were a true definition, the role of the Holy Spirit would be reduced.[8]

At the beginning of the last century J.A. Mohler put forward the definition of the church as the incarnation continued, a definition that was accepted in the nineteenth century and the first half of the twentieth. Vatican II turned away from it, preferring to link the church, in *Lumen Gentium*, to the Holy

Spirit. The continuity of the church rests on the anointing of Christ and the church by the same Holy Spirit (LG 8a).[9]

All the above definitions suffer from the christomonism the Eastern churches accuse us of. Heribert Mühlen has shown that Vatican II rightly tried to base its doctrine of the church on the mission of the Holy Spirit, thereby overturning all previous development in the West.[10] Besides this, *Lumen Gentium* took up an idea derived from the Fathers, in particular St Augustine,[11] emphasized by St Thomas[12] and already put forward in *Mystici Corporis*: that of the Holy Spirit as the soul of the church, performing the functions of the soul in the body. The church is as it were the body vivified by the Spirit as the soul vivifies the body. Of course this analogy has to be used taking account of the very specific meaning given to the concepts of body and soul in medieval scholasticism, unfamiliar to modern parlance. So Vatican II says: "[The Holy Spirit]... vivifies, unifies, and moves the whole body. This he does in such a way that his work could be compared by the holy Fathers with the function which the soul fulfils in the human body" (LG 7h). Here the Council fathers are still refusing to produce a definition of the church, taking the image of the soul as one traditional comparison amongst others, with the underlying intention of emphasizing the function of the Holy Spirit in the church.

The "soul" image does bring out the close union between the Spirit and the church, but it does not shed light on the results of that union. Taken literally, it could mean that everything the church does is equally spiritual. If everything is spiritual, then nothing is; if the Spirit is the "normality" of the church, its presence is no longer meaningful. It can be dispensed with in practice. In fact, having affirmed that the Spirit is the soul of the church, the church has often acted as though the Spirit did not exist. So however interesting the formula of "soul of the church" may be, it fails to inspire a practice. The category "soul" belongs to the language of "substance" typical of the Greek mentality, which defines the eternal and universal essence of things, but ignores history. What concerns us most is the actual and historical repercussion of the presence of the Spirit in the church. If the Holy Spirit is united to the church as the soul is to the body, what does this mean in practice?

(b) The Meaning of the Presence of the Spirit in the Church

If the Holy Spirit is united to the church and present in its life, then the church must be something very different from other forms of human society. Here we can fall into a sort of ecclesiological Nestorianism, which has been the Catholic temptation since the Middle Ages and particularly since Bellarmine: on the one hand, the church would be completely guided and inspired by the Holy Spirit, would be a mysterious reality defined by the presence of the Spirit; on the other hand, it would also be a human society governed by the same laws as govern other human societies. On the one hand it would be like the kingdom of France or the republic of Venice, while on the other it would be an invisible reality. The two sides would be juxtaposed, but the invisible Spirit would have little impact on the church's visible history: the presence of the Spirit would serve to sacralize or authenticate Catholic ecclesiastical society, but nothing of this influence would be visible. Outwardly, the church would act like any other human society.

The other danger is that of ecclesiological Monophysitism, which is the Eastern temptation. This would consist in so idealizing the visible church, the church present in its liturgy above all, that this church would already be living in the heavens, would be heaven brought to earth, literally the kingdom of God on earth. Its actual historical embodiment and its dependence on other historical, economic, political and cultural realities would be lost to sight: the church would be beyond the reach of politics, economics and culture, a sort of piece of heaven on earth.

We need to find a balance between this Monophysitism and this Nestorianism, to discover what the presence of the Spirit in the church really means. Let us first discount certain false interpretations of this presence, then attempt not a full exposition, which would be impossible at the present stage of doctrine on the Spirit and the church, but some pointers toward such an exposition.

(i) What the presence of the Spirit in the church is not. The "Christendom" or *societas christiana* of the Middle Ages provoked many movements of reaction against it, movements

which still persist today and which have produced several schisms. These made a distinction between a spiritual church and a fleshly or material church; they saw the latter as tied to Christendom and all its corruptions; they viewed that church as a new synagogue, a church of law, slaves and temple. Its adversaries saw the Catholic Church as this fleshly church, which they denounced in the name of a spiritual church. Joachim of Flora and his followers are often taken as the precursors of this theology of the spiritual church.[13] In practice, the spiritual church tended to exclude or at least devalue the role of the pope, of the Roman curia, of the bishops and clergy, as well as all the institutions that provided the clergy with the basis and justification for their privileges: the sacraments and "para-sacramental" rites. The spiritual church would be a church without institution, or at least with the minimum possible of institution: Spirit would be the opposite of institution.

The Reformers all sought a spiritual church to some degree, and so all diminished the role of some of the institutions of medieval Christendom.[14] In practice, Protestantism has produced great diversity, depending on the degree to which it has "de-institutionalized" the church. Sometimes it was more a question of emphasis within the institution. So the denominations born in the sixteenth century laid greater stress on the preaching of the word and less on the sacraments, while leaving the institutional nature of the church virtually unchanged.[15]

In practice, making a distinction between Spirit and institution does not get one very far. All human entities are institutional. What we need to know is what changes the presence of the Spirit can bring to institutions. Suppressing the institutional side of the church would be a dream realizable perhaps by angels, but impossible amongst human beings on earth. Besides, the whole of biblical history and Christian history shows that the church has always had institutions. So the abrupt distinction between Spirit and institution has to be discounted: basically, it stems from the Greek opposition between spirit and matter. The Holy Spirit is not outside matter or divorced from it; matter comes from the Spirit and the Spirit is present in it and works through it.

Some Protestant theologians have opposed Spirit and institution on the basis of opposition between event and institution, the latter in this sense meaning everything that is structure, establishment, continuity, while event is something that happens at a particular time. The Spirit would be in event only: this means specifically in the event of conversion and the birth of faith. The Spirit would be in these; the continuation would be subject to the weight of history, which institutionalizes. This distinction also starts from an opposition between spirit and matter, and reveals a fear of matter, as though matter were at the source of evil and corruption, an idea that belongs to the Hellenistic inheritance of the Christian world. This inheritance has provided the dominant temptation for Christianity since the second century.

For example, spiritualizing movements stem from cultural elites. The poor live immersed in matter to such an extent that they can never neglect it. They do not reject matter, but they do reject those historical expressions of Christianity that do so. Consequently, a spiritual church can never be one without institution, nor a church divorced from material things and their historical weight.

Finally, we need to beware of the distortions that arise through using terms from tradition while applying modern meanings to those words. The capitalist mentality sees everything in terms of property; so, if one talks of the "gift" of the Spirit, we tend to see this as acquiring something: what was not "mine" has become "mine." But in the Bible, "gift" means a capacity to do something handed over: those who receive the Spirit are not acquiring a new property but a new capacity for action. If the Spirit is given to one person, it can also be given to others: it is not a sort of personal property. In the same way, if the Spirit lives or resides in the church, this does not mean that the church "possesses" the Spirit; rather that it "is possessed" by the Spirit. Thus neither individuals nor the church can "possess" the Spirit, and we must be careful to remove all traces of unconscious proprietorial feeling with regard to the Holy Spirit.

(ii) The church as human creation. The church was born not just from Christ, but also from the Spirit. How does the Holy Spirit act? Not from outside like Christ, but from inside. The Spirit

penetrates the inner sanctum of human beings and makes its actions spring from there. There is no distinction between human action and the action of the Spirit, because the Spirit is hidden in the multitude of human beings in whom it resides. So what proceeds from the Spirit does so in the form of human action. If the church is of the Spirit, it is born of human beings. Outwardly, everything takes place as though it were a human creation. The word "creation" is appropriate here, since the Spirit is creator: it makes new things be born from old things; it brings new birth. The Spirit is the source of the newness of what begins to exist.

The human activity through which the church is created is slow, prolonged, repetitive, stumbling, with sudden rushes and times of relaxation. Where is the church born of human beings? In little communities, in base groups. The church is born of the Spirit where disciples patiently come together to form a Christian community. All the initiatives, efforts, compromises through which a community is produced and maintained are the creative work of the Spirit. The Spirit creates the church in thousands and millions of different places on earth, in the thousands and millions of places in which communities meet. The creation of the church by the Spirit has been renewed over two thousand years; the church is constantly being born in its multiplicity of communities. Saying the church is born of the Spirit means that it is born of the people. The controversies of some years back over whether the church was born of Christ or of the people were pointless: the church is born at once of Christ and of the people through the Holy Spirit.

The church does not originate at the top and filter down, as nations do from their central power. It originates at the base through small communities. The language employed by canon law can be deceptive. The base communities do not arise from decentralization of parishes; parishes arise from a group of communities. A parish can be "established" by canon law, but if it is to have a real existence this has to come through recognition of the base groups that existed before it. A diocese does not exist because a juridical decree has established it; if it is to be a real local church, it has to be made up of a communion of many base communities. The decree establishing a diocese has to confirm a local church which must have been in existence previously. Law cannot establish an ecclesial reality; it can only recognize its existence, structure it, organize it.

The church is spiritual precisely because it spreads from the base to the top. It differs from human societies which come into existence through the will of a power. The church does not start with a power, but with the communion uniting persons and communities. This communion is persevering and continuous human labour, and the force bringing such a creation about is the Holy Spirit.

(iii) The Church and other religions. I am not attempting here to define Christianity in relation to other religions: this is a task for ecclesiology. I want just to show how the mission of the Spirit is concerned in the matter. If the church is built up through human actions, these are not produced by a pure effort of will. Neither the act of faith nor the solidarity and communion that produce community springs from nothing. Human beings cannot create out of nothing; they can only create from what they have inherited. Their inheritance is their culture, and particularly what always has been and still is the centre of their culture, their religion. Christians can build their faith and religious life only on the basis of their previous religion. The Holy Spirit does not make a complete break with the past. It creates the church out of the material bequeathed by earlier religions. It was already preparing the kingdom of God in the religions of the world. Christianity needed a religion in order to build a church. An ecclesiology based on the Holy Spirit would show how much in present-day Christianity comes from Greco-Roman religion: in doctrine, sacraments and organization.

If people receive Christianity passively and assimilate it just in the shape in which it is presented to them, the church of the Spirit will not have been established in them. This is what happened often in America in the case of the indigenous peoples and the African slaves. They were integrated into a church which they themselves had not created: as a result, their Christianity was artificial and superficial. One could say that over much of America the church is still to be established. It can be established only by the Indians and the blacks: they alone can create it. It is only in them and through them that the Spirit can create the church.[16]

(iv) The historicity of the church and the spirit. If the church were just a creation of Christ, if it had been founded only by Jesus in his mortal life or after his resurrection, it would be simply a continuation of him through history. It would not change, nor could it. Anything history added to it would be casual and valueless; it would have entered history only by accident. It would have remained tangential to history, running alongside it but without penetrating it or being penetrated by it. Many Catholics have indeed seen the church in just this way: an edifice constructed two thousand years ago and unaffected by those years. Christians would be taken up into a church that predated them in every way.

If the church proceeds from the Holy Spirit, however, its condition is different. It springs up in an infinite variety of human situations, as a community made up of communities of faith, hope and mutual love. Each community bears the marks of its historical origin; it springs from the history of those who founded it. Each community is subject to the history of its members and the history of their coming together; each community is made by history. The community of these communities is the flowing together of all the communities that make it up. The one church founded by Christ is also millions of little groups founded by the Spirit throughout history.

Inversely, each community influences history and makes history. The community of communities also influences history, helping to produce a history so complex it is impossible to describe in words. What has been the traditional history of the church has evoked little of the history of the Spirit. It is only recently that some historians have come to discover that the true church has been in the innumerable little communities and their association.

Both historians and theologians have often shown the evolution of the church as constant progress: the history of dogma is that of one progress; the history of the sacraments that of another progress; the history of canon law that of yet

another; and so on. This view of things likens the church to
modern nations. These nations see their history as one of
progress: greater integration, higher GNP, greater power,
would all be forms of progress. But this sort of national progress
can mean regress for at least some of the people who make up
the nation. The same is true in the church: progress in dogma,
the sacraments, ecclesiastical organization, can go with a
regression in the true church. Every development of dogma, of
liturgy, of canon law, has its price: a more evolved and
demanding doctrinal structure can produce greater passivity in
the base communities; progress in the rites of sacraments and
the liturgy can diminish the people's participation in them; each
step forward in ecclesiastical discipline can mean greater
alienation of the poor and ignorant.

The Holy Spirit is not necessarily in this sort of historical
progress; it is rather to be found in the history of the base
communities. This at least is the experience of the base
communities in Latin America.

(v) The church as instrument of the Spirit. Contemporary writers
point to two complementary aspects of the presence of the
Spirit in the church: the ethical aspect and the aesthetic. The
Spirit is there to act and to be enjoyed.

The church is called first to act: to carry out the mission of
the Holy Spirit. The Spirit uses all creatures and acts through
them. But it uses the church more specifically because the
church was made and is being made for this purpose. The Spirit
was sent to bring about the kingdom of God in the world; the
church is there to serve this end.

This means that what is spiritual in the church is the
movement that takes it outwards, beyond its own limits. The
history in which its roots are set tends to make each community
look in on itself. If it expands, this is in order to grow, to
increase its power. It tends to be at the service of its own growth
or survival. The presence of the Holy Spirit in the community
shows itself in outward movement: not designed to gain other
members or other peoples, but to share the gifts of the Spirit
with them. The Spirit is the one who opens doors and windows,
who sends Christians out into the world. The community

exists in order to serve the Spirit in its mission to the world.

This outward movement has another significance as well: every community tends to close in on its past, to accept necessities and abandon the struggle for liberation, to adjust to divisions and forms of oppression, to resign itself to a diminished vitality. The Spirit appears in breaking the bonds and chains that tie the community to an alienating past, bringing greater freedom, more life, more speech, more community, more participation. In this sense, we can say that the ecclesiology of Vatican II was more spiritual than the Council itself realized. Its opening out to greater participation by all, to a greater expression of the word by all, to religious freedom spelt out clearly for the first time, to the advancement of regional and local churches: all this points in the direction of the Spirit. All this spiritualizes the church, makes it a more apt instrument of the Spirit in its action in the world.

"Spiritualizing" does not mean separating from matter, but transforming matter. A freer church is a more spiritual church; a more communitarian church is more spiritual; a church in which everyone speaks is more spiritual; a church that fights for life is more spiritual.

(vi) The church as experience of the Spirit. Western churches accentuate the ethical aspect and Eastern churches the aesthetic. In the East, the church is felt to be an experience of the Spirit. This experience is expressed in praise, thanksgiving and joy. The church lives the resurrection by the gift of the Holy Spirit. Through the Spirit, the church participates in the life of the world to come, anticipating it. Liturgy and continual prayer, public and personal, form a way of life that belongs beyond the limits of this present life.

The coming of the Spirit is the great feast of the church, and the feast of the world. It sums up the whole meaning of festivity; it is the celebration of God's victory through the resurrection of Jesus. The Spirit creates the experience of this victory: inspired by the Spirit, communities celebrate their own victory even in the midst of afflictions and persecutions. They celebrate the victory of the resurrection in martyrdom, in prisons, under torture, through deprivations. The Spirit alone gives the strength to live the resurrection in the midst of this world.

This festive aspect of celebrating victory in the strength of the Spirit lies at the heart of the spirituality of the Christian East and needs to be recovered by the West.[17] This recovery is part of the rediscovery of the Spirit. The festive aspect of the Spirit is clear in St Luke, as it is in the Letters of St Paul.

If the aesthetic approach is not completed by the ethical approach, however, there is a risk of losing sight of the reality of the world. Celebrating victory must not blind us to the continuation of the struggle. The Spirit celebrates the coming of the kingdom, but at the same time feeds hope for the same kingdom.[18]

(c) Church, Spirit and Communion

(i) Traditional teaching. In all that concerns the church and the Spirit, there is no more traditional theme than that of communion. The Spirit makes the church because it produces communion. This communion has its source and model in the communion of the divine Persons. The Spirit is the mediator between the communion of the divine Persons and the communion of the members of the church.[19]

In Byzantine liturgical language the word for communion (*koinonia*) designates the presence of the Spirit in the eucharistic community. Sharing in the divine life means sharing in the intra-divine communion. This is also the teaching of St Basil in his famous treatise on the Holy Spirit.[20]

In the West, St Augustine also made communion the centre of his teaching on the Holy Spirit.[21] "The Father and the Son willed that we should enter into communion among ourselves and with them by means of that which is common to them, and to link us in unity through this Gift which both possess in conjunction, that is, by the Holy Spirit, God and Gift of God."[22] Vatican II took up the same idea: "It is the Holy Spirit, dwelling in those who believe, pervading and ruling over the entire church, who brings about that marvellous communion of the faithful and joins them together so intimately in Christ that he is the principle of the church's unity" (UR 2b).

Human societies present several types of unity. What

concerns us here is the type designated by the word "communion," since the Holy Spirit creates unity but not every type of unity.

(ii) Communion in friendship. The Holy Spirit does not create communion through traditional relationships, which all suppose inequalities and dependencies: the father-son, man-woman, master-servant, authority-subject relationships and so on. The Spirit creates the relationship of friendship which binds communities together.

Friendship is a human relationship that springs from freedom, is based on mutual freedom and preserves this freedom. As Hegel said, it is freedom actualized.[23] Friendship is the relationship Jesus seeks with his followers.[24] St Thomas showed it to be the basis of any new human society.[25] The proper effect of the Spirit is unity founded on friendship.

(iii) Church as community. The friendship of the Spirit exists in a host of actual situations. It generates the basic nucleus of the church, the house community or domestic community.[26] This is made up of the people who meet in one house; this is where the people of God are born, grow and develop. The church is composed of millions of nuclei of friends meeting in one house.

In the early days of Christianity, virtually all church life was spent in houses. For 250 years the church had no other place to meet except people's houses. Whenever the church turns away from people's houses, when public temples take the place of the temples of houses, the church becomes artificial, formalist, devoid of real content. Domestic communities are the basis of Christian faith and charity. They form a network spread over the entire world; without these most basic communities, the church would be nothing. In this respect, the church is the opposite of the modern nation, which springs from a central power and tends to destroy or absorb all intermediary authorities.

If one asks what is spiritual in the church, the answer is that what is spiritual is thoroughly material and solid. Its spiritual element is made up of all the living communities meeting in houses, in which friendship is a practical and daily experience.

These communities are open to one another, and try to live in continual communication with each other. This communication has taken different forms over the years. In modern nations communication between communities has tended to develop into a powerful, all-absorbing bureaucratic apparatus which often stifles the life of the base communities: a distortion which is costing us dearly.

Sociologists have shown how the apparatus of parish and diocese has replaced, discouraged and suppressed the house communities: the parish church demands monopoly in worship as though it were the Temple of Jerusalem. The result has been that the poor have turned away and become alienated from the life of the church. The apparatus has served the interests of the rich and condemned the poor to marginality. But the house communities are the communities and the church of the poor.[27]

(iv) The Spirit and the church of the poor. Those who conform to the movement of the Spirit by forming communities made up of friends meeting in people's houses are the poor. Paul saw this happening in Corinth,[28] and the same can be observed today. The ruling classes want a church organized from the top down; the poor want a church built from the bottom up: they are the ones in conformity with the will of the Spirit.

Structures and organizations are valid as a means of helping ministry in the church, but provided they are there to serve and not to be served. Structures follow sociological laws and become ends in themselves, forgetting the intentions of their founder. The Spirit works by founding new base communities, from which springs new life.

Power structures abuse their cultural, social, political or economic superiority. They have neither the patience nor the humility to listen to the aspirations of the poor. They crush them without even noticing. The age-old struggle between the clergy and popular religion is an example of the weakness of the poor. Yet the Spirit goes on creating the church from communities of the poor; the present experience of Latin America is evidence of this fact.

(v) The Spirit and the wretched of the earth. The Spirit does not bring together only those who meet in base communities.

Experience has shown that the very poorest do not belong to base communities. Those living on the margins of society— tramps, beggars, thieves, prostitutes and other outcasts, most of the unemployed, slum-dwellers, most of those who are hungry or thirsty, who are homeless, who live under arches, who scrounge a living—will not go to public meetings or join formal communities. Are they all outside the church?

The Gospels are quite clear on this point; the marginalized, those who count for nothing, the Lazaruses, the cripples, the blind, beggars, thieves, are the privileged. In reality all these poor make up the other face of the church, and the great bulk of the church. They do not take part in any formal church activity, they do not know the dogmas of faith, they do not frequent the sacraments and they live beyond any contact with a parish or even a house community. The Spirit, however, is with them and brings them together in the people of God.

The clamour of the poor, the cry of the oppressed, rises up from them, and the Spirit is at the source of the cry of the poor (cf Rom. 8:18–27). The church is the huge caravan of the rejected of the earth who call out, cry for justice, invoke a Liberator whose name is often unknown to them.

There are many connections between the church of com- munities and the church of the caravan of the wretched of the earth, all inspired by the Spirit and signs of the presence of the Spirit. The poorest show an admirable solidarity to each other: even if they have no homes to meet in, they help one another along the road, meet each other and exchange tokens of community often more authentic than those exchanged in formally constituted communities. The communities, too, exist to serve the poorest, to liberate and advance the abandoned masses. St Augustine adopted the viewpoint of the great mass of the wretched. Today it is clearer than ever that the great mass of the wretched of the earth is precisely the host of the chosen, whom sometimes Christians themselves do not recog- nize. This is what the Spirit is telling the churches today.

(d) Conclusion

This first section has looked at some old things and some new. It is for ecclesiologists to organize them into a coherent whole, as far as this is possible. Here we have just tried to point out various aspects of the role of the Holy Spirit in the church.

2. THE SPIRIT AND THE MARKS OF THE CHURCH

If the church has its origin in two missions, those of the Son and the Holy Spirit, we can expect that some aspects of its "marks" will be due to the Son and others to the Holy Spirit. It is these latter aspects only that I want to look at here, in particular as they relate to the present experience of the church in Latin America.

(a) The Spirit and the Unity of the Church

The unity of the church stems from unity in Christ; the members of the church are united with one another because they are united in Christ. However, Christ brings its members together in the Spirit, and the Spirit has a special way of bringing people together, a way unlike that of human powers. The unity of the church comes from the Spirit of Christ. "In the one Spirit we were all baptized, Jews as well as Greeks, slaves as well as citizens, and one Spirit was given to us all to drink" (1 Cor. 12:13; cf Eph. 4:5). How do we all become one body in the one Spirit?

The Spirit brings us together in freedom, without coercion, pressure or persuasion. So our unity cannot be uniformity, since this can be brought about only by imposition. The Spirit unites the greatest diversity, while respecting it. Diversity does not contradict unity: the very gifts of the Spirit are diversity. The unity of the Spirit is unity of what is diverse, and this remains diverse. What is diverse—race, language, culture, sex, age, geography, history—does not remain outside unity. The church is not just what is similar among all its members and communities, but precisely the sum of their diversity.[29]

In the Catholic Church we are still suffering the effects of the "state of emergency" established in the period from the pontificate of Pius IX to that of Pius XII, which gave still greater power to some bodies dating from the Middle Ages. The unity of the church was thought to require an absolute uniformity in theology, liturgy and canon law. Scholastic theology, the Roman Missal and Ritual and the *Codex Iuris Canonici* of the Latin Church would be the instruments of this unity. Vatican II began the movement of reaction against this way of thinking, even though the steps it took were still timid ones.

Is the Holy Spirit so weak as to need these forms of coercion? Can the church look after its unity by such powerful human means that everything has to function as though the Spirit did not exist?

The Holy Spirit promotes unity by infusing Christians with a powerful inclination toward others, a movement of friendship which forms the true basis of unity. The church contains a wellspring of friendship which is stronger than all the factors making for dispersion or hostility in it. This friendship is a desire to be together, to reconcile differences.[30] This friendship really exists and can be found in the base communities. The communities themselves look for contacts, for communication with other communities. First Corinthians 13 shows clearly that what is proper to the Spirit is the gift of *agapē*, the power that pushes us toward unity with everyone.

Is this friendship always capable of overcoming cultural and historical separations? Can it bring the separated churches together? Will it be capable of bringing all the nations of the earth together in the bosom of one church? The answer is that we do not yet need the means to bring about complete unity. If ecumenism demanded all or nothing, it would not exist. If complete unity is not possible at the present time, there are many expressions of unity that are possible now. Unity is built up through patience; it advances step by step. It does not shun imperfect communion simply because it is imperfect. If the complete unity of the church is deferred till the end of time, what does it matter? The unity promoted by the Spirit is unity now in everything that is possible now. It does not exclude divergencies and unreconciled differences. We know that today there are divisions within the Catholic Church greater than those between "separated" churches. Yet these divergencies do not prevent unity in all that is possible. Christian unity is not just unity in thought or in religious practices. The unity promoted by the Spirit is also one of a community of material goods. Without material unity there can be no true unity: what happened at the eucharistic celebration in Corinth destroyed the unity of the church there. Unity implies sharing: the sharing-out of goods suggested by Paul (2 Cor. 8) was to be a sign of economic and material unity; it was to "balance out," to re-establish unity between the communities. If some lived in plenty while others went hungry, there was no unity in the church.[31] Here again, the Spirit is not outside matter; it knows that true unity is unity at table, unity that reaches beyond rich and poor, unity in a society of equals.

The Spirit and the Catholicity of the Church

The catholicity of Christianity is vehemently criticized today by non-Western cultures and religions, which see Christianity as irremediably compromised with its Western past, indissolubly bound to the European, white world, the world of conquerors and colonizers. The colonial past is seen as proof that the churches in general and the Catholic church in particular are incapable of breaking their solidarity with colonialism.

In Latin America, similar objections are also raised by blacks and Indians, in Brazil and elsewhere. Even some Christians are asking whether mission is any longer possible among the blacks or indigenous peoples. It is true that many blacks and Indians are baptized and call themselves members of a Christian church. But others consider such Christians traitors to the black or Indian cause, victims of white manipulation.

Today the church has to prove the legitimacy of its universal claim. Can it convert peoples without dominating them, without taking away their culture and personality, without destroying what gives them their identity as a people? If the church were just a human society, a human culture, this would be impossible. On the human level, the Western church, even with the best intentions, cannot have other than dominating or paternalistic attitudes: starting from a position of strength, it oppresses.

Catholicity is possible only by the Spirit, since the Spirit creates the church anew on the basis of the past and personality proper to each people. The Spirit enables these peoples to be creators of their own churches, of new churches. These will seek communion with the old churches, but communion on a basis of equality, based on the fact that they have created their own church by themselves, without being dependent on Western theology, Western liturgy, Western canon law.

So the question is this: will the churches of Western origin, as are the Catholic diocesan churches of Latin America, allow completely free black and Indian churches to be formed, with no coercion in theology, no use of Western languages, no Western liturgy or canon law? At the moment there is no possibility of this happening, so mission is at a standstill. Is it possible to think that mission will one day begin anew? Will the church one day be able to be truly catholic thanks to the Spirit in Latin America?

The universalism of the church brings another problem. Some would claim that because of its universality, the church cannot take sides. The church is for all and therefore cannot intervene in any dispute that brings human beings into opposition with one another. It must therefore be above all parties or causes; the Spirit will keep it outside any of the struggles of the world.

Here we have to make a clear distinction. Whenever human divisions make for competition between powers, the church has no call to intervene. It does not intervene in rivalry between political or economic empires, between nations, cultures or languages. But it does intervene when some groups of people oppress others, when the strong oppress the weak. The Bible is the book that shows how God takes the side of the poor and oppressed. This is not one biblical theme amongst others: it is the basic theme of the whole Bible.

The Spirit is the one who gathers the poor together so as to make them a new people who will challenge all the powers of the earth. The Spirit is the strength of the people of the poor, the strength of those who are weak. Without the Spirit, the poor would not raise their voices and conflict would not raise its head. The antagonism between the people of the oppressed and the powers of this world (cf Eph. 1:13–14; Rom. 8:18–27) exists because the poor exist as a people. The people of the poor cries out for its liberation. The church is this people of the poor crying out for its liberation and rising up against oppressing powers.

(c) The Spirit and the Holiness of the Church

The New Testament shows that the first Christians referred to themselves as "saints." This appelation was not a claim to perfection, but showed their certainty that God was working in them and through them. The holiness of God had appeared in the human world: Jesus was the "Holy One of God." The church is holy because Jesus is in it and it is in Christ, in a unity being brought about by the Spirit.

The New Testament does not call the church holy, but its members: "You have been washed clean, and sanctified, and justified through the name of the Lord Jesus Christ and through the Spirit of our God" (1 Cor. 6:11).[32] The Creeds, the Fathers and Councils always speak of "holy church"; the theme of the "communion of saints" is prominent in tradition and already found in the ancient formulas of the Symbol of the Apostles.[33]

Being holy does not prevent the church from being sinful at the same time. It is holy in what Christ does in it and sinful in what it does against Christ. The theme of the church as at once holy and sinful is as traditional as that of the holiness of the church.[34] So not only do Christians confess their sins, but so does the church itself, as the Council Fathers did at Vatican II and the bishops of Latin America at Puebla.[35] For the oppressed majorities, of course, the church's past shows more sins than holiness. Many do not experience the church as holy, only as powerful. Its holiness still remains to be seen.

If holiness is the effect of the Spirit, it will consist in the fruits of the Spirit. The Spirit ushers in a new humanity and a new life: the poor speak, the oppressed win their freedom, life triumphs over death, friendship gathers communities together. The holiness of the church consists in its participation in the world after the manner of the Spirit, who brings the future world—free, equal, comradely—forward into this world. Everything in the church that helps this process is holiness.

If holiness is the fruit of the Spirit, it cannot be brought about by human powers. Being holy means acting through the powers of the Spirit, freeing oneself from the powers of this world to live by the power of God. The holiness of the Spirit is found in renunciation of the powers of this world. Jesus became little, weak and poor in order to be holy, so as to be God's instrument. The church too has to become weak and poor if it is to be holy.

This way of poverty is one of the most visible signs of the holiness of the church in our days. The Medellín conference stressed this point and Puebla endorsed it.[36] The church has to become poor in order to associate itself with the poor and their clamour for liberation. This is the only way it can serve the cause of liberating the poor without running the risk of taking them over to serve its own greatness. A rich and powerful church could only use the poor to increase its prestige and enhance its social position.

(d) The Spirit and the Apostolicity of the Church

Since the second century, with St Irenaeus as principal proponent, the mark of apostolicity has been used in apologetics against heretics and schismatics: churches that cannot invoke the apostolic succession do not belong to the true church.[37] The same argument is still used today. It is not characteristic of the Spirit, so we do no more than mention it here.

Apostolicity has a wider meaning than its apologetic application.[38] The church is apostolic because it is founded on the witness of the Apostles. This witness is its constant reference; carried along on the currents of history, the church must always return to its apostolic reference point. This is expressed in the New Testament, so saying that the church is apostolic means that the New Testament is its permanent guide. A return to apostolic life has been the call of all reformers in the church.[39]

The witness of the Apostles is a witness to the resurrection as a fact that brought in the "last days." The resurrection changed the world, and the Apostles lived the full consequences of this resurrection. History has not in any way taken away the privilege attaching to apostolic times: there is not a linear progress in the church; there is a privileged reference to the past. The church has gone through periods of decadence in which it has turned away from the apostolic witness, and periods of reform in which it has gone back to the inspiration of the lives of the Apostles.

The apostolic witness culminated in martyrdom. Apostolicity resides in the martyrs. An apostolic church is a church of martyrs. This fact sheds an important light on the church in Latin America, which can show thousands of martyrs since it took the road of liberation at Medellín in 1968.

Apostolicity also means that the church too bears witness. The church is apostolic when it becomes missionary once more, goes out from itself to bear witness before the nations. The theme of the association of the Spirit with witness and martyrdom is present in all the New Testament traditions; there is none more constant.

The Spirit is the one who leads us back to the witness of the Apostles. The Spirit put this witness in writing in the Bible so that it could be a permanent guiding rule. The same Spirit who wrote the Bible helps Christians to listen to its words and receive its witness.[40] In this way, the Spirit is at the source of the apostolicity of the church.

3. THE SPIRIT AND THE MINISTRY OF THE CHURCH

Here the Catholic Church has to respond to the challenge of the Protestant Reformation, as Vatican II began to do. The Reformation accused the Catholic Church of ignoring the Spirit in favour of the prestige of "the flesh." It insisted that salvation was brought by the power of God alone, a free gift of God and in no way the work of human beings. The Reformers saw Catholics as relying on human works, seeking a church strong in human terms so that it could use its power as the instrument of salvation. They did, however, recognize that the Reformed churches could often fall into the temptations of "the flesh," seeking their strength in human strength and not in God's power: this would be true of, for example, the pietistic and rationalist movements of the last century.[41]

In Latin America, the Catholic Church remained set apart from the Protestant challenge for centuries. Till today it has not taken this very seriously, protected as it has been precisely by the power of "the flesh"; the power of the monarchs of Spain and Portugal and the social prestige it still retains from the colonial period.

Protestant concern with avoiding the prestige of the flesh can itself lead to certain excesses. Protestants find it hard to accept that the Spirit can work through the institutions and organizations of the church. They have such an individualistic and spiritualized, or at best personalized, concept of salvation, that they fail to see that God did not just create persons, but matter too, the material nature of humankind and with it all human needs of organization and structures. They see the Spirit working within individuals only. But the Bible and church tradition make no distinction between the inner and outer side of human beings: personal and bodily are the same. The Spirit works in matter and through matter: in the materiality of words, of rites, of structures, of organizations, of systems of government, of the material services Christians carry out for one another. But the Spirit does not act through matter alone; it does not separate matter from the person who is in matter and is matter. The Spirit works through actual persons taken in the fulness of their being: personal, bodily, social.

It is easy to see why Protestants are so worried by the Catholic attitude. The Catholic Church has often given—and still gives—the impression of behaving as though it had the Holy Spirit constantly at its command. It sees itself as a sort of vast warehouse of the Spirit, which it distributes in the form of sacraments, dogmas and acts of authority. Not a church obedient to the Spirit, but one that owns the Spirit, materialized and transformed into a consumer product doled out by the church in accordance with its own market rules.[42]

Protestants give primacy to the ministry of the word. The sacraments come second to this, and are often of very marginal importance (though this is beginning to change under the influence of the ecumenical movement). The Eastern churches go to the opposite extreme and structure their life essentially round the liturgy, giving little prominence to preaching and keeping indeterminate juridical structures. The Catholic Church has laid more emphasis on organization, discipline and law; its sacraments are first and foremost obligatory prescriptions, and its preaching tends to concentrate on dogmas which also have to be accepted. Vatican II tried both to give back to preaching the value assigned to it by the Protestant bodies, and to restore the intrinsic value of the sacraments as the Eastern churches wished. But it is easier to publish texts and issue declarations of intent than it is to change age-old behaviour patterns. The new Code of Canon Law shows that the ruling mentality has still not changed, nor come to accept the intentions of Vatican II. The juridical aspect still predominates in preaching and the sacraments, with emphasis on textual orthodoxy and faithful performance of the prescribed rites.

What concerns us here is the way the Spirit works in the various ministries of the church so as to make them something more than purely human activities that can be exhaustively analyzed by sociology. It cannot be that the church arranges its activities in accordance with the dictates of sociological and historical currents, in the end asking the Spirit to confirm what it has already decided. The problem is: how to ensure that the ministry of the church is truly subordinate to the mission of the Holy Spirit.

(a) The Spirit and the Ministry of the Word

(i) The word in the Bible and today. The churches apply the statements in the Bible on the link between the word and the Spirit to their ways of expressing the word today. Protestants stress preaching, and the pastor's sermon is a key element within their churches. Catholics stress the documents of the magisterium, of the councils, popes, bishops—documents, that is, whose juridical value is decided by canon law. In the extreme form of Catholicism reached during the pontificates of Pius XI and XII it seemed that priests' sermons and theological exposition had no purpose beyond setting out and commenting on the documents produced by the magisterium. Only those priests who preached in such a way were viewed as being recipients of the Spirit and thus able to preach the word. The

Eastern churches, on the other hand, give no value to doctrinal pronouncements after the first seven ecumenical councils, the only ones they consider full, and value the words of the liturgy alone. Both positions are valid in their positive aspect, but become deficient as soon as they seek to be exclusive.

In the New Testament, the word took various forms, adapted to the needs of those who were hearing it. The word of God is not tied to any one literary form. It uses or creates literary forms in order to communicate what the word has to say. So there is no direct translation from the word of the Bible to the words adopted by the churches. The words of the Bible were spoken in a code suitable to their time. They need to be decoded before they can be re-encoded in a form suitable to our times. The literary genres used by the churches came into being as responses to particular challenges that required a new code. Do these traditional codes still communicate their meaning in language accessible to us today? The Spirit is not tied to any particular means of expression; it is tied to the word of God itself, which has to be mediated through human language attuned to the code of the age.

The Spirit speaks through sermons, magisterial documents or the words of the liturgy to the extent that such words actually communicate meaning. It may be that traditional and formalized language no longer communicates anything to Christians, let alone to the rest of the world. If this is so, the Spirit cannot be said to be involved. The Spirit intervenes to make human language in all its forms capable of really communicating the word of God. What the Bible says of the presence of the Spirit in the word[43] applies today only to words that really say something, and something definite. Some sermons teach precisely the opposite of what they should teach: they show God as a tiresome being whom we should be well advised to avoid—or worse.

(ii) The Spirit and understanding of the word. Traditional theology made much of the distinction between the ministry of the Spirit in those who pronounced the word and the ministry of the Spirit in those who heard and understood the word. In church practice, exercise of the word was reserved to a few: the

people listened, but did not speak. This distinction also applied to the action of the Spirit in those who wrote the Bible: the prophets or apostles or "apostolic men" who wrote the Bible under the guidance of the Apostles were seen as proclaimers of the word.[44] This inspiration by the Spirit was part of the wider guidance given by the Spirit to the words and witness of the Apostles.[45] The authority with which the hierarchy of the church spoke was justified by the transmission of the help the Apostles received from the Spirit. Outside this circle were those who were helped by the Spirit to make the act of faith; the Spirit formed faith, maintained it and strengthened it,[46] was present in reception of the word.

All this has always been said, and is quite valid still today. Nevertheless, we need to emphasize some aspects that have become clearer with Vatican II and obvious from contemporary experience in the church, particularly in Latin America.

1. In the church, everyone speaks. All express the word: "The holy People of God shares also in Christ's prophetic office. It spreads abroad a living witness to Him..." (LG 12a). Present-day reality proves the truth of this; the Christian people have learned to read the Bible and to proclaim what they have found in it. Those who proclaim the word of God in the Bible are not just the hierarchical successors of the Apostles: all the faithful are successors of the Apostles when they communicate the words the Apostles left behind them—real successors. Those who are proclaiming the word of the Bible to the world, not formally but really, are the lay people of the communities. In most cases the clergy have been shut off from the world by the curtains of history, so thick that their word cannot get through to their listeners. We are once again witnessing what happened in the early days of the church: it is the poor, the simple, the ignorant of this world who are the evangelizers.[47]

2. It is not only lay people who need to have faith and be born into faith: the hierarchy also receive the Spirit so as to come to faith. They too must obey the Spirit in order to understand the word of God. The meaning of the word is not conveyed by purely human transmission or the laying-on of hands. This does not confer understanding of the word; for this

the hierarchy need to be obedient to the Spirit in the same way as all other Christians.

New sciences and philosophies of language provide grounds for a better understanding of the role of the Spirit in the word. These sciences and philosophies have shown us that when a person speaks or writes, there is no direct transmission from author to hearer or reader—meaning cannot be written; the actual meaning the author seeks to convey is communicated not directly, but through means of signals. How does the reader or hearer understand the meaning, i.e. really receive the word from those signals?

The receiver is not passive: on the contrary, the receiver is more active than the speaker. The act of understanding consists in recreating a meaning, a word, so as to compare it with the signals emitted. Understanding is creating, inventing meaning. This will never be exactly the meaning the speaker had in mind, but the attentive receiver will progressively correct the meaning recreated. Understanding is creating the received word anew. If this task is not performed, we can say that the hearers have received nothing. They will have heard a noise but not received a word—something that happens more often than one might think.

To hear and understand is to speak. Understanding is greatest when the receiver pronounces outwardly what he or she has heard and mastered. There is an intimate relationship between receiving the word and saying it; they are two phases of the same act. Those who speak, really speak—their hearers understand what they are saying. Those who understand are those who say again what they have heard. For this reason, the church is made by the word, born of the word. The church at one and the same time pronounces the word and exists in this act of pronouncing the word of God.

These concepts help us to see how the Spirit relates to the word. After Jesus' death and resurrection, the Apostles had to remember him. This memory was beyond the capacity of purely human powers, since it was not just a question of recalling odd phrases or deeds, but of understanding what had happened. The memory of Jesus was the memory of the meaning of events: the memory of the truth that had been made manifest in Jesus. It was not just an attempt to re-create a past, since Jesus, through his words and deeds, had entrusted the Apostles with a mission. The problem was one of prospective memory: to remember the things that Jesus wished them to do after his death. The Apostles remembered the mission that Jesus had entrusted to them as they understood it.

The New Testament expresses various reconstructions of this memory. It is made up of various creations of meaning, all different, varying understandings of Jesus. It is impossible to reduce these to a single one: the meaning of Jesus is ultimately inaccessible. The guarantors of fidelity among these creations of meaning are Jesus and the Spirit. Those who wrote the New Testament and the Apostles who stood behind them build up various figures, various understandings of Jesus: they were guided by the Spirit. This is what inspiration in the Bible means. It is not a matter of faithfulness to the letter, which would have no value. The Apostles understood spiritually what had come down to them from Jesus.[48]

Following the Apostles, tradition began, and all Christians are active members of this. Tradition is not a matter of repeating the New Testament to the letter, which would be the best way of betraying its meaning. Through its letter, readers and hearers of the Bible have the same mission to create a meaning. This they can do only from within their own human experience. If the word does not speak to their human experience, it cannot be the word of God.

It is the Spirit who guides Christians in their creation of meaning and understanding in the Bible. This is why, as the Fathers always saw, the Christian and authentic meaning of the Bible is its spiritual meaning. The letter kills and the Spirit gives life.[49] The spiritual meaning does not exclude the so-called literal meaning: it uses the literal meaning and holds on to it as a point of reference, but the Spirit alone enables the Bible to be meaningful to men and women of today.

This task of re-creating the meaning of the word of God belongs to all Christians. No one can take the place of believers themselves in this task: neither the hierarchy, nor teachers, nor pastors. The hierarchy can control continuity of meaning in history but are incapable of creating the understanding which the word of God receives in human beings. The Spirit is given to all so that all may actively hear the word and understand it through recreating it.

Since understanding leads ultimately to expressing the word, every believer is a missionary. The Spirit, who is responsible for the construction of the word, is likewise responsible for the expression that produces communication with the world. It is a fact in Latin America today that priests constantly find themselves incapable of finding ways to express the word of God created and used effectively by so many "ignorant" people, unlettered but inspired by the Spirit.

(b) The Spirit and the Sacramental Ministry

The Catholic doctrine of *ex opere operato* lends itself to many confusions and serious objections. Protestants accuse it of destroying the sovereignty of God. Priests would seem to be able to use God's power indiscriminately at will. God would have to submit to the will of men.[50]

In fact not only the theology, but even more the popular understanding of the sacraments has often been ambiguous. We need to be clear that the sacraments are instruments of the Spirit and not the other way round. The sacraments are signs that transmit the Spirit by virtue of the promise made by Jesus, not because the Spirit is at the beck and call of the clergy. We must avoid the materializing that comes from false and facile explanations. The link between Spirit and sacrament is a mystery on which the Bible throws no light, and which the Fathers always approached with a great deal of caution.

The Eastern churches have always exalted the role of the Spirit; their liturgy is a constant reference to the Holy Spirit. They celebrate their liturgy as though they were taking part in a play directed by the Spirit rather than by themselves. They understand that the principal actor in the sacraments is the Holy Spirit.

Western liturgy has given far less emphasis to the role of the Spirit, with the result that sacramental theology in the West has not given the Spirit the value it has in the East. In the West, theology has emphasized the role of the priest as the representative of Christ in the sacramental ministry. The priest celebrates in the name of Christ, takes the place of Christ and does what Christ did. So Christ is thought to act directly in the sacraments using the priest as his instrument. Such a conception leaves no room for the Holy Spirit. The Spirit would appear only in the effects of the sacraments, if at all, since in scholastic theology the concept of grace frequently took its place.

This is not the place for a treatise on the sacraments. I propose to deal only with what concerns the conception of the Spirit in Christian life.

(i) The question of the "epiclesis." Vatican II responded to one of the strongest appeals made by the Eastern churches by including an epiclesis in the eucharistic liturgy. The old Roman Missal, dating from Pius V, contained no epiclesis and Latin theologians had not thought it useful. They rather enhanced the precise moment of transubstantiation, saying that this was produced at the moment when the priest pronounced the words of consecration. If this is the case, what need is there to add an epiclesis asking the Spirit to do what the priest already has the power to do through the words of consecration?

It is now accepted that we should not try to fix the exact moment of transubstantiation, since this leads to a concept of the priest's action as that of a magician producing miraculous effects through the power of "strong" words. It is not the power of the priest that makes the sacrament, but the power of the Spirit. Everyone recognizes the need for the words of consecration—the words instituted in the New Testament. But since the Spirit is the power that effects the sacrament, it is also highly proper that there should be an epiclesis, or invocation of the Spirit, even if in the final analysis the Spirit can act without being invoked.

In the new Ritual all the sacramental rites contain an invocation of the Spirit, thereby indicating that the power present is the Holy Spirit and not a magical power exercised by the priest. The liturgy forms and expresses the faith of the people. If the Spirit is invoked in the liturgy, it will be recognized in the faith of the people.[51]

(ii) The significance of the sacraments. Latin scholastic theology reduced the sacraments to "means of salvation." This means that what mattered was that they should be validly adminis-

tered. The liturgy itself, popular understanding of the liturgy, the meaning of words and gestures, mattered little. The sacraments were reduced to legal status.

We need to relearn the ancient tradition of the church from the Eastern churches. For them, Christianity is somehow entirely present in the liturgy. The liturgy is the fulness of God's word and the fulfilment of the human condition; it places us in the presence of the three divine Persons, introduces us into the communion of the divine Persons. So communion is formed among men and women too. The sacrament makes the connection between both communions, gathering the whole of humanity into the divine communion.

In this way, the Spirit anticipates the eternal life of God. It brings this anticipation about in material form. In the sacraments, matter is spiritualized, impregnated with the Spirit, as in the resurrection or, at least, as a pledge of resurrection. Consequently, the liturgy is eternal life itself. It is more than just a means. It is life itself deified, the very life of God shared. It is the ultimate celebration.[52]

This applies to all the sacraments, but is particularly true of the eucharist. The Eastern churches have always stressed that the church is most fully itself in the eucharist. In this, it realizes the reason for its existence: to introduce humanity into the communion of the Trinity.

The sacraments are all prayers: supplications to the Spirit. Christians know that they are far from the final consummation, that they cannot approach it of themselves, but only through the power of the Spirit. But the Spirit comes to bring a pledge of ultimate happiness. This is why the Eastern liturgy takes the form of insistent supplication. Western liturgy, on the other hand, is like a gesture of command made by the priest, which carries the risk of trivializing God's part, of making God an object in men's hands. Eastern supplication manages both to underline the distance between us and God and stress the help brought by the Spirit.

Since Catholic liturgy, even the semi-renewed liturgy of Vatican II, now arouses boredom more than anything else, it may well be that Westerners and the whites of the Latin world are ultimately incapable of reshaping the sacraments so that they really give faith. This could be the task of non-Western peoples, including the blacks and Indians of Latin America.

(c) The Spirit and the Ministry of Service

The church's ministry is also one of service to humanity, the practice of "charity," that is, of active solidarity both within and outside the community. Vatican II says: "There is only one Spirit who, according to his own richness and the needs of the ministries, distributes his different gifts for the welfare of the church (cf 1 Cor. 12:1–11). ... Giving the body unity through himself and through his power and through the internal cohesion of its members, this same Spirit produces and urges love among the believers. Consequently, if one member suffers anything, all the members suffer it too, and if one member is honored, all the members rejoice together (cf 1 Cor. 12:26)" (LG 7c).

One of the outstanding aspects of the ecclesiology of Vatican II was its rediscovery of charisms. All these are expressions of charity, because everything inspired by the Spirit is service to our neighbour. Charity is the greatest charism and the one that inspires all the others. Through charisms, the Spirit has recuperated a ministry it had lost in Catholic theology.

There are three aspects of charisms that need to be picked out here:

1. They all proceed from the Spirit, and if they proceed from the Spirit, they must be recognized and accepted by the church.

2. Charisms are diverse: the Spirit has infinite possibilities of varying its gifts.

3. All believers receive charisms; they are not reserved to certain privileged categories, such as the clergy or religious. Lay people are also given charisms. The Council tells priests that they should "acknowledge with joy, and foster with diligence the various humble and exalted charisms of the laity" (PO 9d).[53]

Throughout the course of history, the Spirit has inspired innumerable initiatives of service to one's neighbour, some recorded in written history, but the vast majority forgotten. The history of charity deserves to have said of it what the author of the Fourth Gospel wrote: the whole world is not big enough to contain the books that could be written about it.

There is no space here to comment on this history. I should like just to make some observations that relate to the situation today, to bring up some questions posed by the presence of the Spirit as the origin of charisms:

1. In recent centuries the hierarchy have increasingly organized the activities of lay people both inside the church and outside it: they have taken responsibility for works of education, health, assistance to the needy, even forming huge administrative complexes to carry these works out. Millions of lay people collaborate in these undertakings. But how can these lay people experience their collaboration as a charism from the Spirit? Their experience is often rather of complete subordination to administrative or functional criteria. Is there still room for the Spirit in such constructs?

2. The control of charisms by the clergy and the hierarchy often has the effect of being radically selective and thereby eliminating very useful gifts. As a general rule, the clergy have eliminated everything that did not originate with them or did not fit in with their plans—made without consulting the laity.

It suffices to listen to oral history—which does not get written down for obvious reasons—to discover that priests have destroyed many lay initiatives. Parish priests, for example, abolish all the offices that existed before their arrival: they suppress "wise women," healers, counsellors. They eliminate all manifestations of services and charisms proceeding from lay people, as though clericalism needed to make a *tabula rasa* of everything done by the laity.

If one looks at the history of the workers' movement, or of liberation movements in the Third World, one sees that the clergy have tried to take over the leadership of all church participation and have cut short many initiatives that might have shown the church the right way to proceed. Like all bureaucracies, the clergy tend to simplify, to rationalize, to cut down diversity. Bureaucracy hates variety. The famous decree of the Fourth Council of the Lateran in 1215 forbidding the formation of new religious orders is a good expression of the bureaucratic spirit: its consequences were dramatic. Among these consequences was that in the fourteenth century it became impossible to formulate any solution to the question of the Franciscan Spirituals, a situation that provoked their persecution at the hands of popes and the burning of good religious by the Inquisition. Similar measures have been repeated at various moments of history and are still in effect today. New bans are continually being pronounced, on what priests and religious can do, on what lay people can do even in their secular lives.

Surely limiting new experiences in advance without checking their content is going against the Holy Spirit and beyond the gift of discernment reserved to the hierarchy?

3. Organizations created in order to serve can come to have very great social and economic power. Does the power to save placed in the hands of the heads of such organizations tend to awaken ambitions to power as such? The accusation of seeking power under the guise of service has been made so often that it must have some basis. What should be service to the poor becomes a source of riches. In the past, when the church was very wealthy, it justified this wealth as being for service of the poor. Is it not rather true that power accumulated for the practice of charity always turns against this very charity? What does the Spirit say about power in the church? Are the words of the New Testament about poverty and weakness no longer applicable?

4. THE SPIRIT AND MINISTERIAL OFFICE

The definition and attributes of the various ministerial offices will be examined in the volume of this series dealing with the life of the church. Here I shall limit myself to clarifying what ministerial office owes to the Holy Spirit. We shall see first that ministerial offices really do proceed from the Holy Spirit, then look at the qualities that derive from this origin in the Spirit and finally draw some conclusions from these facts about the Catholic Church's current theology of ministerial office, particularly as it applies to Latin America.

(a) The Spirit and Ministerial Office in General

By "ministerial office" I mean here those offices and services to which some degree of authority in the church is attached.

The Holy Spirit confers real power on certain persons: a power of convincing, directing, leading, governing; it confers real authority preceding any juridical authority. So St Paul had the capacity to evangelize with power; he was effective in his office, and this effectiveness came from the Spirit: "Far from relying on any power of my own, I came among you in great fear and trembling, and in my speeches and the sermons that I gave, there were none of the arguments that belong to philosphy; only a demonstration of the power of the Spirit. And I did this so that your faith should not depend on human philosophy but on the power of God" (1 Cor. 2:4–5). So the Apostle's authority was founded on a deeper knowledge, on a greater penetration into the workings of God.

Authority in the church does not derive from purely administrative decrees, nor from being drafted into a civil service, as in modern states. One sometimes has the impression that authorities in the church are based on the same criteria as those used by the state in electing its officers. If this were the case, the church could count only on human power and not on the power of God; then its effectiveness would be limited and it could produce neither faith in its own people nor the conversion of others.

This is why election to ministerial office must follow the indications of the Spirit. Neither the community nor the hierarchy can choose those to hold ministerial office in accordance with purely human interests, for the sake of administrative convenience or organizational requirements. The Spirit has already chosen those persons who are clothed with a power. It is not mere juridical appointment that confers power.

It can happen—and often has—that those elected to the office of priest, bishop or even pope have been incapable of exercising authority. They have left problems unsolved, their flocks abandoned with no course to follow, evils uncorrected and the church without leadership. They received a power they were incapable of applying. Those whom the Spirit wanted were not chosen.

The church is not administered like a state, which can rely on force, on the ability to impose its will. Authority in the church has no force at its command. Even if it could use coercion, it would not be opportune for it to do so, since this would scatter the flock instead of uniting it. Authority in the church requires a very different quality: the capacity to guide through persuasion in freedom. If it is not capable of doing this, the church enters a period of dispersion; its members leave. Bad government is the greatest destroyer of the church; bad government prevents peoples from being converted. So it is vital that those who are accepted and juridically confirmed in authority are those who receive power from the Spirit.

Authority in the church is a spiritual power above all else: the power of increasing the faith of the community, of guiding prayer, of making the liturgy an experience of the kingdom of God, of stimulating works of charity, of awakening all to a sense of responsibility. Authority has its administrative side, but this is very secondary and should not furnish criteria of selection. A bishop who is no good at administration can easily find a good secretary; a bishop who does not know how to evangelize the poor cannot get anyone else to do this for him: he will be incapable of exercising the power of God.

(b) The Spiritual Attributes of Authority

(i) Authority as service. The Puebla Final Document says: "Pastors are within the Family of God and at its service. They are brothers called upon to serve the life that the Spirit freely sparks in their other brethren. Pastors must respect, accept, foster, and give direction to that life, even though it may have arisen independently of their own initiative" (249). And again: "Since Vatican II and the Medellín Conference, a great change can be noted in Latin America in the way that authority is exercised within the Church. Greater emphasis has been put on its character as service and sacrament and on the dimension of collegial concern" (260).

At Puebla, the bishops returned to the inspiration of St Paul: "For it is not ourselves that we are preaching, but Christ Jesus as the Lord, and ourselves as your servants for Jesus' sake" (2 Cor. 4:5). This does not mean apostles do what all the members of the church want them to do, since their service is service of

Christ, service of the growth of Christ in the members: "People must think of us as Christ's servants" (1 Cor. 4:1).[54]

(ii) The humiliation of ministers of authority. The difference between the condition of authority in the church and in the world was set out incomparably by St Paul. The authority of an apostle, instead of bringing honour and dignity, privileges and rewards, brings humiliations, persecutions, displeasure and suffering. Apostles are humiliated, and this humiliation is part of their service. Because of the apostles' sufferings, the people grow in faith, hope and charity. Spiritual ministry renounces all worldly grandeur.

"It seems to me, God has put us apostles at the end of his parade, with the men sentenced to death; it is true—we have been put on show in front of the whole universe, angels as well as men. Here we are, fools for the sake of Christ, while you are the learned men in Christ; we have no power, but you are influential; you are celebrities, we are nobodies. To this day, we go without food and drink and clothes; we are beaten and have no homes; we work for our living with our own hands. When we are cursed, we answer with a blessing; when we are hounded, we put up with it; we are insulted and we answer politely. We are treated as the offal of the world, still to this day, the scum of the earth" (1 Cor. 4:9–13; cf Cor. 1:5–6; Gal. 2:20; Phil. 3:7–10). "We are only the earthenware jars that hold this treasure, to make it clear that such an overwhelming power comes from God and not from us. We are in difficulties on all sides, but never cornered; we see no answer to our problems, but never despair; we have been persecuted but never deserted; knocked down, but never killed; always, wherever we may be, we carry with us in our body the death of Jesus, so that the life of Jesus, too, may always be seen in our body. Indeed, while we are still alive, we are consigned to our death every day, for the sake of Jesus, so that in our mortal flesh the life of Jesus, too, may be openly shown. So death is at work in us, but life in you" (2 Cor. 4:7–12).

Here is the spiritual portrait of those who hold power in the church. This is the portrait that was shown in Latin America in the persons of the martyr-bishops Oscar Romero,[55] Eduardo

Angelelli and Gerard Valencia; in so many other prophetic and persecuted bishops; in so many priests, deacons and ministers of the word. The power of the Spirit has shown itself and still shows itself on this continent in the weakness of the flesh, in the agony and the cross of Christ. This is the sign of the Spirit in authority.

(c) Two Shapes of Authority in the Church

The church proceeds from Christ and from the Spirit. Authority in the church likewise derives from Christ and the Spirit. At present, authority is seen as being derived from Christ alone, which gives it a particular shape. If it is seen as deriving from the Spirit alone, it takes another shape. Both are valid, but are complementary, not mutually exclusive, and both are needed, since each corrects the extremes of the other.

If we start from Christ alone, we see authority as permeating from the top downward. Christ delegated his authority to the Apostles; these in turn handed it on to their successors, and so on. The successors of the Apostles confer a share in their authority on lesser ministers. Everything stems from Christ: teaching, sacramental grace, government. The Apostles received from Christ, the priests receive from the bishops, the laity receive from the priests. Authority is the source of everything. Church activities are defined as sharing in the activities of the clergy, who hold the authority; lay people have nothing to create or invent; they just apply what they have been taught and told. If the church derived solely from Christ without the Spirit, this is the shape it would take.

But the Spirit is there too, and the second view of authority in the church emphasizes that our only access to Christ is through the Spirit. Now the Spirit has been sent to everyone in the church, enabling all to rediscover Christ. All the faithful create, invent their faith, their prayer, their life in common. The Spirit co-ordinates and unifies this wealth of diversity. The Spirit also inspires ministers and maintains authority in the church. But the role of this authority is to discern, to maintain visible unity in the outward organization of the church, to assure continuity with tradition in a right reading of the Bible.

The hierarchy help, but they are not the driving force. We are all prophets, priests and kings (cf LG 10, 12). The hierarchy maintain visible unity, but they have no more initiative than any other Christians.

The two shapes are complementary. It is a fact that Catholic theology has taken account of the first only and ignored the second. Chapter 3 of *Lumen Gentium* itself is still moulded to the first shape; the distortion continues. Fortunately, since then, a new practice has begun to emerge in the church in Latin America. This practice still awaits its theology and official recognition, though it has already found its biographers.[56]

CONCLUSION

The Bible and tradition firmly unite church and Spirit. Unfortunately the theological tradition of the Latin Church has not kept such a strong sense of the presence of the Spirit as has the Eastern tradition. Vatican II started a process of recovery of the integral tradition, but it has still not penetrated the consciousness of the Western church.

Because the church proceeds from the Spirit, it is at once profoundly different from human societies and profoundly human—more human than secular societies in history. Through the Spirit who is sent to all its members, the church is a human creation that is built up from the cultures and religions which provided building materials and that is transformed and spiritualized. The church is totally historical; it comes from history and changes history. Through the Spirit, the church is diversity united in full freedom in a truly human unity, respectful of human values. Diversity is reconciled in friendship through the formation of communities and communities of communities. These are not built on the powers of this world, but on the weakness of the poor and oppressed.

All the marks of the church need to be reinterpreted in the light of the Spirit if they are to be full marks, since traditional Latin ecclesiology has been one-sided.

The church's ministries are directed by the Spirit. The ministry of the word is the work of the Spirit, from the inspiration of the Bible to the formation of the faith of the humblest Christian. The liturgy is the work of the Spirit, an anticipation of the kingdom of God here on earth. The works of charity performed by the church are inspired and empowered by the Spirit. The Spirit, then, is not something immaterial, alien to material realities. It transfigures material by making it the material of the kingdom of God. Authority itself is spiritualized; power in the church is different from power in secular society—different in origin, in essence, in its attributes, in the way it is exercised.

When Bellarmine compared the church to the kingdom of France or the republic of Venice, he was using very dangerous categories. The triumph of his ideas—something he never foresaw—produced an ecclesiology without the Spirit, or with a Spirit summoned merely to consecrate a society built on the model of the societies of this world. Step by painful step we are emerging from this ecclesiology, following and extending the path marked out by Vatican II.

Chapter IV
The Holy Spirit in Persons

The object of this chapter is not to look at what the Holy Spirit produces in persons, but at how the Spirit shows itself through what it does in them. This might at first sight seem easy enough, but there are two problems. The first is the inheritance of Western theology, in which the churches of Latin America—or at least the Catholic and mainstream Protestant churches—share. Since the end of the Middle Ages, there has in the West been a separation between theology and spirituality.

Theology has neglected the Holy Spirit. Due to the force of the inertia of Greek philosophy, theology examined revelation starting from the category of "substance," into which the Holy Spirit did not fit. Scholastic theology spoke of actual grace, the effect of God on the soul. The theology of grace formed the centre of both Catholic and Protestant theology after the end of the Middle Ages, and this hid the Holy Spirit. The mysticism that developed at the same time was unable to call on the aid of theology on this point, since the theology of grace shed no light on mysticism. So the mystics ignored theology and did not feel they were missing out on anything. They formulated representations of their experiences based on a dawning psychology (which they helped to bring into being), but they could not find any concepts that might have shed light on their way in traditional theology. They did not know the Holy Spirit was at work in them, nor did they know the whole patristic and Eastern tradition that could have showed them what was happening to them.

The spiritual tradition of Latin America owes virtually everything to the Spanish mystics of the sixteenth century—St Teresa of Avila and St John of the Cross—and to St Ignatius and the Jesuits and the Franciscan and Dominican reformers of the period. So Latin American spirituality likewise grew up without theology and without the Holy Spirit. This Western tradition is still influential today, and this explains why the new spirituality has not till now been accompanied by a theology of the Holy Spirit. The new spirituality cannot find helpful concepts for developing its insights in the old schools of Spain and Portugal, and it does not know the Eastern and patristic traditions.[1]

One way of presenting the Holy Spirit came with the charismatic renewal movement.[2] This way passes through a very narrow gate: at least as far as the Catholic charismatic movement is concerned, it is very limited in its spread and its approach; it seems bound to repeat what has been said and written in Europe and the United States. If it continues thereby to remain outside the great challenges facing the continent at the present, it cannot be innovative nor produce a spirituality that truly expresses the spiritual reality of Latin America.[3] So we can say that in the main spirituality still follows the Western tradition: it has not blended with a theology of the Holy Spirit as it has in the East.

The second problem facing us at the outset of this chapter is that spirituality has been of direct and explicit concern to the new theology of Latin America only since the beginning of the eighties.[4] Our spiritual renewal has come about without much theology, still following the old tradition: spirituality deals with spiritual experiences, while the theology of grace speaks of a reality that cannot be experienced.

So on the one hand we have spiritual experiences with no theological references, and on the other a theology of grace without reference to experience. Such a separation between the invisible and the visible, between the gift of God and Christian experience, harms both theology and spirituality. There is no space here to attempt an outline of spiritual theology for our times in the light of the old patristic or Eastern tradition, merely to put forward some pointers to an eventual spiritual theology of the future.

We are now in a fruitful period of spiritual experiences in Latin America.[5] This is producing a renewed understanding of how the Spirit works in human beings. While the theology of the Holy Spirit remains separate from spiritual experiences, theology will lack the renewal it needs, and experiences will not be integrated into the continuance of the great Catholic tradition.

1. THE CRISIS OF MODELS FOR THE ACTION OF THE SPIRIT

(a) Two Models in Crisis

There are two basic models for interpreting the action of the Spirit in human beings: the Eastern and the Western. Both are now in crisis; both are in a double crisis: from the modern age itself, and from the crisis of the modern age.

(i) The Eastern model. This never held much sway in the West. Nor would it be possible to reintroduce it as a simple alternative to a decadent Western model, since it is in its own crisis.

The Eastern concept is that the work of the Spirit is to divinize humankind. This world is transfigured, "caught up," by the kingdom of God, gradually enlightened by divine forces. Spiritual life is a progressive assimilation into the process by which the Spirit divinizes us. This process also follows the path of the sacraments and the liturgy; people are spiritualized by taking part in the liturgy, transformed into praying beings. Human beings follow an itinerary along which they are carried by the enlightenment of the liturgy till they become identified with the celebration of the glory of God and unending thanksgiving. The ascetic and mystical life is no different from the liturgical life; individuals become fused with the people in prayer and find their greatest vitality in this identification with the divine fire.[6]

In the words of a contemporary exponent of Orthodox theology:

> There is a strict correspondence between the sacramental itinerary and the life of the soul in Christ. Initiation through baptism and anointing reaches perfection in the eucharist

and... [that itinerary is] one with the height of mystic endeavour: *theiosis*. Both are mutually enlightening, present the same event, are mystically identical. This is the realization of the golden rule of all patristic thought: "God became man so that man might become God," and reaches to the heart of Orthodox spirituality: "Man becomes through grace what God is by nature."[7]

The profundity of this model is evident. It has been for many and still is for some an admirable interpretation of the good news of the Holy Spirit in the New Testament. But today we can see that it is not the only possible model. What it contains is not to be rejected; it needs to be taken up into a more all-embracing model, but in itself it is no longer viable. What it lacks is any reference to the history of this world. The world of today, in the peripheral nations perhaps even more than in the central ones, was born of history and cannot now forget the fact.

(ii) The Western model. This derives from St Augustine. It has been re-fashioned and developed many times since then, but always on the same lines. Its starting-point is the basic experience of sin: humanity aspires to salvation from the sin that holds it prisoner to evil, to the flesh, to death. Creatures cannot be saved by their own efforts; the Spirit is the source of the path of liberation from sin, which calls itself justification, or regeneration, or sanctification.[8] Liberation from sin is a totally gratuitous grace from God. Yet in some way it includes a certain human activity and postulates a certain human freedom. The relationship between grace and freedom as they relate to justification was to be the object of interminable discussions among the different church confessions and within each.

In this view, the gospel message was "save your soul," meaning saving it from sin. Sin was seen as an individual reality, the one thing human beings had of their own. Salvation was also an individual process. One can see why the Western model reached its most extreme expression in Protestantism, in which grace is above all individual.[9]

This model was another interpretation of the New Testament texts. Like the Eastern model, it also needs to have its positive aspects absorbed into a more all-embracing model. In itself it is no longer viable. It is actually dead.

(b) Conditions for a New Model

It is not up to us to show the Holy Spirit what direction to take. We are not going to set out a new model and then ask the Spirit to deign to use it in carrying out its mission among us today. Nevertheless, history teaches us that the Holy Spirit inspires models that correspond to the basic aspirations of a culture. While it is true that we cannot create a theoretical model believing it to be valid for our times, we can infer the probable ways of the Spirit from the culture of our times.

Life in the Holy Spirit does not depend on theoretical models: saints do not follow theological schemes. On the contrary, life comes first and theory about life follows. Spiritual experiences come first, then the building of the theoretical model to which these experiences correspond.

Conditions, or the "signs of the times," today enable us—as the conditions of the past did for early Latin American spiritual experience—to infer some probable characteristics of a new model of how the Holy Spirit acts in human beings today.

(i) Alienation and liberation. The point of departure for men and women in Latin America today is their experience of an integral alienation, both external and internal. This alienation results from the situation of generalized dependence described in the Puebla Final Document and still obtaining today.[10]

Alienation involves both frustration of external action and internal personality disorder. The personality is attracted by, confused by and finally emptied of identity by the forces of the dominant culture. Alienation affects the masses of the poor and also the ruling classes who collaborate in dependence.

Alienation goes very deep and reaches to the foundations of personality. It produces a corruption of the will and of the understanding. A new reading of chapter 7 of the Letter to the Romans could be applied to it.[11] It is a new embodiment of the dominion of death, of sin, of the flesh and the Law, the starting-point for Paul's message in Romans and Galatians.

The situation of Latin America cannot be resolved simply by political, economic and social change. It needs all of these, but much more still. It needs a complete change or reversal of oppressed personalities, a transformation from people who submit to integral alienation into people who free themselves from this integral alienation and struggle in all aspects of their existence.

If liberation is not taken up by individual men and women, no induced transformation from outside them can be effective. Integral liberation requires a process through which every man and woman liberates himself and herself, loosing all the bonds that tie them to the past, so as to retie the bonds that bind a free society together.[12]

(ii) Alienation and the modern age. Liberation from alienation has been and is the great theme of modern times. The gospel of the age consists in proclaiming a liberation without or even from religions, and in particular without or even from Christianity. Liberation from alienations is to be brought about through science and technology, in a purely secular process. Any spirituality would be superfluous, or even harmful.[13]

Latin American culture is being deeply penetrated by the spirit of the modern age. The ruling classes learn it in their colleges through the "scientific approach" which is taught there, both explicitly and—above all—implicitly. The masses of the people assimilate modern culture through television. Some adopt some of its most acute manifestations in political or revolutionary movements: Marxism is the spirit of the age adapted to conditions of dependence and oppression.

The challenge is this: must the struggle for liberation necessarily fall into modernity and secularism, or can it be the point of departure for a new spiritual journey? The outcome will certainly depend on the Holy Spirit, but it also depends on us.

(c) Steps Toward a New Spirituality

The Spirit is at work among the people of Latin America, working on two levels: the level of the poor who are awakening to their liberation and beginning to act with new spirit; and the level of those among the privileged who are giving up their privileges to take part in the struggle of the poor for their liberation. In both these groups there are signs of the active presence of the Spirit working toward the formation of a new spirituality.

(i) The spirituality of the elite. Puebla addressed itself to religious in particular: "Pastoral openness in one's labors and a preferential option for the poor represent the most noticeable tendency of religious life in Latin America" (733). There is now a new relationship of religious "with the poverty of the marginalized. Now this does not imply simply interior detachment and community austerity; it also implies solidarity with the poor, sharing with them, and in some cases living alongside them" (734).[14]

(ii) The spirituality of the poor. Their new spirituality is a conversion of their traditional religiosity. That religiosity already provided a sound basis: "This is why the religiosity of the Latin American people often is turned into a cry for true liberation" (Puebla 452). Because this desire for liberation has a spiritual basis, Puebla could say that, "In a word, our people yearn for a full and integral liberation, one not confined to the realm of temporal existence. It extends beyond that to full communion with God and with one's brothers and sisters in eternity. And that communion is already beginning to be realized, however imperfectly, in history" (141).

In the base communities above all, a spiritual path is opening up, starting from the religious inheritance of the people and leading to new expressions of it and new subjects for it, making it the equipment for a really new spiritual journey.[15]

(iii) A quest in the dark. Christians trying to walk in the ways of the Spirit are questing in the dark. They feel that the old ways, the methodologies they once learned, no longer work. They sense that the old spiritualities are in decline. They can see that many give up through discouragement because they are disorientated and have lost confidence. There is a general impression that the old certainties no longer hold.

What Christian history teaches is that the Holy Spirit is present in just such situations. The Pauline opposition between Spirit and law or letter has been proved by spiritual men and women of all times. The new spiritualities always arise out of a feeling that the old ones have failed.[16] When all spiritual paths have become choked, then the Holy Spirit is active. This experience of deprivation and incapacity is needed to hack out a new path. Not only is the Spirit not a prisoner of the past; the Spirit always surpasses the past.

Life in the Spirit does not unfold in the calm of the already known; it is a life of risk-taking, accepting the challenges of the unknown. The world of Latin American liberation is a spiritually unknown world because it is a response to actual situations. It is an attempt to create a new model on top of the ruins of the old one. This is why the greatest personalities of the church in Latin America give such an impression of creativity and inventiveness. They are not reproducing existing models. There can be few times when there has been such an upsurge of outstanding personalities in the church. This applies equally to bishops, priests, religious, sisters and lay people.

The sign of the presence of the Spirit is accepting this quest in the darkness, in insecurity; it is faithfulness to the quest even when its direction is unclear; it is persevering with confidence. In the end, strong personalities appear, torch-bearers who shed the light of the presence of Christ, who appear as new Christs in the midst of the people.[17] The great nights are spent in struggles for liberation and in confronting the new challenges they pose for everyone.

(iv) Back to basics. When traditional recipes, models and rules fail, the Spirit takes us back to our origins, that is, to the two models provided in the New Testament: the disciples' following of Jesus and the early communities.

The following of Jesus stems from Jesus' own actions among his people: these were public actions, which have also—perhaps polemically—been called political. Jesus' spiritual journey encompassed his option for the poor, his total dedication to the outcasts of society, his controversies with all power groups, his public witness in Jerusalem, and finally his death on the cross.

It is the quality of public action in Jesus' behaviour that provides the basis for today's liberating option for the poor.[18] This is why Puebla says: "Hence service to the poor is the privileged, though not the exclusive, gauge of our following of Christ" (1145).

For their part, the base communities "are rediscovering also the brotherly and sisterly experience of the early communities, which met for prayer and the breaking of bread, which shared their goods and lived united in one heart and one soul."[19] In them too spirituality starts from a recognition of the public and political significance of the early Christian communities.

Of course the objection has been raised that classical spiritualities never took their inspiration from an explicitly political understanding of Jesus or the early church. This is true, but there is nothing to be inferred from that. All contemporary exegesis, at least for the past twenty years, has concentrated on the social, economic and political underlying structure of the Bible. It emphasizes the Old Testament roots of the New; it denounces the illusions of a falsely spiritual exegesis, divorced from matter and taken out of the material context of the sacred texts.

The new spirituality is now guiding New Testament exegesis. If people are trying to live in the Spirit in the midst of the real world, with its economic and social structures, its politics, it is only natural that they should try to find in the Bible the aspect that sheds light on their spiritual quest. Any new spirituality is based on a new reading of the Bible.[20] The Holy Spirit leads us back to the Bible first, because it contains the light that brightens our journey.

(v) The new reading of the good news of the Spirit. St Paul gives the most complete account of this good news in chapter 8 of his Letter to the Romans. This chapter is coming true in a most impressive way at the present time: "The law of the spirit of life in Christ Jesus has set you free from the law of sin and death" (Rom. 8:2). We were living under regimes of sin and death; now, with the Spirit, we are entering into a new world that sets us free from these regimes. We are living under the regime of the Spirit who is life: "not according to the flesh but according

to the Spirit" (Rom. 8:4). "The flesh" here means the regime that Paul had before his eyes—the Judaic and pagan worlds. It also means the regimes we have before our eyes. "All those moved by the Spirit of God are children of God" (v. 14): they are those who allow themselves to be led in insecurity through the darkness, through doubts, conflicts, divisions, through the dark nights of the senses and the soul; these are the true children of God, not those installed in what they consider perfection.

"From the beginning till now the whole creation, as we know, has been groaning in one great act of giving birth; and not only creation, but all of us who possess the first-fruits of the Spirit, we too groan inwardly as we wait for our bodies to be set free" (vv 22–3).[21] We are now being set free through endless struggles; this land is the setting for almost despairing struggles, in which the enslaved poor groan and hope. The Spirit is present in these groans and hopes. At the same time the Spirit has always been the proclamation of victory, and this proclamation is itself a first victory. When the forces of the flesh and the world disappear, the power of the Spirit is still present.

We must be "guided by the Spirit" (Gal. 5:16); "If you are led by the Spirit no law can touch you" (5:18). In this world in revolution, the old codes are falling away. The law of the Spirit stands. The new spirituality is allowing itself to be led by the Spirit.

Conclusion

Every spirituality is conditioned by the political situation of the church and of Christians in its time. Eastern spirituality was and is monastic, cut off from political life. It concurred in the Eastern dream—of Byzantium and Russia—that the empire was already Christian and had entered upon a transformed world. Western spirituality is basically individual and supposes a separation between religion and politics of which Luther's doctrine of the two kingdoms represents the extreme formulation. In Latin America today our situation is the challenge to live according to the Spirit in the midst of the oppressed Christian people's struggles for their liberation. A new spirituality will have to take this situation into account.

We have already said that establishing a new spirituality does not depend on men and women alone. The Spirit blows where it wills and when it wills. Nevertheless, such eminently spiritual figures have already appeared that we would seem to be able to talk of the Spirit creating a new model of Christian life. This new model of the Spirit in action has been most evident in a pleiad of bishops such as have seldom appeared in history. Their only comparison is with the Fathers of the fourth and fifth centuries, with the bishops martyred in the evangelization of Latin America in the sixteenth,[22] or perhaps the bishops of the barbarian period of the dawn of Europe in the sixth and seventh centuries. The names of these bishops are well-known to their people, and it can only add to the dangers they face to mention them here. Those who have already been martyred have been mentioned.

The bishops, of course, are only the summit of the mountain. There are thousands upon thousands of ordinary Christians who have sought and made new roads in their struggles for liberation. We mention bishops because their example gives greater credibility to the new spirituality.

2. COMPONENTS OF THE NEW SPIRITUALITY

Let us think of some traditional components of the action of the Spirit in people: contemplation, ascesis, prayer, paschal joy. Each of these components has been in a way re-invented in the current experience of the people of Latin America. It is always the same Spirit who produces different fruits appropriate to each age. These fruits are at once different and the same. In their own way they fulfil the promises of the Spirit made by Jesus and made present in the apostolic churches.

(a) The Spirit and Contemplation

The Holy Spirit is the source of faith. This faith unfolds in contemplation of the "mystery" of God. It constitutes a wisdom, a higher knowledge becoming ever deeper. This is what the New Testament texts say: the Spirit allows us to penetrate into the secret of the words and deeds of Jesus.

"The Advocate, the Holy Spirit whom the Father will send in my name, will teach you everything and remind you of all I have said to you" (John 14:26). "The things that no eye has seen and no ear has heard, things beyond the mind of man, all that God has prepared for those who love him. These are the very things that God has revealed to us through the Spirit, for the Spirit reaches the depths of everything, even the depths of God... Now instead of the spirit of the world, we have received the Spirit that comes from God, to teach us to understand the gifts that he has given us" (1 Cor. 2:9–10,12). "If you read my words you will have some idea of the depths that I see in the mystery of Christ. This mystery that has now been revealed through the Spirit to his holy apostles and prophets was unknown to any men in past generations" (Eph. 3:4–5).

A long tradition of monasticism and mysticism has explored every nook and cranny of this contemplation without ever being able to exhaust its riches. Let us quote just one example, from the greatest Byzantine theologian, Simeon the New Theologian: "In charity the Holy Spirit comes to us and enlightens us; he regenerates us, makes us sons of God, clothes us in Christ, lights the lamp of the soul, makes us sons of light, dispels the darkness in our souls, and makes us know that henceforth we participate in eternal life."[23]

We can ask: where does this experience of the wisdom of God come about? Where and how can we know the mystery of God? What is this mystery?

The mystery of God is that God's love is shown in the option for the poor. The Son became poor, "taking on the condition of a slave." The Father became like the poor by giving his Son over to poverty. As a result, it is in the poor that we see the face of God; it is in the poor that the Spirit shows us the face of Christ. The voice of the poor is the voice of God and the cry of the poor is the cry of Jesus. Wisdom, penetrating the mystery of God, consists in discovering this paradoxical and incomprehensible reality: that God has chosen what is weak in this world to confound the strong (1 Cor. 1:27).

The folly of the cross is clearly seen in this, however hard to accept: God revealed to the poor, dedicated to them, choosing them to usher in a new world of freedom, solidarity, reciprocity.

The mystery of God does not reside in some ethereal sphere

above this world, nor does it consist in some theorem that only the cleverest can understand. The mystery of God is a reality at our side, but hidden from the eyes of this world: this world ignores or despises the poor, expects nothing from them, arouses nothing in them. In the new spirituality, the folly of the cross is more than ever central to the message. No one can see this all at once; it is easy to speak or write about the poor, but accepting them, living together with them, working alongside them in the same poverty, these require a wisdom that can come only from continual enlightenment by the Spirit. It is not an intellectual barrier that stands in the way of Christian wisdom; it is our instinctive, natural and culturally-induced aversion to poverty: an aversion the poor themselves share, since they live and die of shame at being poor.[24]

The lives of the great leaders of the church in Latin America this century reveal the history of their discovery of God in the poor: their spiritual journey has been a series of steps along this road. The life of Archbishop Romero himself is a good illustration of this spiritual way.[25]

(b) The Spirit and Ascesis

The progress of Christian life includes a struggle against the evil that dwells within a person; this struggle is called ascesis. The Spirit guides this struggle, the goal of which is liberty in the full sense given to the word in the New Testament.

(i) Ascesis. Liberty is both a calling and something that has to be won: "My brothers, you were called, as you know, to liberty; but be careful, or this liberty will provide the opening for self-indulgence. Serve one another, rather, in works of love" (Gal. 5:13). This verse shows the dynamic of how liberty is to be won. It is won against the domination of "the flesh" and its seductions; it leads to service of others: "Walk by the Spirit and do not gratify the desires of the flesh" (5:16). These "desires of the flesh" are enumerated in verses 19–21; they are opposed by the fruits of the Spirit (v 22). Of course the passage from flesh to Spirit is a long one. The Spirit is the pilot showing the way.

In practice, the meaning of winning liberty against the tendencies of the flesh takes on different aspects at different stages of the development of Christianity. There is an old ascetic tradition built up over the centuries by monks. This interpreted the struggle of the Spirit in each Christian in a manner applicable to monastic life, and within a Hellenistic cultural context. Such an interpretation is subject to evolution in time, and the Spirit can produce other interpretations suited to each age.

The themes of traditional ascesis are well-known. The goal of the ascetic struggle is inner freedom: in the monastic tradition this was reinterpreted as *apatheia* (impassivity), which was often translated as "indifference." This does not mean a passive indifference composed of insensitivity or self-centredness—an attitude that easily leads to Stoicism, which had a considerable influence on early Christian spirituality. It means an active indifference, an openness to being guided in any direction in accordance with spiritual inspiration.[26]

This state of indifference is reached through struggling against "the passions," the spontaneous inclinations of the body or the mind, whether innate or culturally conditioned. Again, it is not a matter of extinguishing these spontaneous inclinations, but of working to direct them toward the fulfilment of the kingdom of God.[27] This struggle against the passions leads to the "divesting" of oneself, to a fight against one's natural egocentricity.

In the traditional interpretation of ascesis, the Spirit adopted many ideas from classical pagan wisdom, giving them a new meaning compatible with the new life in Christ. This means that tradition does not constitute the indispensable and only possible model for the ascetic life.

The same applies to ascesis as to all life in Christ: it is not by our initiative that we find new ways. The Spirit finds these through the ways taken by those who entrust themselves to the Spirit. In today's world, the Spirit is producing new ways of ascesis as well as of contemplation. These will not negate the traditional means to ascesis, but will produce a new way of putting these means into practice. This is not something that can be worked out theoretically, since practice does not derive from theory. On the contrary; practice comes first, then we work out a theory of this practice.

(ii) Ascesis in the liberation of the poor. As for the poor themselves, their lives are one long ascesis. No pattern of ascetic life devised by religious can begin to rival the level of "divesting" and deprivation on which the poor of Latin America live. They belong to the kingdom of God because of what they are, and have no need to plan a course of ascesis. Like the poor Lazarus in the parable, they already have a place reserved for them in the future kingdom of God.

Nevertheless, the poor are sensitive to the trappings of riches. When they have the opportunity of observing a "higher" culture, they are easily fascinated. Witness the addiction of the poor to TV soap operas. In many places, the community of the poor has died with the advent of television. To miss an episode of *"Champagne"* or the like for the sake of a community meeting requires true heroism.

Ascesis applies to people whose education can afford them a higher level of life than poverty. If these are to commit themselves to the liberation of the poor, they need to be ascetics. There is no need for them to look for methods of "divesting" themselves, mortifying their passions or struggling against selfishness: sharing the lives of the poor will implacably do all this for them. What characterizes this ascesis is that it is not a method applied by the person who practises it, but one imposed from outside, by the environment.

Sharing the lives of the poor is a mortification of the body: it brings problems of food and water, insects, mud, lack of space, filth, excesses of heat and cold—discomforts of every sort imaginable. Sharing the lives of the poor requires patience and perseverance equal to the exercises set by the anchorites of old.[28]

It also requires another level of ascesis: mental and intellectual ascesis to enable one to live with people whose mentality is different, who have different values, different criteria governing their personal and social lives. The poor devise their own culture, one fitted to the conditions in which they live.[29] Those who wish to commit themselves to the poor have to accept their culture and make it the instrument of their evangelizing work. This mental ascesis is even more difficult than the physical ascesis required.[30]

Finally, those who commit themselves to the poor will be persecuted not only by the ruling classes and the economic, social and political authorities, but also by elements within the church itself. Incomprehension, hostility, the most painful denunciations, often come from their own colleagues, members of their own religious order, their own diocese or parish. Those who side with the poor are forever despised by anyone of any "importance," are put down, mistrusted. Those who commit themselves to the poor are virtually "excommunicated" from the society in which they were born and grew up. This is the most demanding ascesis of all: there are few who can stand being "rejected."

So a new way is being opened up, a new imitation of the cross of Christ. No one can find this way alone. It comes of its own accord, brought by the Holy Spirit.

(c) The Spirit and Prayer

(i) The Spirit in prayer. Just like contemplation and ascesis, so prayer comes from the Spirit: we cannot invent it. The Spirit creates it in every age using the resources of the culture of that age. So prayer for today will be a new creation of the prayer of Christ. The Our Father is not a formula: the meaning its words convey is constantly being renewed. There is a new Our Father in Latin America, still the same, but still new.[31]

"When we cannot choose words in order to pray properly, the Spirit himself expresses our plea in a way that could never be put into words, and God who knows everything in our hearts knows perfectly well what he means" (Rom. 8:26–7). "The proof that you are sons is that God has sent the Spirit of his Son into our hearts: the Spirit that cries 'Abba, Father'" (Gal. 4:6).

"Be filled with the Spirit. Sing the words and tunes of the psalms and hymns when you are together, and go on singing and chanting to the Lord in your hearts, so that always and everywhere you are giving thanks to God" (Eph. 5:18–20).

(ii) The new prayer in the Spirit. The base communities are rediscovering prayer. By giving the word back to the laity and the poor they are opening themselves to the inspiration of all their members. There is no incompatibility between physical struggles and prayer. Those who organize themselves and those who pray are the same people with the same needs and the same hope.[32]

Their prayer springs from their situation of weakness and insecurity on one hand, and from their confidence in the Father on the other. It reinterprets the Our Father: it asks for the kingdom of God to come; this kingdom has clearly definable outlines when hoped for by those who have been oppressed for centuries. The same applies when they ask for their daily bread, or for the forgiveness of sins.[33]

Nor is there incompatibility between asking and working. Human beings alone cannot bring in the reign of God, but if God is to reign, men and women must help through their work.

At the same time a prayer of praise and thanksgiving rises up. Signs of the presence of the Father, of the coming of the Son and the Holy Spirit, can be seen clearly in the world of the poor. Those who share the lives of the poor give thanks to God for the marvels they are privileged to witness.

True prayer is not prayer that needs to be forced out, but prayer that springs naturally from the reality of life. This has been true of all the great periods of mysticism. Something of this is springing up in our world: the dawning of an age of mysticism comparable to those recognized in the past. This is one of the signs that the Spirit is active.[34]

(d) Joy in the Spirit

"The kingdom of God... means... joy brought by the Holy Spirit" (Rom. 14:17). "You were led to become imitators of us, and of the Lord; and it was with the joy of the Holy Spirit that you took to the gospel, in spite of the great opposition all round you" (1 Thess. 1:6). Only in the Spirit is joy possible in the midst of so much suffering. Paul who wrote this had experienced extreme suffering and joy in the Spirit: he knew what he was talking about. I would not dare to talk of the Spirit today unless this had been my experience in daily life.

The joy of the poor is always somewhat austere because they know where it comes from, and they know what threatens them. But it is a spontaneous joy, with no second thoughts, an open joy, no threat to anyone. It is a joy without victims, an innocent joy.

Joy comes from certainty of future victory. "I have told you this so that my own joy may be in you and your joy be complete" (John 15:11). This is the joy of the eve of martyrdom. It is a joy of which we have some experience in our time: it is the joy found in chains and prisons, in concentration camps. It is the joy of certainty of victory, and of the conviction that our liberty, our solidarity, our present friendship, are the beginning, now, of what is waiting for us.[35] "For I am certain of this: neither death nor life, no angel, no prince, nothing that exists, nothing still to come, not any power, or height, or depth, nor any created thing, can ever come between us and the love of God made visible in Christ Jesus our Lord" (Rom. 8:38–9).

This is what Bishop Angelelli wrote to two of his priests who had been taken captive: "I share your suffering and your joy, and those of so many others. Those who believe must be witnesses to the joy of Easter. Don't worry if your compatriots laugh at this. Use your detention to meditate on the word of God in the Bible I am sending you, which you asked for as the only thing you want to possess at this time."[36]

Conclusion

Each person is called to a complete transformation in the Spirit (Eph. 4:22), to leave the old human being and put on the new one who is Christ. This new humanity is a different reality in each person, an infinitely diverse reality. It is always Christ, but there are an infinite number of personal embodiments of Christ.

Each person is called on to build himself or herself anew; all men and women have their own way of putting on this newness. No one can copy an earlier model. It is not a matter of obeying general rules, universally applicable in equal measure. It is not a matter of personifying a pattern of typical "humanity," as the elites of olden times thought and as the elites of our world still think today.

It is the Spirit who guides our discernment of what is needed to become new men and women.[37] Discerning means reading the signs and finding a vocation in them, a vocation that will always be personal and unique. We cannot build our lives out of nothing; we create using the material that God has placed at our disposal. But the figure of the new human being is not insribed in material form; it is a creation of the Spirit. We have to go on guessing at it, reconstituting it little by little till the last day of our earthly journey.

Forming our new being is the ground of the freedom to which we are called.[38] Freedom means making something new, thereby sharing in God's creativity. Being free means being capable of producing something never seen before, so projecting a unique personality, and forming it by this very projection.

Freedoms do not drive one away from others. Human newness consists in friendship with other people. Human inventiveness is to find human relationships. The new things we create are not merely material realities, but above all social realities. Freedom creates the new community. In this way individual and church come together.

Building the new being is a long task. It is the synthesis of a long journey of contemplation and ascesis. Since this is a journey to the Father undertaken in the New Man who is Christ, a journey moved by the Spirit, prayer goes with us on our journey. Our road is not a lonely one; we share it in solidarity with the communities and furthermore in the company of Christ under the gaze of the Father who is at its end. The Spirit teaches this permanent prayer, which is like the breathing of new beings.[39]

The Spirit leads the new beings through their Exodus: we each have our Exodus, our Exile and our return from exile. We each have our Easter. The Spirit is in the cross and in the resurrection. The Spirit is present to recapitulate, as it were, at each moment the whole weight of existence, to recapitulate the whole of our past, to recapitulate all our aspirations for the future in one hope. *Veni, Creator Spiritus*: all prayers to the Spirit have always struck this note.[40] Filled with the Spirit, we look to the same Spirit to be our guide on the journey, which is always being undertaken anew, always into the unknown, ever dangerous and joyful.

Chapter V
The Two Hands of God

The phrase comes from St Irenaeus: The Father works through his two hands, the Word and the Holy Spirit. Both hands have equal strength and equal value. Both hands work together. But they are not identical; each has its own sphere of operations. One complements the other, and between them they produce one finished result.

The Son works through incarnation. Through his incarnation, the Son is present in one single human being, one chosen from among billions: present in one particular place and at one particular moment in the history of humanity. The Son forms one point in this history. The Word pronounces certain words, spoken in a particular language, and written down in one linguistic form. The gospel is addressed to all men and women, but it starts from one specific and unique point in history and geography. For all other human beings, the gospel comes to them from outside themselves, and strikes them as something that challenges their whole being. The Son generates attitudes signified by words such as: hearing, listening, following, imitating, obeying. There is a unity proceeding from the Word of God, going out to meet human diversity so as to integrate it, bring it together in unity.

The model of church which prevailed in the West from the Middle Ages, and even more so since the sixteenth century, in both its Protestant and Catholic embodiments, proceeds from this Christ considered in isolation. Protestants obey Christ present in the word of the Bible; Catholics obey Christ present in the hierarchy. This at least has been the prevailing model.

The mission of the Holy Spirit, however, is every bit as important as the mission of the Son. The Holy Spirit is not incarnated in one individual. It is not tied to any one person, nor to a particular moment in time or space. The Holy Spirit is sent to all places at all times. It is present in the whole of humanity, it works in everyone, of whatever culture or religion. The Holy Spirit dwells in multiplicity, takes on diversity, creating a movement of communion and convergence from within the immensity of human diversity.

There is another difference. The Son became incarnate in one human person and in this way formed a perfect person, far surpassing all other human beings. The Holy Spirit, on the other hand, exists in the imperfection of countless individuals seeking light through the darkness that encompasses them and liberation in the midst of the sin that besets them. The Holy Spirit produces a great movement of communion and converg-ence of a humanity that is sinful, corrupt, subjected to evil. The Son is incarnate in a person who is already the end of this movement, who anticipates the coming of the new humanity toward which the throng led by the Holy Spirit is making its way.

Despite the differences, the Son and the Holy Spirit work in perfect harmony. There are not two religions, two churches, two evolutions of humanity. The Father frees his people through the convergent action of the Son and the Holy Spirit.

It is the same Spirit who was sent to Jesus and to the rest of humanity. The same Spirit enfolds the head and members in a single body. The same Spirit moves Christ and all created peoples into the same overall being. Nor does the Spirit detract from Jesus, but carries everyone and everything to him. On the one hand, "this Lord is the Spirit" (2 Cor. 3:17); on the other: "No one can be speaking under the influence of the Holy Spirit and say 'Curse Jesus,' and... no one can say 'Jesus is Lord' unless he is under the influence of the Holy Spirit" (1 Cor. 12:3). The Spirit leads to Jesus and nowhere else.

This is why the Spirit does not produce dispersion, but creates unity out of dispersion. The Spirit does not keep individuals isolated in themselves, but opens them out to a universal communion whose centre is Jesus. For his part, Jesus does not work on other human beings simply through human

means, which would lead to uniformity, submission, renunciation of one's own nature; Jesus brings humanity together
according to the way the Spirit works: that is, starting from the
proper nature of every individual, and of every human
collectivity.

This chapter has four sections: the first looks at the two hands
of the Father at work in Jesus; the second shows the ways in
which Word and Spirit come together to produce one single
effect: the renewal of the world. The third section applies these
concepts to the church, which proceeds simultaneously from
Christ and the Spirit; the fourth draws some conclusions for
mission from the Father working through two hands.

1. THE SON AND THE SPIRIT IN JESUS

The theme of Jesus' anointing by the Holy Spirit has been
rediscovered, rehabilitated and reintroduced into Catholic
theology in recent years mainly through the persuasive and
persevering work of one man: Heribert Mühlen.[1] The reintro-
duction of this idea has led to a long task of correcting and
complementing traditional Catholic christology, a task that is
still not finished. Vatican II mentions the theme of Jesus'
anointing by the Spirit at the beginning of its Constitution on
the Liturgy, but did not go on to make it the basis of any
theological elaboration.

(a) The Limitations of Traditional Western Christology

In one of his last books on the Holy Spirit,[2] Yves Congar, great
Thomist and fervent admirer of the christology of St Thomas
though he was, recognizes and clearly defines the limitations of
this christology, which had become the basic component of the
ordinary teaching of the Catholic Church. The Holy Spirit is
mentioned in Thomist christology, but plays no significant part
in it. Everything revolves round the mystery of the incarnation
of the Word in one human nature.

According to St Thomas, Jesus was formed in the full dignity
completeness of his being from the moment of the incarnation.
From this moment on, he was what he would always be, since

everything that he was derived from the incarnation. From then on, Jesus possessed the various forms of actual grace which were the consequences of the incarnation of the Son: sanctifying grace in all its fulness and special grace as head of the new humanity. As a result, Jesus' history on earth added nothing to him; in itself, this history had no value. Its events brought him nothing new and changed nothing in the perfection he possessed from the moment of his conception in Mary's womb.

Thomist christology describes God coming down to humankind: the Son of God became man and transformed human individuality by uniting it to the person of the Son of God. What it left out of account was the other face of the mystery, the elevation of the human being Jesus into God: Jesus as the story of the integration of a human being into God. Such a christology makes it appear that the human being Jesus lost his historicity in Christ. Such a human being would have no prehistory in his people or his family, his country or his culture. He would have no history in his education or in his sharing in the life of the people. The events narrated in the Gospels would merely repeat the same fundamental mystery of the incarnation in different forms, but would not tell any significant story.

By concentrating all its attention on the "God-Man," St Thomas' christology and the Catholic christology deriving from it ignored Jesus the Messiah-Liberator. But Jesus' human actions make up a history, and this history was understood and explained by the evangelists in the light of biblical concepts, of which the most important were the various concepts of the Messiah. This is why Latin American christology concentrates primarily on the Messiahship of Jesus, and why at first sight it seems so alien to traditional christology.

Jesus' Messiahship is bound up with the presence of the Spirit in him. It is the Holy Spirit who invests Jesus with his messianic mission. This did not happen all at once, but by degrees. This is why the Gospels show a series of comings of the Spirit on Jesus, each one corresponding to the launching of a new stage in his messianic mission. Seen from the standpoint of Jesus' messianic mission, his pre-history, his history on earth, and his history after the resurrection take on their true meaning.

Through his messianic mission, Jesus enters into history and creates history. He ceases to be a unique phenomenon, virtually estranged from and alien to the history of humanity.

A form of integralist Catholicism in vogue in the nineteenth century delighted in the idea of a Christ removed from any contact with our world: one more application of the *"Credo quia absurdum."* Such a christology is quite simply not Christian: it is not what the Gospels and the whole New Testament teach. On the contrary, the Bible shows Jesus' presence as the culmination of human history at the end of the slow process of the preparation of Israel.

The Holy Spirit made Jesus Messiah, forming him gradually through historical events particular to a specific time and place. It is not enough to consider the human nature of Jesus through the changes brought about in it by the incarnation; we need to follow the New Testament as it shows Jesus in action, working in historical time, changing as he did so. His role was that of Messiah-Liberator; his actions in historical time were determined by the comings of the Spirit on him; the changes in him accompanied each new stage of his confrontation with the world.

(b) The Stages of the Coming of the Spirit on Jesus

(i) The form of a slave and glory. St Paul clearly distinguishes two stages in Jesus' Messiahship. Before his death and resurrection, Jesus was a hidden Messiah, humiliated, in the form of a slave. After the resurrection, he was clothed in power and received the fulness of his messianic mission, which he carried out through the power of the Spirit.[3] It was with his resurrection that Jesus, "in the order of the spirit, the spirit of holiness that was in him, was proclaimed Son of God in all his power" (Rom. 1:4).[4]

St Peter, as shown by his discourses related in the Acts of the Apostles, preached the same doctrine: "Now raised to the heights by God's right hand, he has received from the Father the Holy Spirit, who was promised, and what you see and hear is the outpouring of that Spirit" (Acts 2:33; compare 13: 32–3). St John teaches the same: it was only after the resurrection that

Jesus received the Spirit so as to pour it out: this was a new stage, bringing such abundance of the Spirit that Jesus could pour it out, something he could not do before. The fulness of his anointing with the Spirit came about in his resurrection and ascension, and at Pentecost. His interventions after the resurrection show that he could not have the full anointing till he had gone back to the Father (cf John 20:17).

This is why the Spirit remained somewhat hidden during Jesus' earthly mission. It was only in the light of the resurrection that the disciples understood that this earthly mission had been promoted by the Holy Spirit, and identified the earlier stages of Jesus' anointing with the Spirit. They themselves had not seen this at the time. After Pentecost everything became progressively clearer: Jesus' life on earth had been messianic and inspired by the Spirit.

(ii) Anointing in baptism. In his address in the house of Cornelius, Peter was referring to Jesus' baptism when he said: "God had anointed him with the Holy Spirit and with power, and because God was with him, Jesus went about doing good and curing all who had fallen into the power of the devil" (Acts 10:38). He went on to say that he had been witness to everything Jesus had done in his mission stemming from his anointing—curing the sick and casting out devils. This activity in fact started with Jesus' baptism. All the evangelists state that Jesus' messianic activity began with his baptism, or rather, with what happened on the occasion of his baptism.

Each of the evangelists tells the story of this baptism in his own way. The earliest version, that of Mark, says that only Jesus saw the Spirit at the time. This version in fact corresponds to the old idea that the disciples had not recognized Jesus as Messiah while he was carrying out his mission in Palestine, but only at a later stage.

The Father's words and the presence of the Spirit clearly show that Jesus' anointing took place here, that Jesus was made Messiah at this moment.[5] At the same time, the allusions to Old Testament texts show the direction his messianic activity was to take: that of the Servant of God according to Isaiah. The effect of Jesus' anointing showed then in his victory over Satan (Luke

4:14). Following this, he began to evangelize with the power of the Spirit (Luke 4:18).

2. THE SPIRIT AND THE WORD

The unity between the actions of the Son and those of the Spirit is shown in the mutual implication of word and Spirit. Christ is the Word; St Irenaeus said: "The church has its pillar and support in the Gospel and the Spirit of Life."[6] This association is already clear in the Bible and was a constant theme of tradition, which presented it in different lights at different times. Today we are beginning to see it in a renewed light, different from traditional forms, but equally valid.

(a) Spirit and Word in the Bible

The Old Testament already demonstrated the association between word and spirit: "By the word of Yahweh the heavens were made, their whole array by the breath of his mouth" (Ps. 33:6; cf Gen. 1:2ff). In the prophetic genre that began at the time of the Exile, with Isaiah and Ezekiel, Spirit and word act together: "My spirit with which I endowed you, and the words that I have put in your mouth, will not disappear from your mouth" (Isa. 59:21); "As he said these words, the spirit came into me" (Ezek. 2:2).[7]

There are few references to the Spirit in the Synoptics, but they are associated with words: "It is not you who will be speaking; it will be the Holy Spirit" (Mark 13:11; Matt. 10:19–20; Luke 12:11–12). "Elizabeth was filled with the Holy Spirit. She gave a loud cry" (Luke 1:41–2). "The Spirit of the Lord has been given to me. . . . He has sent me to bring the good news to the poor" (Luke 4:18).

In the fourth Gospel, the unity between word and Spirit is treated systematically.[8] "He whom God has sent speaks God's own words: God gives him the Spirit without reserve" (John 3:34). "God is spirit, and those who worship must worship in spirit and truth" (4:24). "Truth" is the good news announced by Jesus, the reality of salvation proclaimed in the gospel: "The words I have spoken to you are spirit and they are life" (6:63).[9]

The two hands of God are very clearly present in Paul's

message: "When we brought the Good News to you, it came to you not only as words, but as power and as the Holy Spirit" (1 Thess. 1:5). "In my speeches and the sermons that I gave, there were none of the arguments that belong to philosophy; only a demonstration of the power of the Spirit" (1 Cor. 2:4).[10]

In the Acts of the Apostles, the association between the two is continually emphasized: "You will receive power when the Holy Spirit comes on you, and then you will be my witnesses" (Acts 1:8). "They were all filled with the Holy Spirit, and began to speak foreign languages as the Spirit gave them the gift of speech" (2:4).[11]

The letters in Revelation proceed equally from Christ and the Spirit (Rev. 2:1, 7, etc.).[12]

What all these texts are saying is that the gospel on its own is not enough. What gives it power and efficacy is the Holy Spirit. For its part, the Holy Spirit does not inspire any sort of word, but only the word of Christ. This is why Paul shows such concern over the gift of tongues that might not say anything intelligible to the Christian community; he prefers the gift of prophecy, which builds up the community, the body of Christ. The true gospel of Christ is that which speaks the truth about Christ, preaching the gospel of the cross (1 Cor. 14).

It is true that the presence of the Spirit can be interpreted in an inadequate manner. The Spirit can be invoked merely to support words formed without it, to set a seal of approval on discourse, confer authenticity or give strength. But then the Spirit remains external to the words themselves, with no part in their composition or expression; it is just used as a prop. This sort of interpretation has often been a prevalent practice in the West. The "gospel" was seen as simply the letter of the Bible, or the teaching of the magisterium. Such interpretations derive from purely circumstantial factors, and fail to restore true meaning to the Bible through the association between Spirit and word. The word must come from the Spirit and be worked by the Spirit, both in its emission and its reception.

(b) Spirit and Word in Tradition

Tradition has kept some aspects of the close association between Spirit and word, without exhausting all its implications.

(i) Spirit and word in reception of the word. Tradition, above
all in the West, has stressed reception of the word. The word
has been seen as proceeding directly from the Word of God.
Insistence has been laid on the continuity between the Christ-
word and the words present in the church—the written word of
the Bible, the spoken word of preaching, the solemn word of
the magisterium, defining, proclaiming or condemning. The
role reserved to the Spirit in this process was to ensure
reception of this word in true faith.

It is traditional teaching that it would be impossible to receive
the word of the gospel with true faith without being enlightened
by the Holy Spirit. Like the Ephesians, we need "a spirit of
wisdom and perception of what is revealed, to bring [us] to full
knowledge of him" (Eph. 1:17). The need for the Holy Spirit
in order to be able to make a true act of faith was solemnly
proclaimed by the Second Council of Orange in 529, in its
canon 7: it is impossible to reach the stage of making an act of
faith "without the enlightenment and inspiration of the Holy
Spirit" (DS 377).

Human response to the word of God is listening. Listening is
the great task of the people of God. Indeed, listening and
obeying are one and the same. Listening has to be an active,
working process; this is, obedience: "Listen, Israel" (Deut.
6:4).[13] "If only you would listen to him today, 'Do not harden
your hearts as at Meribah...'"(Ps. 95:8). Listening is a gift of
the Spirit.

The theme of listening was given its most complete expression by St Augustine in his idea of the "inner master."[14] An
outer master teaches and an inner master gives understanding
of the outer word. This inner master is the Holy Spirit. This
idea of the inner master passed down Western tradition through
St Gregory the Great, St Thomas Aquinas and *The Imitation
of Christ*, enriching its spirituality and its theology.[15]

The same idea lies behind an ancient practice regarding
sermons; the practice goes back as far as St John Chrysostom,
who asked that the Holy Spirit be invoked before beginning a
sermon. The word of God has its own power, but it needs to
be pierced by the Holy Spirit for those who hear it to assimilate
it. There is also a very ancient rite in the consecration of bishops

which unites the word of the gospel with the Holy Spirit: placing the book of the Gospels on the head and shoulders of the candidate while invoking the Holy Spirit.[16] In the same line, there is an old adage which says that, in order to understand the written word of the Bible, we need the Spirit who wrote it.[17]

The doctrine that the word of Christ is taught by the Spirit belongs to all branches of the Christian church. Eastern theologians give it special weight.[18] In the West, Luther elaborated it forcefully in his disputes against extremists and Catholics. No one insisted more than he on obedience to the word of the Bible; he would not admit that the doctrine of inner enlightenment by the Spirit could stand in the way of submission to the written word of the Bible.[19] He accused Müntzer and other theologians of the sixteenth century revolution of appealing to the Spirit against Christ.

Calvin further developed the doctrine of the need for inner enlightenment by the Spirit in order to understand the Bible.[20]

This enlightenment by the Spirit which stands at the origin of faith and of understanding the word does not exclude human and material mediations. It is not a purely individual matter; it is not a contact between the Holy Spirit and the individual mind disconnected from historical realities. The same Spirit who enlightens minds also makes them communicate with one another. It uses the communion of believers for the mutual enlightenment of the faithful. This is how the Holy Spirit directs and guides tradition, which is not simply a product of sociological factors. There is a communion among believers that goes beyond natural ties. The Spirit creates a chain of transmission from generation to generation, reaching across time and space, and this is tradition. As Vatican II stated: "This tradition which comes from the apostles develops in the Church with the help of the Holy Spirit. . . . The Holy Spirit, through whom the living voice of the gospel resounds in the Church, and through her, in the world, leads unto all truth those who believe and makes the word of Christ dwell abundantly in them" (DV 8b, c).

The active memory of the words of Christ revealed by Jesus in his farewell discourse begets this tradition. The Holy Spirit enlightens individuals through their insertion in this living tradition, ever renewed, rediscovered, revivified. The church's mediation prolongs that of tradition. The Spirit begets faith through community. The word of Christ is received in the church and through the church; each individual receives it through this ecclesial reception and in communion and dialogue with it. This is why there are not an infinite number of different meanings of the word, but one common, basic perception, though differentiated. There is an ecclesial voyage of discovery of the word of God, in which all have their proper part to play, but never separately from each other. Vatican II called this voyage the "sense of faith" of the people of God. The people of God teaches infallibly when it teaches with universal consensus. The faith of each individual is enlightened by this common sense in the church: "For, by this sense of faith which is aroused and sustained by the Spirit of truth, God's People accepts not the word of men but the very word of God" (LG 12b).

Put like this, this teaching would seem to be acceptable to Catholics and Protestants alike, but Vatican II adds a note: "The fact that the faithful as a whole bear witness to the gospel does not make superfluous the teaching of the hierarchy. To them it falls to shepherd the whole flock by clear, authoritative doctrine." This role of the hierarchical magisterium in guiding the sense of the faithful lies at the root of Catholic-Protestant disagreement. For Protestants, the very authority of the hierarchy is a rejection of the sovereignty of the word of God. There is room here for many long debates yet.[21] Catholic teaching was set out in the Constitution on Divine Revelation: "The task of authentically interpreting the word of God, whether written or handed on, has been entrusted exclusively to the living teaching office of the Church, whose authority is exercised in the name of Jesus Christ. The teaching office is not above the word of God, but serves it, teaching only what has been handed on, listening to it devoutly, guarding it scrupulously, and explaining it faithfully by divine commission and with the help of the Holy Spirit" (DV 10b). The magisterium ("teaching office") is not above the word it interprets. The magisterium cannot be thought of as something outside the church; it is within the church and within the sense of faith of the people of God. There are not two Spirits: one for the people and one for the magisterium. The same Spirit teaches both the people of God and the magisterium. Despite this, there have been problems in practice in the Catholic Church, particularly since its nineteenth-century rejection of the world. Nevertheless, it is clear that the magisterium is not called to impose an interpretation of the word of God on the people if the people do not hold this interpretation to be true in any way.

It has to be said that the Catholic theology developed in the last century has sometimes tended to champion a situation in which the people are obliged to bow down in blind obedience before a magisterium capable of seeing clearly what no one else can see. This is certainly not the meaning of enlightenment by the Holy Spirit.

(ii) Spirit and word in emission of the word. The word of truth is Christ. He alone speaks with authority. All the words spoken by the church and in the church have their rule, norm and meaning in Christ. Yet, the letter kills and the Spirit gives life. Christian preaching of the word does not consist in indefinite repetition of the actual words written down in the Bible or contained in the dogmas defined by the magisterium.

There was an office of the letter: Moses' office. There is an office of the Spirit: that of the Apostles and all their successors.[22] The office of the Spirit follows in the line of the old office of the prophets and brings in the prophetic office of the church. The Spirit inspires a powerful word; through the Spirit, the word that is preached has the power of God.

Till recently, not much importance was given to the spiritual or prophetic office. Protestants insisted on radical obedience to the word of the Bible, Catholics on radical obedience to the magisterium. Now, we see another aspect: in the New Testament, the office of the word is spiritual; St Paul, St John and St Luke all emphasize the role of prophets in the church. Prophets are bearers of the word. They are strong; they exhort, insist, persuade, awaken people to faith, to conversion, to service to the community: they build community.[23]

In the early days of Christianity, prophets were somehow institutionalized, showing that there was no opposition between prophecy and institution. Paul, John and Luke all speak of prophets as an established category, with official status in the church. The prophets were not isolated figures; they belonged to a large family, followed a definite tradition. But they did not just repeat words: the words they spoke were pertinent, words that penetrated and transformed those who heard them.[24] Charism and institution came together in the prophets. And the church recognized prophets as a class within it and rewarded them with its attention and esteem.

Prophets have to be faithful to the word of him who sent them out to speak. But they are also profoundly personal, and in a sense recreate the word they have received. Prophets make the word of God a deeply personal and community word, a word capable of penetrating and convincing. Prophets are at once inventive, creative and totally obedient. They combine submission to the message they have received with a capacity to express this message in a comprehensible manner. They make the word of God be a real word for the human situation they are addressing. The word of Christ is really from Christ if it is both the same and different for every individual and every culture.

Today we are again beginning to give the name of prophet to those who are able to hand on the word of Christ in human language endowed with real meaning.[25] How then does prophecy relate to the instituted office of the hierarchy? Since Vatican II we no longer uphold the one-sided "verticalist" view of revelation worked out by medieval scholasticism and generally accepted in the Catholic Church after the Council of Trent. In this view, prophecy would have disappeared forever from the church after the third century. The word of Christ would have been handed over to the Apostles, who would have handed on the totality of revelation to the hierarchy, who would in turn communicate the tradition they had received to the Christian people.

Such a scheme never corresponded to the reality of the Catholic Church at any time in its history. It is a theoretical construct, taken by some as an ideal to be achieved. It never was. At all periods, people have been raised up by the Spirit to exercise a decisive spiritual influence independently of the hierarchy, which usually recognized their inspiration, at least in practice. These were martyrs, monks or nuns, spiritual writers, mystics, founders of religious orders or institutes carrying out social or evangelizing works, founders of communities or associations. The vitality of the church has always owed much more to their initiatives than to the far more formal preaching of the clergy.

Christian history has in fact always shown two poles in the preaching office. One is the instituted pole of the hierarchy, extended down through presbyters and deacons. This pole is mainly concerned to transmit a literal concept of tradition. The hierarchy keeps the "deposit" contained in the Bible and traditional interpretations, without taking many initiatives in the direction of renewing, adapting the message to current needs. Its chief concern is not to deviate from the path of continuity. The hierarchy guarantees connection with the origins and with the traditions of the past; it guarantees fidelity.

The danger for the hierarchy is the literalism that can result from seeking to be faithful to revelation by repeating the old words literally, without taking account of the fact that these same words today either no longer have any meaning, or that history has given them a very different sense from that originally intended. Also, up to the pontificate of Pius XII, it was held that tradition could not be handed on in other than a scholastic formulation. This led to the hierarchy identifying tradition with one school of theology, one whose limitations are now becoming ever more obvious.

The other pole is formed by a prophetic tradition, by people who may be members of the hierarchy, but more often are not. These people have a special gift which enables them to find contemporary human words which better convey the meaning of the gospel words to an audience conditioned by history and geography. Vatican II recognized the legitimacy of the prophetic tradition in the church, especially in its declarations on charisms.[26]

There is a distinction between the two poles, but not necessarily opposition, since there cannot be two Spirits, nor two Christs. All must submit to the word of Christ. All recognize the limitations of human words in translating the words of Christ and of the Bible.

The prophetic tradition does not reject the hierarchy; it recognizes that the bishops have a duty to submit contemporary expressions of the word to the criteria of continuity. The hierarchy is the guarantor of continuity between the message of former times and the message of today. There may be temporary opposition and conflict between the two, but in the end, in the Catholic tradition, prophets submit to the declarations of councils, popes and the episcopal magisterium in general.

For its part, the hierarchy is not a gift of the Holy Spirit, nor the source of all truth. It does not usually take the initiative, but intervenes in the second instance following initiatives taken by the prophets. The hierarchy has to be attentive to the voice of prophets, since it too comes from the Spirit. Bishops receive the sacrament of orders, which infuses the Spirit. Episcopacy is also a charism; bishops are not conservative scribes of a fixed dead word. They need sufficient spiritual sensitivity to recognize the Spirit at work among prophets.

The ideal would be to have an adequate number of prophets among the ranks of bishops. They would facilitate cross-fertilization between the hierarchical pole and the prophetic pole. This has happened at various junctures in history. It would certainly seem to apply to Latin America today: hence Medellín and Puebla. Despite this, there are grounds for fearing for the future. There seems to be a change in the criteria used in Rome for appointing bishops: lawyers and administrators are being preferred, prophets avoided. The history of the church in the eighteenth and nineteenth centuries shows what happened when bishops were almost completely lacking in prophetic spirit and were content to exercise the virtues of good scribes. Are the troubles so much lamented by Cardinal Ratzinger today not a result of bishops exercising a prophetic role and refusing merely to be scribes? What the modern world is rejecting is the church built by the clergy of the eighteenth and nineteenth centuries, the church that refused to face up to the problems of the emergent new world.

(c) Spirit and Word Today

Christianity is today, as it always has been, a cross-fertilization between the mission of the word and the mission of the Holy Spirit. But the two traditional roots of this cross-fertilization have lost their validity.

In the tradition that took root in the West, the word of God has always been closely linked to human words, whether the words of preaching or those of dogmatic definitions. Jesus appeared in the human discourse of the hierarchy and of theologians. The task of the Holy Spirit was seen as encouraging the faithful to be obedient to these words. Faith was mental obedience to a system composed of human words. Today, after two centuries of criticism, the identity between the word of God and human discourse no longer looks so evident.

In the Eastern tradition, the word was always seen mainly as doxology: words are praise, thanksgiving, proclamation of the glory of the Father through the Son. The Holy Spirit associates the people with these words through the liturgy. Faith is an enlightenment of the mind which finds itself participating in the heavenly liturgy as an anticipation of the kingdom of God. This model excludes earthly history from both the word and the Holy Spirit, and in that form the model has now become incomprehensible.

Today we are returning to a more biblical concept of the word. The word is found in action. The eternal Word became human word through acting in our history. Jesus spoke through the actions of his life. His "sayings" comment on his life and would be meaningless without that life. The Holy Spirit enables us to understand Jesus' life, his actions.

Now Jesus' actions can only be understood through following him. Those who do not follow him cannot understand him. The praxis of imitation of Jesus is the starting-point for an understanding of him. We cannot understand Jesus' words if we start with them alone, using a dictionary, a grammar and the tools of literary criticism. We understand his words by taking part in the actions to which the words refer. The Gospels themselves affirm the primacy of action over words on every page. It is only from within a liberating praxis that Jesus' words can be understood.

What part does the Spirit play in this process? The Spirit creates the liberating praxis that follows the lines laid down by Christ. The Spirit discovers how to live in true obedience to Jesus: by imitating his actions. In the twentieth century, it is not possible to copy materially what Jesus did in Galilee in the first century. What is needed is a new historical creation. But this has to be faithful: the Spirit cannot separate itself from Jesus. A purely human creation would necessarily be different: the same creation cannot span twenty centuries. The Spirit alone can assure continuity across such a distance in time.

Given that words in the form of discourse originate in praxis, the second part played by the Spirit is to guide the creation of a new language, of a new discourse that today can faithfully represent the discourse of the Gospels. It would be ingenuous to think that we could translate the discourse of the New Testament into today's language through literary or purely intellectual disciplines. The lesson of two hundred years of "scientific" exegesis is that the intellectual road leads to a Christian archaeology. Biblical theology failed to progress beyond this archaeology; it proved incapable of developing an evangelizing discourse, of speaking to our contemporaries. This is why Vatican II proved incapable of suggesting any form of discourse that would be capable of evangelizing. It returned to the biblical language of the first century, but could not speak to our contemporaries. Biblical theology cannot do this because it creates no new praxis, and words without praxis to lend them support are empty of substance.

The Holy Spirit who recreates Jesus' praxis also inspires a language capable of explaining and commenting on the new praxis. This language does not need to be eloquent with human eloquence: suffice that it be capable of demonstrating an eloquent reality.

3. CHRIST AND THE SPIRIT IN THE CHURCH

In the church too the two hands of God work together, constructing a living synthesis. This is the truth that lay hidden for so long under the ecclesiology that prevailed since Trent.

This started from the idea that Christ was the founder of the church. The assumption here is that Christ founded the church as a hierarchical society endowed with all the means necessary for salvation. J.A. Möhler has summed up the ecclesiology he was taught in these words: "God founded the hierarchy and thereby provided all that would be needed till the end of time." All the Holy Spirit could do was confirm the work done by Jesus. The imbalance in such a conception is obvious: Christ does everything and the Holy Spirit is virtually superfluous. Rediscovering the Holy Spirit leads to a new balance in our conception of the church. It means understanding how the Word and the Spirit work together.

(a) The Relative Autonomy of the Spirit in the Church

The idea that the church was founded by Christ is true in part, but it must not be made the whole truth. The history of the church since the Reformation shows a series of phenomena indicating the intervention of God—in the here and now God was at work in the origins of churches and movements. Under cover of the greater freedom of the Reformation, many Christian groups and movements arose proclaiming their direct dependence on the initiative of the Holy Spirit. Examples would be the conversion of George Fox and the founding of the Society of Friends (Quakers), the Pietist movement, Wesley and the great adventure of Methodism, the revivals of the eighteenth century, which saw the birth of the Pentecostal movement which eventually worked its way into the traditional Protestant churches and the Catholic Church itself.[27]

All this shows that what is happening in the church today already has a long history. In the Catholic Church, reaction against the Reformation gave rise to what has been called a "mystique of obedience."[28] Obedience to the hierarchy became virtually the only criterion of the value of Christian life. Such an unbalanced position could not last indefinitely.

Beside fidelity to what was revealed to the Apostles and handed on from them, there is a spiritual structure of the church. Life does not spring from mere repetition of the past. Even under a mystique of obedience, life is made up of initiatives, struggles to overcome obstacles, personal choices, inventiveness and creativity. From the point of view of the hierarchy, everything that happens at the grassroots can seem obvious and devoid of problems. From the point of view of the hierarchy, the essential thing is that all movements should take place within the framework of continuity. The members of the hierarchy do not know how much work it takes to develop new initiatives.

The church is charismatic because everything that really happens in it derives from the gifts of the Spirit. If these gifts are not recognized and respected, life leaves the church and the institution is left hollow. This is what is happening today. Those churches that still have a rigid institutional system complain that their followers are deserting them. At the same time, however, thousands of new movements are growing from the grassroots, charismatic communities fearful of being manipulated by powerful systems.

If the hierarchy is a regulating principle, it is not a source of life. Life comes from the Spirit, and the Spirit blows where it will, how it will and when it will. It does not follow the lines laid down by bureaucrats.

(b) The Subordination of the Church to Christ

There is no opposition between Christ and the Spirit. The Spirit does not depart from what Jesus did and said. On the contrary, all its gifts lead to a new encounter with what Jesus did and said. Besides this, Jesus did not define in advance everything that his church should say and do: his basic founding act with regard to the church was to send the Holy Spirit to be the guarantor of continuity with him.

Christ left the Twelve as a reference. But the Twelve were themselves charismatics, not scribes repeating words or worrying over the establishment of the institution. The Apostles invented: they left four different Gospels, and allowed other apostles, such as Paul, to present their own version of the good news.

In tradition, the hierarchy does not act alone. Hierarchy and the Christian people with their charisms act together, influencing each other and carrying the church forward in a movement combining inventiveness and spontaneity with continuity with the origins. This is what the Constitution on Divine Revelation says: "In holding to, practising, and professing the heritage of the faith, there results on the part of the bishops and faithful a remarkable common effort" (DV 10a).[29] It would be illusory to suppose that a literal conservation of the same word forms could be a true guarantee of continuity with Christ. In fact literal repetition could be the worst sort of betrayal of real faithfulness.

The danger, of course, lies in confusing the Holy Spirit with purely human initiatives wrongly attributed to the Spirit. Without some form of effective control, religious movements can fall into the hands of unbalanced enthusiasts. Religious sentiments lend themselves more than most to deviations and confusion. Religion has always served to cloak the worst aberrations: the prophets are continually denouncing false religions. The present secular liberalism and climate of religious freedom greatly favour the multiplication of religious subjectiv- isms and inconsistent sects. Faced with this uncontrolled effervescence, the hierarchy has to act as a secure defensive system. This, however, must not hinder spontaneity and initiative.

4. CHRIST AND THE SPIRIT IN EVANGELIZATION

We all know that evangelization as it has been carried out in the past is now being severely criticized and harshly judged. In the Third World—not only in Africa and Asia, but also among black and indigenous movements in the Americas—and among anthropologists the world over any form of Christian mission is widely seen as being nothing other than a renewal of colonial- ism. This is because it tends to destroy ancestral religions, replacing them with a religion that will inevitably be under Western and white control. Those who become Christians are effectively surrendering to white supremacy. The "inculturation"[30] preached by the church today is merely denounced as a more subtle form of ideological colonialism.

In the face of such accusations, missionaries are asking themselves whether the very proclamation of Christ as the one means necessary to salvation is not in itself a form of domination and cultural imposition. They are asking if evangelization can continue to preach the uniqueness of Christ, whether it might not be better to limit it to preaching God. But then which God would this be? Is there any point in evangelization proclaiming something that is already common to all cultures?[31]

So in the end one has to ask the question: is it still lawful to evangelize in the present context? Should we not rather wait for a new historical configuration, for the fall of the West?

Missionaries have already put forward a number of suggestions by way of reply to their adversaries. The first would be to concentrate more on practice than on a formal message. Christianity is better communicated through deeds, actions, attitudes, sharing in people's lives, than through sermons or explanations of religious concepts. In fact, this suggestion is merely reinforcing a practice that has been in effect for a long time: missionaries have usually been practical rather than intellectual and have spent more of their time in material work than in theoretical teaching.

Another suggestion has to do with dialogue. Evangelization should not be a direct call to conversion, but primarily an interchange, a theoretical and practical dialogue with other world religions through cultural exchanges. In such dialogues, missionaries should be prepared to learn, since there can be no dialogue without reciprocity; if one of the interlocutors is convinced he or she possesses the full truth, that person will not be receptive, but merely prepared to tolerate others speaking before repeating his or her own views.

The third suggestion goes beyond religious dialogue. It claims that the meeting between religions has to come about within the context of a joint praxis of liberation. Religions divide, but liberating action unites. Through action, religious men and women can come to a proper appreciation of the religious message of their co-workers, and through progressing together can come to ad hoc agreements. The hope underlying this suggestion is that a liberating praxis will show the superiority of Christ and Christianity over other world religious figure-heads and teachings.

The Holy Spirit has been little invoked in missionary debate. This is a reflection of the absence of the Holy Spirit from Western theology. But the mutual implication of Son and Holy Spirit has to be the rule in mission as much as in any other aspect of Christianity. The Christian message is not a proclamation of Christ alone, but of the Holy Spirit too. Now the Spirit has been acting in pagan peoples and in all religions since humanity began. The Spirit leads peoples and religions in directions we cannot know in advance. All we can do is observe the signs of the Spirit at work and go along with it. There is no way we can anticipate it. If the Spirit leads nations to Christ, we do not know what steps or ways it has actually taken; about this we are as ignorant as pagans. We in fact know less than them, since the signs of the Spirit were given to them first and not to us. We have to learn from them how the Spirit has acted in their evolution.

The Spirit is preparing the church in the midst of the nations. But we do not know in advance how this church will come about, or how it will differ from those that already exist. Therefore we cannot embark on mission with a ready-made concept of what the church is, nor with a message fully worked out. We should not pretend to know how to bring about a synthesis between the old churches and the new churches to come before it happens. We start out from what we are and have, and embark on a process of discovering new churches yet to come into existence. As this process unfolds, we ourselves will be changed through dialogue. We shall probably never understand exactly what the Spirit is doing in others. No matter: the dream of a universal ecclesial consciousness bringing the faith of all the churches together in an overall synthesis is the expression of a superhuman pride. Such a synthesis is not within the grasp of human creatures. The ambition to know both what the gospel is for us and what it is for others goes beyond human bounds. Not even ecumenical councils have claimed this much. If our partners in dialogue see us claiming this, the only thing they can do is reject our pretentious pride.

It is the Spirit who shows Christ to the nations. We preach him, but do not know how they will understand him. The important thing is to present Christ in the same way as he presented himself: the way of humility and the cross. Christ sprang from poverty, from the midst of poor people. He presented himself as one without power. The revelation of Christ is the revelation of his cross experienced as the true way. The good news of Christ is not discourse about Christ, but manifesting Christ made into a slave and crucified. It is the Spirit who directs us in this way of humiliation. So the Christ of mission will not be human discourse on Christ, but a living, real presence of Jesus made poor and powerless, in such a way that he can reach the hearts of the poor of all nations.

In this way, Christ and the Spirit are united in mission too, and it is only their unity in mission that makes mission possible at this juncture of human history.

CONCLUSION

Not only do Christ and the Spirit complement one another, but the mission of one sheds light on that of the other. The absence of the Holy Spirit from the consciousness of the churches of the West has produced historical distortions which led to situations from which there is now no way forward: one-sided emphasis on discourse about Christ which no one understands any longer; a church fuelled by a mystique of obedience that has become socially and culturally oppressive; a mission alternating between disheartenment and insecurity and blind activism. We are not advocating opposing a spiritual church to a hierarchical one, but returning to a balanced church in which the two poles blend into each other and complement one another. Christ is Spirit and the Spirit is Christ. Christ cannot be known through rigid formulas like those of a Torah; Christ is known through praxis led by the Spirit. And the Spirit does not inspire just anything dreamed up by the imagination of Christians. The Spirit leads Christians to submit to the criteria of the Bible and of tradition, and also to the judgment of the magisterium made in the name of these criteria.

Chapter VI
The Holy Spirit and the Trinity

The mission of the Holy Spirit in creation shows its reality as a Person of the Holy Trinity. Till now, we have been looking at the mission of the Holy Spirit in the world. In a way, all that we have seen so far can be summed up in an overall view of the Spirit in the Trinity. Here, of course, we are entering into the secret of God, and all that we can say stops short of the reality of God, which is inaccessible to us. Nevertheless, we have the words of God's own revelation, and these we should contemplate. Total silence is undervaluing the revelation given by the Father through Christ in the Holy Spirit, not to mention the intelligence we have been given in God's creation.

The relationship between the different Persons of the Trinity is dealt with in Leonardo Boff's *Trinity and Society* in this series, and here I want to pick out just some aspects referring specifically to the theology of the Holy Spirit. There will inevitably be some overlap, but we should not close a book devoted to the Holy Spirit without seeing how the whole mission of the Spirit tends to manifest its relationship to the Father and the Son. The Holy Spirit was sent to lead us to Christ, and Christ leads us to the Father.

The first section of this chapter deals with specific questions of the Holy Spirit in the Trinity. The second examines those properties of the Spirit most often contemplated by Christian tradition.

1. THE SPIRIT IN RELATION TO THE FATHER AND THE SON

The Holy Spirit is God, equal and consubstantial to the Father and the Son. This teaching was defined in the fourth century and has remained unshaken. Nevertheless, there is a discrepancy between the understanding of the Western and Eastern churches concerning the relation of the Spirit to the Son: the well-known *Filioque* question. Without claiming to introduce new elements into the controversy, let us at least examine the current state of the question.

(a) The Divinity of the Spirit

The "Symbol" of faith, or Creed, promulgated at the Council of Nicaea in 325 merely mentioned the Holy Spirit without qualifying it in any way. At that time, theological debate revolved round the relationship between the Father and the Son, due to the Arian heresy. During the course of the fourth century, some Christians came to deny the divinity of the Holy Spirit. Then the Cappadocian Fathers—Saints Basil, Gregory of Nyssa and Gregory Nazianzen—took up the "cause," as it were, of the Holy Spirit, and their efforts finally bore fruit in the new Creed that completed the Nicene Creed. The Council of Chalcedon and tradition gave this new Creed the name "Constantinopolitan," attributing it to the Council of Constantinople in 381, the records of which have been lost. This new Creed was introduced into the liturgy, where it is still used, and from that time on became the most solemn and official rule of faith for Christianity, both East and West.

The Niceno-Constantinopolitan Creed did not call the Holy Spirit "God," nor did it use the term "consubstantial" (Greek *homoousios*), used of the Son and upheld through innumerable and tragic debates. The fact is that the New Testament nowhere says that the Holy Spirit is "God." The council fathers did not want to go beyond the language of the Bible, for fear of alienating from the church those who refused to use words not attributed in the Bible. Consequently, they refrained from giving the qualification "consubstantial" explicitly to the Spirit. But the sense of the Creed is, without any doubt, to give the Spirit divine attributes and to affirm its equality with the Father and the Son, though in different words.

The Creed calls the Spirit "Lord and giver of life." Using

functional rather than essential language, it also says that the Spirit, "together with the Father and Son, is worshipped and glorified," and that the Spirit "proceeds from the Father." Tradition is unanimous, and the words used are designed to teach that the Father, Son and Holy Spirit are equal to one another.

The meaning of this equality is clear from the arguments put forward at the time in order to formulate the expressions of the Creed. These arguments feature in the works of the Cappadocians, particularly St Basil. His first argument derives from the baptismal formula: if baptism is conferred in the name of the Father and of the Son and of the Holy Spirit, then the Holy Spirit has the same value as the other divine Persons. His second argument is drawn from the "economy" of salvation (the way God works in history). St Athanasius had used the argument before: if the Holy Spirit is not God, it cannot transform us according to the image of the Son so as to unite us to the Father. If the Spirit is not God, the Spirit cannot divinize us.[1]

This produced the formula that in the East has become the synthesis of Christianity: the Holy Spirit gathers men and women into the Body of Christ who is one with the Father. The Father sent the Son; the Son sent the Holy Spirit; the Holy Spirit integrates creation into the Son, and the Son bears the whole of creation within himself to the Father. This is the mystery we celebrate in the sacraments, above all in the eucharist, and in the whole church as the great sacrament of God's plan. The Greek Fathers and Eastern theologians tirelessly repeated such expressions, finding in them the most incontrovertible argument for demonstrating the equality of the Persons of the Trinity against all the pseudo-philosophical reasonings advanced against the faith of the people of God.

The Holy Spirit is the neighbour God, the Person closest to us. The Spirit is God in us, the God who has been preparing us since the creation of the world, God working in creation since the beginning of time so as to lead us to Christ. The Holy Spirit produces the link between us and the Son, and it is through the Son that we go to the Father.

(b) The "Filioque" Question

The *Filioque* question is the main source of doctrinal debate between East and West. It expresses and symbolizes the difference in both temperament and tradition between the two parts of historical Christianity in the first two millennia.

Some Eastern theologians have regarded the introduction of the *Filioque* into the Creed in the West as a basic heresy and the source of all theoretical and practical distortions in the churches of the West: Vladimir Lossky[2] and Nissiotis[3] are examples of this view. Others, such as Paul Evdokimov[4] and Sergei Bulgakov,[5] take a more lenient view and regard the problem as one not of heresy but just of theology. They would accept the conclusions of the agenda drawn up by Boris Bolotov for a meeting in 1892 between Orthodox and Old Catholics; Bolotov said that the divergence between East and West on the *Filioque* question should not be seen as a Western heresy.[6] In the West, for their part, many Catholic theologians of the Middle Ages and even modern times have regarded the rejection of the *Filioque* by Eastern Christians as heresy,[7] so recriminations on this score have been mutual. Today, however, there are equally many in the West, Catholics and others, who would not consider the Eastern rejection of *Filioque* to belong to the realm of heresy.[8]

The problem is basically this: the Niceno-Constaninopolitan Creed, in accordance with John 15:26 and 14:26, states that the Spirit "proceeds from the Father." It says nothing on the relationship between the Spirit and the Son. Neither does John say that the Spirit proceeds from the Son; what he does say is that the Spirit "takes" from the Son (16:14). The Creed does not allude to this text, nor to the other idea, found in several places in the Fathers, that the Spirit "rests" on the Son.

In 431 the Council of Ephesus had the opportunity to add something on the relationship between the Son and the Spirit, but did not do so. On the contrary, it pronounced an "anathema" on anyone who dared to add anything to the Nicene Creed. The Council of Chalcedon in 451 and the Third Council of Constantinople in 680–1 renewed this anathema and added nothing to the Creed concerning the relationship of the Holy Spirit to the Son.

Meanwhile, in Spain, the Third Synod of Toledo in 589 had produced the formula "who proceeds from the Father *and the Son [Filioque]*." Following this, the Visigoth King Recaredo, a recent convert from Arianism, ordered that the word *Filioque* should be added to the Creed. The Fourth Synod of Toledo approved this in 633. The Visigoths saw the addition of *Filioque* as a refutation of Arianism, since, if the Spirit proceeds from the Father *and* the Son, this proves the complete equality between the Father and the Son. Their intention was to assert this equality.

The great protagonist of the *Filioque* was the Emperor Charlemagne, who resolved to make it a weapon in his struggle against the Eastern empire. As emperor in the West, he determined to show that the East was heretical on account of its omission of *Filioque* from the Creed. He summoned a council in 807 to condemn the empire in the East, and the inclusion of the *Filioque* in the Creed used in the empire in the West dates from that event. Pope Leo III refused to include the *Filioque* and ordered the traditional Creed to be upheld; the church in Rome held out for two hundred years. Finally, in 1014, the Germanic Emperor Henry II came to Rome to be crowned by Pope Benedict VIII, and insisted that the Germanic rite, with the *Filioque*, be used in the mass. This was the first time the Creed with the *Filioque* was chanted in Rome, but once introduced, it stayed. In the ninth century, Patriarch Photius of Constantinople had reacted violently against *Filioque*, and propounded an Eastern theology against it, condemning it as heretical and defending the expression "proceeds from the Father *alone*." In 1054, the papal legate Cardinal Humbertus solemnly excommunicated the Eastern church, in Constantinople, in the name of the pope, accusing it of suppressing the *Filioque* from the Creed, which, not unnaturally, exasperated the Greeks. Since then we have not found a way out of the impasse, despite two attempts at reconciliation, by the Councils of Lyon in 1274 and Florence in 1439. No real reconciliation was achieved: the Greeks see the Latins as having changed the Creed without consulting the Eastern half of the church, and view the change as being contrary to the anathemas of the Ecumenical Councils and as having no scriptural basis; the Latins see the *Filioque* as an obvious deduction from a correct understanding of the Trinity, accusing the Greeks of obstinacy and bad faith.

One cannot attempt a new solution to the problem in a few pages. This has been essayed by Yves Congar, probably the greatest Catholic expert on the matter, so I should just like to summarize his conclusions. In Latin America, the question of the Eastern Churches does not loom very large, but it is nevertheless very important for Catholics of this continent to understand Eastern sensibilities, since the Catholic Church in Latin America has inherited the distortions of the church in Western Europe, without appreciating the origin or even the existence of such distortions.

Congar concludes his investigations in the form of nine theses, which I shall summarize as briefly as possible.[9]

1. Faith in the Holy Spirit is the same in East and West, though expressed differently. There was a time when Eastern and Western Christians engaged in mutual condemnation. But as long ago as the Middle Ages, there were major theologians who held that the difference was one of formulation, not of faith. St Anslem, Abelard, Richard of St Victor, Hugh of St Cher, St Thomas Aquinas himself,[10] and many Franciscans, including St Bonaventure and Duns Scotus, held that the difference was one of expression, not of meaning.[11] Equally, in the East, theologians have not been lacking who accept the orthodoxy of the West. Paul Evdokimov says that "in practice, one can find no difference in worship of the Holy Spirit. The lack of practical consequences shows the dogmatic inadequacy of the opposing formulas."[12] The problem is the difficulty in formulating faith: the actual faith, however, is the same, since faith is expressed in practice rather than in words.

2. The Trinity is a mystery which surpasses human understanding. Eastern Christians accuse Western ones of using rational—not biblical— principles, of trying to rationalize the mystery of God, thereby offending against God's transcendence. They do not accept St Augustine's principle of defining

the Persons of the Trinity by their relationship.[13] Nor do they accept St Anselm's maxim: *"in Deo omnia sunt unum, ubi not obviat relationis oppositio"* (everything in God is common to the three Persons, except where this is prevented by opposition of relationships).[14] They look with the deepest suspicion on the scholastic principle insisted on by Karl Rahner: "The economic Trinity is the immanent Trinity and vice-versa" (meaning that the relationship between the divine Persons shown in the salvation of creation expresses the relationship between them in the divine mystery).[15] Eastern Christians claim a stricter adherence to biblical formulas and will not easily move beyond them. Any process of logical reasoning strikes them as an attack on the transcendence of God, as trying to pry into the inner sanctum of the divine essence.

3. We should recognize the strength of the model of the Trinity constructed in Eastern theology. There, the starting-point is the position of the three Persons shown in the biblical texts. So to distinguish the Son from the Spirit, it suffices to use the different terms the New Testament applies to each: the Son comes from the Father through begetting, or generation; the Spirit proceeds from the Father. This is enough to show that they are accepted as different; there is no need for any opposition between the Son and the Spirit, nor for any relationship, since the Persons are not defined by their relationship. Both the Son and the Holy Spirit simultaneously receive the divine essence from the Father. For the Greeks, the unifying principle in God is not the divine nature, but the Father, from whom both the Son and the Spirit receive the same nature. Nevertheless, the Son and the Spirit are not without communication: far from it. There is a circulation among the divine Persons, known as *perichoresis* (translated into Latin as *circumincessio*): the Father is in the Son and the Son in the Father. The Father is in the Son giving him the Holy Spirit. The Father is in the Holy Spirit with the Son. The Holy Spirit is in the Father with the Son. The three Persons are in permanent communication: two are already in the third.[16]

The Eastern churches do not accept the *Filioque* formula, which implies that the Spirit proceeds from the Father and the Son as from one single source or origin (*"tamquam ab uno principio*" in the Latin scholastic formulation). For them, this formula supposes that God is defined first by God's common nature and that the Persons are defined by means of their relationships to one another within this common nature. The churches of the West, however, reject this as an interpretation of their theology. Furthermore, the Eastern churches claim, if the Spirit proceeds from the Father and the Son, as from a single source, this source can only be the divine nature. This would then distinguish the Holy Spirit from the divine nature, which is absurd. It would suggest several sources in God: the Father, the Son and the divine nature. The East insists that the source has to be one: the single source is the Father.

What Eastern theology fails to explain well is why the Son is placed second and the Holy Spirit third in the lists in the Bible, as well as in the baptismal formula.

4. Various Greek Fathers express some form of participation by the Son in the production of the Holy Spirit. Examples are to be found in Didymus the Blind, head of the Alexandrian school, St Basil, St Gregory of Nyssa and St Gregory Nazianzen, but above all Sts Cyril of Alexandria and John Damascene.[17] None of the expressions of these Fathers can be interpreted in the same sense as the Latin *Filioque*, but neither do they exclude some intervention by the Son in the production of the Holy Spirit. The usual Eastern explanation, that these texts refer to pure "economy," does not seem adequate.[18] Especially since the radical polemics of Photius, the Greeks insist that if the Son does send the Spirit, this is only in the order of the "economy" of salvation, but reveals nothing about the inner mystery of God. Against this, the Western church maintains that the relationships between the Persons evident from the "economy" of salvation reveal relationships within the inner nature of God, since they proceed from them.

The fact is that the texts from the Greek Fathers mentioned above do not seem to reduce the relationship between the Son and the Holy Spirit to one of pure "economy." Several Eastern theologians accept that something within the inner nature of God requires a certain "special relationship" between the Son and the Spirit. They express this something by a preposition used several times by the Fathers: "through" (Greek *dia*). So they say that the Spirit proceeds from the Father through the Son (as if passing through the Son, involving the Son). This formula was accepted by the Greek representatives at the Council of Florence. It was officially held to be the Greek equivalent of *Filioque*, as though it meant the same thing, which seems somewhat excessive. In any case this development at the Council of Florence did not make a lasting mark on the Eastern churches, and they did not recognize the proceedings at Florence as an Ecumenical Council. Nevertheless, the formula "through the Son" used by the Greek Fathers would seem to offer a basis for unity.[19]

5. There is basic agreement between some elements in the Western churches and the theology of the school of Gregory Palamas, the fourteenth-century monk of Mount Athos who was the major figure of medieval Byzantine theology and spirituality. This medieval Byzantine theology marks the high point of theology of the Holy Spirit.

Gregory Palamas and Palamism distinguish between divine essence and divine *energia*, claiming thereby to assure both the transcendence of God and the "divinization" of human beings, the perennial axis of Eastern theology. The essence of God would be the incommunicable part of God, that which is totally inaccessible. The energies of God would be the accessible part of God. Because they are given by God these energies are divine, but express what in God is within reach of human beings. In divinization, it is not the essence of God that is communicated, but the energies of the Father, through the Son in the Holy Spirit. There is an order in the energies as there is an order in the essence—or rather, there is an order among the Persons on the level of essence and another on the level of energies. In the order of energies, the Son shares in the character of the Father as source: this is the sense in which "through the Son" is interpreted, and some Palamists would allow that in reference to the divine energies *Filioque* in a sense is equivalent with "through the Son."[20]

Several Catholic theologians see the school of Gregory Palamas as compatible with the *faith* held by the Catholic Church, if not with Western *theologies*.[21]

6. In the Western manner of presenting the Trinity, the

Filioque is necessary to safeguard (a) the distinction between the Son and the Holy Spirit and (b) the consubstantiality of the Father and the Son. The Western model stems from St Augustine and his conception of the relationship between the three Persons: the only thing that differentiates them is the relationship that distinguishes one from the other. What makes the Father Father is his relationship to the Son. What makes the Son Son is his relationship to the Father. St Thomas defined Augustine's thought by calling the divine Persons "subsistent relations."

As far as the Father and the Son are concerned, this is clear enough. The problem arises with the Holy Spirit. If a relationship (of procession) opposes it to the Father, the Holy Spirit becomes a Person. Procession distinguishes it from the Father. But if the Holy Spirit has no relationship opposing it to the Son, it does not become distinct from the Son and so is confused with the Son. So the solution consists in saying that the Holy Spirit proceeds from the Father and also from the Son. But how is it possible for the Father and the Son to appear as opposite poles to one other Person, while the Spirit is one pole opposite two Persons? Is this not using two different formulas to define the divine Persons? No, according to Augustine and Western tradition, because the Father and the Son are joint authors of the procession of the Holy Spirit. The Holy Spirit proceeds from Father-and-Son as from a single source. Besides, if the Father were the sole author of the Holy Spirit, then the Father would have something the Son does not, besides his fatherhood, and have this as a divine Person. The Son would then no longer be equal or consubstantial with the Father.

Clearly, what makes the *Filioque* necessary is the definition of the Trinity as subsistent relations. But this is not a directly biblical concept; it is a reasoned, theological one. This is why the Greeks objected to it, apart from the fact that it negated the exclusivity of the Father as source. St Augustine in fact said that the Spirit proceeds "principally" from the Father, but this distinction did not survive in Western tradition.

The Western theory received its most complete expression in St Thomas Aquinas, though this expression did not convince the Eastern churches. Once the principle of subsistent relations was accepted, it was compelled as belief. But what faith compels as belief is the equality between the Persons and their complete distinctiveness. Once we start using theological principles we enter a zone of insecurity and indefinition, however clear the concepts.[22]

7. The *Filioque* was professed by the Latin Fathers and by Latin Councils before the separation, when West and East were still united in one communion, and Eastern churches, who knew about the *Filioque*, made no objection to it. Among the Fathers, the earliest quoted are St Ambrose, St Augustine, St Hilary and St Leo the Great. In following centuries, many saints and doctors professed the same doctrine, among them St Gregory the Great and St Isidore of Seville.[23] The Councils include the Third and Fourth Councils of Toledo (589 and 633), as well as others held in Toledo in the seventh century. At this time the Eastern churches were aware of what was being taught and made no protest.

The dispute began when Charlemagne condemned the Council of Nicaea of 787 for proposing the cult of images. At the Council held in Frankfurt in 794, Charlemagne also condemned the absence of *Filioque* from Eastern professions of faith. The Eastern churches began to argue back, and Photius' teaching in its most radical form was ever more widely accepted.

From the standpoint of faith, rather than of politics, the most significant aspect is that for centuries the Eastern churches, while not using the *Filioque*, did not condemn it either. They accepted a plurality of expressions, believing this to be compatible with the unity of the faith.[24]

8. The earliest testimony of agreement comes from St Maximus the Confessor, widely respected in both East and West, in a letter written in 655. This is positive evidence, more than just the silence of the Eastern church.[25] In it, St Maximus says that the Latins use *Filioque* to express what he himself expresses by "through [*dia*] the Son."

It is worth recording that a supplementary difficulty arose from the difference between Latin and Greek vocabularies. While Latin has the one verb *procedere*, Greek has several near equivalents, making a distinction between *ekporeuesthai* and *proienai.* The first means "to have its origin, to proceed as from a source that is truly the initiator of the process": it is therefore applied to the Father alone. The second means "to come from" without indicating the original source: this is applied to the Son. What the Greeks could not accept was the application of the same verb *ekporeuesthai* to both Father and Son, since this destroyed the Father's quality of source, principle or origin; they wanted two different verbs. They argued that the Son cannot bear the same relationshop to the Holy Spirit as the Father does.

9. The Council of Florence began a forward movement, seeking to equate *Filioque* in meaning to *per Filium*, so as to show that the Father and Son do not act in precisely the same way in the procession of the Holy Spirit, while still maintaining that the Son participates actively in the process and is not just a passive channel through which the Holy Spirit is produced. It is possible to imagine a new, truly ecumenical council, representing East and West, studying the problem afresh on the basis of John 15:16 and 16:14–15. The Catholic Church could withdraw *Filioque* from its Creed, since it was introduced by an irregular route, without consulting the Eastern church. This could remove the legitimate worries of the churches in both East and West.

From the standpoint of the church in Latin America, the question may seem marginal. Nevertheless, it is not wise for the church in Latin America to ignore the Eastern churches and their theology. It would be possible for the Catholic Church in Latin America unconsciously to prolong a harmful exclusive reliance on Latin thought. Latin American theology needs deep contact with the tradition of the Christian East, since the Western tendency to christomonism is even more marked in Latin America than in Europe. The heritage bequeathed by Spain and Portugal owed little to the East; colonial Christianity was an isolated Christianity, cut off from communication with the other great centres of Christendom. Although the massive immigration of the past hundred years has brought Christians from many parts to Latin America, this has produced little Eastern influence on the broad outlook of the church, which is still markedly Latinate. So the trinitarian questions that divide

East and West are important for the church in Latin America, which is in fact advantageously placed to take an ecumenical initiative in the matter.

2. SOME IMPORTANT ASPECTS OF TRADITION

Rather than attempt to summarize all the interesting aspects of theology of the Holy Spirit developed in Christian tradition, I want to take just three, which seem most applicable to the present situation in Latin America. These are the Holy Spirit considered as love (or "charity"), gift and life. The first two belong to the Latin tradition, the third to the Eastern, more specifically Syriac, tradition.

(a) The Spirit as Love

As do so many aspects of trinitarian theology, this one derives from St Augustine. God, he said, is love, love in three forms: "there is the love of one who loves him to whom he gave being, the love of one for the one from whom he received his being, and there is this very love in itself" (*De Trinitate* VI, 5, 7). If God is love, how can this title be given to the Holy Spirit in a way peculiar to it: is it not common to all three Persons? St Augustine replies that the Holy Spirit is the substantial communion of the Father and the Son; being common to the Father and the Son, the Holy Spirit is given all the names that are common to both (*De Trinitate* XV, 19, 37).

A second stage of development of the theology of the Spirit-Love was reached in the Abbey of St Victor in the twelfth century, where Richard wrote his treatise *De Trinitate*. In God, he says, there is the greatest possible perfection. Now, loving oneself can never be the greatest love, so love for another Person cannot be lacking in God. Hence the supremely lovable Son, who is equal in perfection to the Father and whom the Father can love with all the strength of his love. Then, Richard adds, the true excellence of love consists in wanting another person to be loved with the same love. So the Son needs the Holy Spirit to feel that the Spirit receives the same love (the Spirit is called *condilectus*).

St Bonaventure took up the Spirit-Love theme: the Holy Spirit is the mutual, reciprocal love between the Father and the Son. Bonaventure saw the perfection of love as being in its reciprocity, so the title "Love" is especially appropriate to the Holy Spirit, since it is reciprocity itself.

St Thomas Aquinas also expresses the theme of mutual love and the Spirit as union between the Father and the Son.[26] But he does not attribute special importance to it, since his metaphysic did not allow him to deduce the Holy Spirit from this concept. He reworks St Augustine and St Anselm, who viewed the Holy Spirit as being derived from the Father and the Son by the way of will or love. Just as the Son proceeds from the Father by way of the knowledge the Father has of himself, so the Holy Spirit proceeds from the love the Father has for the Son. St Thomas gave no decisive function to the idea of reciprocity. There are excellent books examining St Thomas' exposition of the derivation of the Holy Spirit according to the way of love, so there is no need to examine the issue at greater length here.[27]

Despite St Thomas' reservations on the subject, the concept of the Spirit as mutual love has produced strong echoes in modern and contemporary theology, thanks to the chords it strikes in modern Western psychology. But the concept is still completely alien to Eastern understanding.

(b) The Spirit as Gift

In the Scriptures, the Holy Spirit is the gift above all others. The Spirit is the one "promised" by the Father and the Son.[28] It is the presence of the kingdom of God in anticipation, the first-fruits of the resurrection.[29] The title of "gift" appears in several places: St Peter promises it in his Pentecost address: "you will receive the gift of the Holy Spirit" (Acts 2:38); after the conversion of Cornelius, the witnesses are astonished at "the gift of the Holy Spirit" (Acts 10:45). And surely "what God is offering," as Jesus proposes to the woman of Samaria (John 4:10), is the Holy Spirit? The Spirit is the gift that Simon hoped to buy with money (Acts 8:20). In many places it is the complement to the verbs "give" or "receive."[30]

The Fathers enlarged on the idea, especially the Latin Fathers, with St Augustine again foremost among them.[31] He makes "Gift" the proper name of the Holy Spirit. The givers are everlastingly the Father and the Son. The Gift is the Holy Spirit. What is given in the Holy Spirit is the very God in the form of Gift.[32]

St Thomas emphasizes two names proper to the Holy Spirit: love and gift (*Summa Theol.* Ia, q. 37 & 38). If the Holy Spirit is gift, this is to be understood as being God's communication with creatures. The Holy Spirit is the opening of God out from God's self. The movement that is God tends to ever greater expansion. Every gift is gratuitous; therefore, God's gift to creatures is gratuitous. But the gift God makes to creatures is in perfect concordance with God's nature of expansion; the gift is of God's self. The Spirit itself shows that God is projection of God's self outside that self.

(c) The Spirit as Life

The attribute of life is the proper name of the Spirit in the tradition of the Syriac Church, which continues that of the Patriarchate of Antioch.[33] St John Chrysostom said that the Spirit was life because the church could not live without it.[34] The community can begin to live only with the life the Holy Spirit infuses into it. The Spirit is the source of the church, bestowing on it existence and fruitfulness. The three basic symbols applied to the Spirit in the Bible, breath (or wind), water and fire, all refer to life.

Syriac liturgy celebrates life in the Spirit: "Honour, glory, power and exaltation to the Holy and Consubstantial Trinity: Father, Son and Holy Spirit who are Being, Word and Life."[35] Syriac theology is lyrical and liturgical rather than highly developed. It endlessly acclaims the Spirit as author of life, while at the same time being a hymn to life.

Latin American theology also tends to be a proclamation of life, in prophetic rather than liturgical tones,[36] but in a movement similar to that found in the old Syriac Church. By combining liturgy and doxology with prophecy, we shall come to a resounding proclamation of the triumph of the Holy Spirit.

General Conclusion

Vatican II occasionally mentions the Holy Spirit in conjunction with Mary, but without working out a theology of the relationship between the two. Yet we can say that in Mary, the Holy Spirit somehow finds the centre-point of its mission in the world. Contact between the Son of God and humanity came about through Mary. In Mary, the Holy Spirit, through the incarnation, brought about unity between the whole of humanity and the word of God. The incarnation does not represent just the raising up of a single individual in the Person of the Son of God, but the integration of humanity to form the Body of this Son of God. This integration comes about in a material, fleshly manner, in a particular embodiment of our humanity— Mary, the new Eve, mother of the human species renewed and integrated into Christ. This is why Mary can be called the "temple of the Holy Spirit" (LG 53a). She was prepared for her mission by being "fashioned by the Holy Spirit into a...new creature" (LG 56b).

The whole history of humanity comes to a head in Mary, since the nations of the earth prepared the way for the coming and choice of Israel, and the people of Israel lived in hope of and preparation for their Messiah who was to be born from one of its daughters.[1] The Holy Spirit was present in the peoples of the earth from the beginning, preparing them to receive their saviour. Peoples do not receive their liberation in passivity; on the contrary, their liberation by the Messiah coincides with their maximum activity. It is in their reception of the liberation brought by Christ that peoples reach their pinnacle of dynamism. Since the beginning, the Holy Spirit has been preparing active faith, the transforming conversion that will constitute the active participation peoples must bring to their effective liberation by Christ. The Spirit follows the long, slow, inter-weaving, multiple roads of history. It does not impose itself on history, but adapts to its rhythm, which seems so slow to us. Our lives are short and we want to see the end of history before we have to leave this earth. But the Spirit is eternal and acts with the slowness of history, for which a generation is barely an instant.

The Holy Spirit prepares the communion that makes com-munity within the body of Christ, preparing it through the evolution of clans, tribes, peoples, the community of the poor, the solidarity of the oppressed. The first community grouped around Mary in Jerusalem was a historical miracle in which thousands of years of human history were summed up. The Holy Spirit does not create this community out of nothing, but had been creating it since the origins of humanity. Bringing together all the threads of history to weave them into this rich, strong, harmonious tapestry, the Spirit made Pentecost a sign of its irruption, though this irruption had been maturing for thousands of years.

In this long course of preparation, Mary stands at the high point of evolution, in a way at the end of history. All the actions of the Holy Spirit since the beginning of time were concentrated in her. She handed over to Christ humanity's long, patient endeavour, embodying it in her person, in which personal faith blended with perfect hope and total love, to bring about the link between the age-long work of the Spirit in humanity and the action of the Spirit on the Son.

So, we might ask, why did Mary not come at the end of time, to crown history? Why was Christ not incarnate at the end of time, to sum up humanity's whole long march in himself? Why did they come so early, when humanity was still so little evolved, with probably less than a tenth of the number of people that are living today, with so few possibilities for action in relation to the material world or in the social sphere? Why did the Spirit make such an early link between the history of humanity it led and the incarnation of the Son? Why not leave this till the end of time?

The truth is that the Spirit has been calling and clamouring since the beginning. The Spirit and the Bride have been saying "Come!" (Rev. 22:17) since the beginning. This is the cry of the oppressed, and its foundation is the Holy Spirit. The reply was: "I shall indeed be with you soon" (Rev. 22:20). The Son did not resist. The Father did not resist, and brought forward the mission of Christ.

The Son came to share the condition of the oppressed who called on him. The Father and the Son could not leave humanity in the power of the oppressors and abandoned to its wretched fate. The Son came to take on the condition of the poor and to share their lot. He knew what it was to be without power: those who had it killed him. Humanity could not take up the challenge he brought; it was neither ready, nor willing.

All the same, the Father did not leave the Son abandoned to the apparent triumph of his oppressors. The Father raised him to life and installed him as Messiah and Saviour from then onward. The enthronement of Christ from that point on had to bring consequences. The risen Christ was empowered to send the Spirit then as the first-fruits of the kingdom of God. The kingdom began before its time and right in the middle of a hostile and unprepared world.

Since then, the Spirit has been coming by two routes, carrying out two phases of its mission at once. The Holy Spirit continues working in all peoples, preparing them so they can actively receive Christ. And the Holy Spirit already anticipates the peace, happiness and communion of the end of time in some nuclei that have emerged from the people of Israel. Everything stems from Galilee and from Jerusalem. St Luke in Acts gives us a picture of a typical start in Jerusalem, showing the Spirit bringing the first community, mother of all later communities, to life.

The evolution of the world and the history of communities follow a convergent course, since there are not two Spirits, but only one. Yet the Spirit does not do violence to history; its two courses of action often run in parallel, coming together only at certain moments of history. These moments cannot be discerned by us in advance: the convergence will be apparent in the Spirit's time. The historical obstacles are immense. Their historical embodiments often make communities hide more of Christ than they reveal. Christ came to respond to the cry of the poor and oppressed, and still comes for this purpose, but church communities show another face of Christ, so that the poor often do not recognize him in them. But the Spirit is patient and persevering, and bides its time.

Starting from the preparation made by the peoples, the Spirit creates the church. The church has to go on being born till the end of history: it is born again each time a new community appears. Each new community is a new creation, a new beginning, a new Pentecost; what happened in Jerusalem happens once more. Wherever the Spirit forms a people into a new community, there the church begins once more.

This is because the church is not a sociological organism that grows by absorbing new generations or groups of people it has "won." The church does not absorb people into itself, but opens itself to welcome the new church. The old church opens out to new ones, make room for them, even disappear in order to give them room. At present we are witnessing the death of an old church of Christendom. This church must die so that the new communities can have space to breathe and live.

This does not break continuity in the church. The communities are united in time as well as in space. They are not just united invisibly through being inspired by the same Spirit; the Spirit works in material ways and arranges physical links between the communities: the ministry of the apostolic succession, the tie of union with the successor of Peter, the continuity of the sacraments, the traditional expressions of faith as found in the Creeds, and above all the Bible, maintain a union between the communities of all ages. We, however, should not add to the links arranged by the Spirit by laying down any conditions that might be an obstacle to the birth of new churches.

The Holy Spirit is more active than ever. It is not just acting in invisible ways. It is showing itself. Whenever new churches are born, the presence of the Holy Spirit can be more directly felt, the signs of its presence become more obvious. There is no doubt that at this time we are receiving experiences of the

Spirit such as have been known on very few occasions in history. This explosion of the Spirit in its obvious manifestations coincides with the end of one type of society and one type of church, and serves to bring in another type of society and another type of church.

The Spirit is now active among peoples, particularly among those peoples who are at the stage of their full awakening. In Latin America the blacks and indigenous tribes are awakening, as well as all the poor who have always been downtrodden and marginalized. One day, community will be born among such peoples: it is already happening in many places. It is always the same church, but it is always being born anew. The new communities do not break with the old, but neither are they subordinate to them. Each community has the right to be what it is, different from any that existed before. Institutional ties between communities in time and space cannot constitute limitations, nor forms of domination.

Christ's followers bring their whole inheritance, redeemed by the Holy Spirit, to the founding of communities. All that is good, all that works for unity, is material for building community. The Spirit discerns what is good, as do we with the Spirit: "Never try to suppress the Spirit, or treat the gift of prophecy with contempt; think before you do anything—hold on to what is good" (1 Thess. 5:19–20).

The Spirit leads all peoples in ways that are hidden from us. At its due time in history it raises up new communities, and the time of the Spirit is always the time of the irruption of the poor. The Spirit works in the old churches so that they can open ways, make space for and allow new churches to be recognized. In this way, God is present in humanity. The God closest to us, because amongst us and in us, is the Spirit. The Spirit forms our history, and forms us for our history. The Spirit leads us to Christ, integrating us in our communities and in Christ. The Spirit was sent by Christ to bring us to him. In Christ, the Spirit makes us the people of the Father, presenting us as "a holy sacrifice, truly pleasing to God" (Rom. 12:1). Our final end will be to become the result of the permanent appeal the Spirit makes to us: "Do not model yourselves on the behaviour of the world around you, but let your behaviour change, modelled by your new mind. This is the only way to discover the will of God and know what is good, what it is that God wants, what is the perfect thing to do" (Rom. 12:2).

Summary

1. Christianity has two sources: the "Jesus event" and experience of the Spirit—Easter and Pentecost. The two events are intimately bound up in one another, but neither can absorb or reduce the other. The tradition of Western Christianity has never given enough importance to the Spirit. There was one Easter; there are millions of Pentecosts.

2. The New Testament shows experience of the Spirit as the point of departure for the Christian event, above all in the teachings of St Paul, St Luke and St John. At the outset of Christianity, the presence of the Spirit was always something experienced: faith was not separated from experience. This separation came after the second century; till then, the Holy Spirit was the first thing known, an immediate reference to which Christians could appeal.

3. We are now witnessing an unforseen renewal of experience of the Spirit: the Pentecostal phenomenon is the most noteworthy development in Christianity today. In its first phase, this laid much stress on certain spectacular phenomena, similar to those found in Corinth. With maturing experience in time, discernment of spiritual experience has come about, renewing the discernment enjoined by St Paul.

4. Among the signs of the times that allowed Vatican II to proclaim a new age for the church of God is the end of a rationalized, intellectualized and institutionalized Christianity modelled on great human organizations. The nation can no longer offer any model to a church living experience of the Spirit in thousands upon thousands of small groups.

5. In the struggle for liberation, experience of God is

experience of the Holy Spirit: experience of action, freedom, word, community and life.

6. In Latin theology, the chain Father-Son-church took the place of the old patristic order Father-Son-Holy Spirit. Henceforth, the Spirit was invoked only as a prop for everything the hierarchical church had already decided.

7. The Spirit has been at work in the world since its beginning, preparing it for a resurrection, for the kingdom of God, a new creation, the birth of a new humanity. Pentecost brought about a spiritual explosion, announcing the full and final realization. The first-fruits of eternal life are now present. Before Pentecost, however, the Spirit was already at work, just as it still continues at work in the midst of nations on which the Spirit has not yet been fully poured out.

8. The Holy Spirit lies at the root of the cry of the poor. The Spirit is the strength of those who have no strength. It leads the struggle for the emancipation and fulfillment of the people of the oppressed. The Spirit acts in history and through history. It does not take the place of history, but enters into history through men and women who carry the Spirit in themselves.

9. The signs of the action of the Spirit in the world are clear: the Spirit is present wherever the poor are awakening to action, to freedom, to speaking out, to community, to life.

10. Scripture and tradition endlessly repeat St Irenaeus' phrase: "Where the church is, there too is the Spirit of God." The Spirit "dwells" in the church. The presence of the Spirit does not exclude the material, institutional, historical aspects of the church. The Spirit is present in the human body—individual and social—to be as it were its "soul," as a traditional theological concept would put it.

11. The presence of the Spirit in the church means that the church starts with groups of people gathering in communities, is borne up by historical forces and subject to the rhythms and criteria of history. It is not dominated by the history its task is to transform, but neither can it prescind from it.

12. The Spirit is the source of the unity, catholicity, holiness and apostolicity of the church. None of these marks is the result of purely human forces, nor of a strategy based on criteria drawn from human arts and sciences.

13. The Holy Spirit inspires the church in its three offices: it confers its strength and sheds its light on the office of the word, the liturgical office and the office of service to the community and the world.

14. Ministries, particularly those that include authority, are not outside the Spirit's sphere of action. The Spirit is present in them too, competing with psychological, sociological and anthropological tendencies.

15. A new spirituality is being born under the impulse of the Spirit, among elites placing themselves at the service of the poor, and among the poor themselves who are irrupting on to the stage of history. This spirituality includes a new form of contemplation, ascesis and prayer, whose first signs are already well apparent.

16. Traditional theology has not valued Jesus' Messiahship, preferring to define Jesus by the incarnation and from the moment of his conception. The new theology of the Spirit values his anointing by the Spirit and the progressive stages of Jesus' journey to his Father.

17. Spirit and word are in active collaboration. Classical theology failed to attach sufficient value to the actions of the Spirit because it was distorted by Greek intellectualism. Theologians thought in terms of immediate contact between us and Christ made through the purely human word handed on by tradition. They failed to understand that the word has meaning only from the activity of the Spirit, because all meaning is received starting from a praxis and within a praxis.

18. The Holy Spirit is God, equal to and consubstantial with the Father and the Son.

19. It is possible to see a way out of the quarrel between East and West concerning the relationship between the Son and the Holy Spirit within the Trinity.

20. All attributes of the Spirit denote movement: the Spirit is giving, loving, living. The Spirit comes at the end of movement in God, but the beginning of God's going-out to creation. It is at the start of creation's road back to the Father.

Glossary

AGAPĒ: There is no satisfactory translation of this term in modern languages. The traditional Latin and derived translation was "charity," but this term has acquired a progressively narrower, and even pejorative, meaning in contemporary usage. Another translation is "love," but this suffers from its predominant emotional and subjective charge. Another translation could be "solidarity," but this is not yet widely accepted. *Agapē* is the bond existing among members of the same family, the same clan, the same community. It is the formative attitude of the biblical people of Israel. *Agapē* makes people treat one another as brothers and sisters.

CHARISM: A particular gift of the Spirit designed to promote a specific type of activity.

CHRISTOMONISM: A theological system placing exclusive value on Christ's mission in the salvation of humanity to the detriment of the Holy Spirit. It is an accusation levelled against Western theology by some Orthodox theologians.

EPICLESIS: The prayer to the Holy Spirit which Eastern liturgy places at the centre of the celebration of the eucharist to ask that the bread and wine be changed into the body and blood of Christ. The liturgical reform of Vatican II made the Latin Church introduce an *epiclesis*, which had till then been absent from the Roman liturgy.

FILIOQUE: A word added by the Western church to the Creed known as the Nicene Creed, provoking constant protests from the Eastern churches. *Filioque* means "and from the Son," so the Western churches say that the Holy Spirit "proceeds from the Father and the Son," whereas the Eastern churches hold that the Spirit proceeds from the Father alone.

MONTANISM: A religious movement led by one Montanus, of whom little is known, who wanted a prophetic church with no hierarchical structure but only a spiritual structure, less immersed in the world. Tertullian is the best known adherent of Montanism.

SPIRITUALS: A movement within the Franciscan Order in the late thirteenth and early fourteenth centuries. The Spirituals sought to return to the true spirit of St Francis, and preached a more "spiritual" church, one less contaminated by money and the quest for power.

Notes

I. Experience of the Holy Spirit

1. Cf also Rom. 5:5; 1 Thess. 5:19
2. Cf W. Schmithals, "Experiencia del Espíritu como experiencia de Cristo", in C. Heitmann and H. Mühlen, eds., *Experiencia y teología del Espíritu Santo* (Salamanca, 1978), p. 158: Span. trans. of *Erfahrung und Theologie des Heiligen Geistes* (Hamburg-Munich, 1974).
3. St Paul uses the word "rejoice" 28 times and the word "joy" 22. These words are nearly always used to refer to a feeling of the presence of the Spirit.
4. As, for example, in the lives of St Francis of Assisi, St Teresa of Avila and St Ignatius of Loyola.
5. The two aspects of the presence of the Spirit are not separated in Acts: the Spirit is the presence of the beginning of the kingdom and the strength for mission. Mission belongs to the "last times". The times of the Spirit are not ones of enjoyment, rest, leisure, but of struggle, work and weariness in the midst of joy.
6. Cf Mark 4:40; 6:50; 7:18; 8:16–18, 33; 9:28, 33–7, 38–9; 10:13, 32, 35–45; 14:27–31, 37–41, 50, 66–72; 16:11, 13, 14.
7. In English see, e.g., H. Mühlen, *A Charismatic Theology: Initiation in the Spirit* (London and New York, 1978); F. Sullivan, *Charisma and Charismatic Renewal: A Biblical Theological Study* (Dublin, 1982), with bibliography; Ch. Duquoc and C. Floristán, eds., *Charisms in the Church* (*Concilium* 109, 1977).
8. H. Mühlen, "Espíritu, carisma, liberacíon," in *Experiencia y teologia*, pp. 65ff.
9. Cf Fr. Cartaxo Rolim, *Pentecostais no Brasil. Una interpretação sócio-religiosa* (Petrópolis, 1985); R. Reyes Novaes, *Os escolhidos de Deus. Pente-costais, trabalhadores e cidadania* (Rio de Janeiro, 1985).
10. See the discussion in Reyes Novaes, *Os escolhidos*, pp. 139–54.
11. Cf G. Gutiérrez, *Beber en su propio pozo* (Lima, 1982). Eng. trans., *We Drink from Our Own Wells* (Maryknoll, N.Y., 1984); *El Dios de la vida* (Lima, 1982).

12. See the commentaries in Mühlen, "Espíritu, carisma," pp. 41–52.
13. Ibid., pp. 53–69.
14. Cf C. Mesters, "Como se faz teologia bíblica hoje no Brasil," *Estudos bíblicos* 1 (1984), pp. 7–19; C. and L. Boff, *Como se faz teologia de libertação* (Petrópolis, 1986): Eng. trans., *Introducing Liberation Theology* (Tunbridge Wells and Maryknoll, N.Y., 1987), pp. 32–5.
15. Cf H. Crouzel, *Origène* (Paris, 1985), pp. 91–120.
16. Cf C. Mesters and P. Richard, *A Bíblia a partir dos pobres* (Petrópolis, 1987).
17. Gutiérrez, *We Drink*.
18. Cf L. Boff, *A Trindade e a sociedade* (Petrópolis, 1987): Eng. trans. in this series *Trinity and Society* (Tunbridge Wells and Maryknoll, N.Y., 1988), ch. 3.
19. Cf H. Mühlen, "Experiencia social del Espíritu como respuesta a una doctrina unilateral sobre Dios," in *Experiencia y teología*, pp. 339–64.
20. N. Berdyaev, *Freedom and the Spirit* (London, 1948).
21. Y. Congar, *La parole et le souffle* (Paris, 1984), p. 181.
22. K. Rahner, "La vivencia carismático-entusiástica en confrontación con la experiencia graciosa de la Transcendencia," in *Experiencia y teología*, pp. 102–5.
23. Cf O. Dilschneider, "La necesidad de nuevas respuestas a preguntas nuevas," in *Experiencia y teología*, p. 224; G. Sauter, "Certeza extática o seguridad de acercioramento?" in *Experiencia y teología*, pp. 264ff.
24. Rahner, "La vivencia." pp. 99–120.
25. Cf Y. Congar, *Je crois en l'Esprit Saint* (Paris, 3 vols, 1979–80).
26. Such as the joint works by Heitmann and Mühlen, *Experiencia y teología* and *L'expérience de Dieu et le Saint Esprit* (Paris, 1985).
27. Cf A. González Montes, "'Nostalgia del Espíritu' en la crisis actual de la fe," in *Experiencia y teología*, pp. 13–27.
28. See, e.g., Frei Betto, *Fidel e a religião* (São Paulo, 1985).
29. See the report of the National Commission on "disappeared" people, published as *Informe de la Comisión Nacional sobre la desaparición de personas* (Buenos Aires, 1984), with its eloquent testimony to the state of human rights in Latin America and Argentina specifically. In Brazil, a similar document, *Brasil nunca mais*, was published by Vozes in 1985, with an introduction by Card. Paulo Evaristo Arns.
30. Cf the publications of the Brazilian Episcopal Conference (CNBB) for the "brotherhood campaign" of 1986.

31. Cf L. Fernández, *Como se faz uma comunidad eclesial de base* (Petrópolis, 1984).

32. CNBB, *Nordeste, desafio à missão de Igreja no Brasil* (São Paulo, 1984).

33. See the sections on "Justice" and "Peace" in the Medellín document, and the "Final Document" from Puebla, nn. 15–20.

34. Cf J. Marins, T. Trevisan and C. Chanona, *Martirio, memória perigrosa na América Latina hoje* (São Paulo, 1984).

35. For examples of the commentary on the Bible made by the poor, Cf E. Cardenal, *The Gospel in Solentiname*, 4 vols. (Maryknoll, N.Y., 1976–82).

36. J. Comblin, "O novo ministério de missionário na America Latina," REB 40 (1980), pp. 625–55.

37. *Comunidades eclesiais de base na Igreja do Brasil*, CNBB doc. 25 (São Paulo, 1984); *Comunidades eclesiais de base no Brasil*, CNBB studies no. 23 (São Paulo, 1984).

38. Cf. J. de Santa Ana, *Pelas trilhas do mundo a caminho do Reino* (S. Bernardo do Campo, 1985).

39. For a vivid account in English see J. Kramer, "Letter from the Elysian Fields," *The New Yorker*, Mar. 2, 1987, pp. 40–75 [TRANS.].

40. Gutiérrez, *We Drink*.

41. Cf C. Rodrigues Brandão, *Os deuses do povo* (São Paulo, 1980); *Memória do sagrado: Estudos de religião e ritual* (São Paulo, 1985); cf also *Popular Religion* (*Concilium* 186, 1986).

42. Cf Schmithals, "Experiencia del Espíritu," pp. 159–61.

43. Cf K. Schelke, *Theologie des neuen Testaments*, 4 vols. (Düsseldorf, 1968–70). Eng. trans., *Theology of the New Testament* (Collegeville, Minn. 1971–4).

44. Cf G. Thiessen, *Sociologie der Jesusbewegung* (Munich, 1977): Eng. trans., *The First Followers of Jesus: a Sociological Analysis of the Earliest Christianity* (London, 1978).

45. Cf R. Brown, *The Community of the Beloved Disciple* (London, 1982).

46. Compare 1 Tim. 4:1; 2 Tim. 1:7, 14; 1 John 4:1, 2, 3, 6, 13; *Didache* 11–13.

47. Y. Congar, *Je crois en l'Esprit Saint*, vol 1 (Paris, 1979), pp. 95–105. Eng. trans., *I believe in the Holy Spirit*, vol. 1 (London and New York, 1983).

48. *Adv. Haer.* II, XXXII, 4.

49. Ibid.

50. See the article by G. Bardy, in *Dict. de Théol. Cath.* X, 2355–70; short def. in K. Rahner and H. Vorgrimler, *Concise Theological Dict.*

(London and New York, 1965) and in R. Eno, *New Dict. of Theol.* (New York and Dublin, 1987), p. 676.

51. Refs. in Congar, *I Believe*, vol 1.

52. B. Bartmann, *Die Erlösung* (Paderborn, 1938).

53. *Adv. Haer.* III, XXIV, 1.

54. J. Meyendorff, *Initiation à la théologie byzantine* (Paris, 1975), p. 283; cf also his *Byzantine Theology: Historical Trends and Doctrinal Themes* (New York, 1974), with bibliog.

55. Meyendorff, *Initiation*, pp. 281–95.

56. W. Ullmann, *The Growth of the Papal Government in the Middle Ages* (London, 1955), p. 440.

57. There is now an abundant literature on Joachim of Flora. Cf H. de Lubac, *La posterité spirituelle de Joachim de Flore* (Paris, 1979), pp. 13–121.

58. Ibid., pp. 140–60.

59. Cf H. Müller-Schwefe, "¿Razón productiva o Espíritu divino de transformación?" in *Experiencia y teología*, pp. 377ff.

60. Ibid., p. 376.

61. Cf L. Russell, *Human Liberation in a Feminist Perspective – A Theology* (Philadelphia, 1974), p. 102.

62. Cf F. Mayer, "La unilateralidad de la doctrina tradicional sobre Dios," in *Experiencia y teología*, pp. 324–30.

63. Mühlen, "Espíritu," pp. 53–66.

64. Cf P. Ribeiro de Oliveira, *Religião y dominação de clases* (Petró-polis, 1985).

65. Mühlen, "Espíritu," pp. 53–70.

II. The Holy Spirit in the World

1. Cf P. Nautin, *Je crois à l'Esprit Saint dans la Sainte Eglise pour la résurrection de la chair* (Paris, 1947), pp. 48–72.

2. *Adv. Haer.* V, XII, 4.

3. *Adv. Haer.* V, XIII, 4.

4. St Irenaeus, "Proof of the Apostolic Preaching," in *Ancient Christian Writers* XVI.

5. Particularly on the first two centuries, see Nautin, *Je crois*, pp. 28–42.

6. Translations of the Bible often hesitate between "Spirit" and "spirit". There is a continuity in the Bible between the Holy Spirit, the divine Person, and everything that proceeds from the Holy Spirit and is spiritual in creation. All that is spirit is somehow related to the Spirit.

7. Cf J. Meyendorff, *Initiation à la théologie byzantine* (Paris, 1975), p. 227.

8. Cf G. Haya Prats, *L'Esprit force de l'Eglise* (Paris, 1975), pp. 53–72.

9. Cf. J. Comblin, *O Espíritu no mundo* (Petrópolis, 1978), pp. 76–89.

10. See Jesus' farewell discourse in John 3:4–6; 4:10, 13, 14, 23; 6:63; 7:37–9.

11. C. Barrett, *The Holy Spirit in the Gospel Tradition* (London, 1966), pp. 15ff.

12. What is at issue here is not the original meaning and later evolution of meanings of OT texts referring to the Holy Spirit, but the interpretation given to these texts by Christian tradition.

13. Cf Y. Congar, *La parole et le souffle* (Paris, 1984), p. 192, n. 2.

14. Meyendorff, *Initiation*, p. 227.

15. Ibid., pp. 227ff.

16. Barrett, *Holy Spirit*, pp. 23–52.

17. Ibid., pp. 53–83.

18. Cf J. Dupont, "La nouvelle Pentecôte," *Nouvelles études sur les Actes des Apôtres* (Paris, 1984), pp. 193–8.

19. Cf H. Cazelles, "L'Esprit Saint dans les textes de Vatican II," in *Le mystère de L'Esprit Saint* (Tours, 1968), pp. 163ff.

20. Cf Y. Congar, *Je crois en l'Esprit Saint*, vol. 3 (Paris, 1980), pp. 206–18; L. Bouyer, *Le Consolateur* (Paris, 1980), pp. 365–8.

21. Congar, *Je crois*, vol. 3, pp. 211ff.

22. Ibid., p. 209.

23. Cf E. Dussel, *Historia general de la Iglesia en América Latina* I/1 (Salamanca, 1983), p. 153, quoting M. Eliade's classic *A History of Religious Ideas* (Chicago and London, 1979).

24. Cf Dussel, *Historia*, pp. 336–46.

25. Congar, *Je crois*, vol. 1, pp. 224–6.

26. With one exception: IIa IIae, q. 88, a. 11 ad 1, where St Thomas refers to pilgrimage to the Holy Land.

27. Cf S. Gameleira Soares, "Reler os Profetas," *Estudos bíblicos* 4 (1985), pp. 8–32.

28. See 1 Cor. 1:26–2:16.

29. In view of the importance of this subject, those prepared to study further might look at: J. le Goff and others, *Hérésies et sociétés dans l'Europe pré-industrielle, 11e–18e siècles* (Paris and The Hague, 1968); E. Benz, *Ecclesia spiritualis* (Stuttgart, 1964); G. Leff, *Heresy in the Middle Ages*, 2 vols, (New York, 1967); M. Mollat, dir., *Etudes sur l'histoire de la pauvreté*, 2 vols. (Paris, 1974); for a brief account, see J. Leclercq and others, *The Spirituality of the Middle Ages* (London and New York, 1968), p. 264.

30. Cf *Franciscains d'Oc. Les Spirituels ca 1280–1324* (Toulouse, 1975).

194   *The Holy Spirit and Liberation*

31. W. Van Dijk, "Le réprésentation de Saint François d'Assise dans les écrits des Spirituels," *Franciscains d'Oc*, pp. 203–30.

32. This sad story is given in Leff, *Heresy*, vol. 1, pp. 51–255.

33. Various, "Polémiques autour de la notion de pauvreté spirituelle," *Etudes sur l'histoire*, vol. 1, pp. 347–459.

34. Cf Pope John XXII, Const. *Gloriosam Ecclesiam*, 23 Jan. 1318, no. 14, DS 911.

35. Cf M. Walzer, *The Revolution of the Saints* (New York, 1974).

36. Cf the article "Cola de Rienzo," LThK 2, 1252ff.

37. Cf A. Ducellier, *Le drame de Byzance* (Paris, 1976), pp. 109–84.

38. It was E. Käsemann who propounded this thesis that apocalyptic is the mother of Christian theology. Cf P. Gisel, *Vérité et histoire* (Paris, 1977), pp. 221–92.

39. E. Käsemann, *Perspectives on Paul* (London, 1971).

40. Meyendorff, *Initiation*, pp. 281–7.

41. Cf A. Dempf, *Sacrum Imperium* (1929, n.e. Darmstadt, 1954); R. Foiz, *L'idée d'empire en Occident du Vme au XIVme siècle* (Paris, 1953).

42. Cf F. Héer, *Europa, Mutter der Revolution* (Stuttgart, 1964).

43. Cf P. Engelhardt, *Versöhnung und Erlösung* (Freiburg, 1982), pp. 144–9.

44. Cf ibid., pp. 150–4; in general see the authors referred to and commented on in P. Anderson, *A crise da crise do marxismo* (São Paulo, 1984), particularly the Frenchmen C. Lefort and C. Castoriadis.

45. Cf J. Guichard, *Eglise, luttes des classes et stratégies politiques* (Paris, 1972).

46. Cf G. Fessard, *De l'actualité historique*, 2 vols. (Paris, 1960).

47. Cf E. Peterson, "Die Kirche aus Juden und Heiden," *Theologische Traktate* (Munich, 1951), pp. 239–92.

48. See Eph. 2:14–22; Col. 1:19–22.

49. Cf J. Danélou, *Origène* (Paris, 1948), p. 167: Eng. trans., *Origen* (London and New York, 1955).

50. See the application to Nazism and communism in the works of G. Fessard, n. 46 above.

51. Cf J. Robinson, *The New Reformation* (London, 1966).

52. The recent *Instruction on Christian Freedom and Liberation*, issued by the Congregation for the Doctrine of the Faith on 22 March 1986, though it marks a step forward from earlier positions, is still not the response needed to present-day longings.

53. S. Lyonnet, "Christian Freedom and the Law of the Spirit in St Paul," I. de la Potterie and S. Lyonnet, *The Christian Lives by the*

Spirit (New York, 1971); Käsemann, *Perspectives*; see "Freedom" in *New Dict. of Theology* (New York and Dublin, 1987), pp. 404–6.

54. See the quotes from St Thomas in Lyonnet, "Christian Freedom."

55. Cf J.-M. González Ruiz, *Epístola de San Pablo a los Gálatas* (Madrid, 1971), pp. 229–61.

56. N. Berdyaev, *Freedom and the Spirit* (London, 1948), ch. 4, "The Freedom of the Spirit."

57. Meyendorff, *Initiation*, pp. 235–8.

58. Hence the culture of guilt that has so strongly marked Western history and is so forcefully rejected today. Cf J. Delumeau, *Le péché et la peur. La culpabilisation en Occident. XIIIe-XVIIIe siècles* (Paris, 1983).

59. Cf Berdyaev, *Freedom*, ch. 4.

60. Cf L. Dumont, *O individualismo. Uma perspectiva antropológica da ideologia moderna* (Rio de Janeiro, 1985).

61. Cf J. Comblin, *O clamor dos oprimidos, o clamor de Jesus* (Petrópolis, 1985): Eng. trans., *Cry of the Oppressed, Cry of Jesus* (Maryknoll, N.Y., 1988).

62. Cf S. Gameleira Soares, "Reler os Profetas," *Estudos biblícos* 4 (1985), pp. 8–52.

63. The Niceno-Constantinopolitan Creed says, "We believe in the Holy Spirit . . . who has spoken through the prophets."

64. There is an obvious disparity in size between what the group who received the Spirit in Jerusalem represents and all nations.

65. Cf S. Lyonnet, "The Fundamental Law of the Apostolate as Formulated and Lived by St Paul (2 Cor. 12:9)," in *The Christian Lives*, pp. 245–65.

66. Cf F. Porsch, *Pneuma und Wort. Ein exegetischer Beitrag zur Pneumatologie des Johannesevangelium* (Frankfurt, 1974).

67. Origen, *Contra Celsum* III, 55; cf ch. 2 of E. Hoornaert, *The Memory of the Christian People*, in preparation for this series.

68. Cf Barrett, *The Holy Spirit*, pp. 200ff.

69. See Judg. 13:25; 14:6; 1 Sam. 10:10; 11:6; 16:13; 2 Sam. 23:2.

70. Cf Barrett, *The Holy Spirit*, pp. 75–84.

71. See 1 Cor. 2:4–5, 10–16.

72. Cf G. Haya Prats, *L'esprit force*, pp. 53–72.

73. Cf J. Trocmé, "Le Saint-Esprit et l'Eglise d'après le livre des Actes," in *L'Esprit-Saint et L'Eglise* (Paris, 1969), p. 20.

74. Cf Käsemann, *Perspectives*, pp. 9–41.

75. "It is . . . through the gift of the Holy Spirit that man comes by faith to the contemplation and appreciation of the divine plan" (GS

15e). "The same Holy Spirit constantly brings faith to completion by his gifts" (DV 5). See also LG 12–14.

III. The Holy Spirit in the Church

1. *Adv. Haer.* III, 24, 1. On the birth of the church through the Holy Spirit, with special reference to Pentecost, the encyclical *Dominum et Vivificantem* takes up the teaching of Vatican II and strongly upholds it (nos. 25–6).

2. Cf A. Benoît, "Le Saint-Esprit et L'Eglise dans la théologie patristique," *L'Esprit-Saint et l'Eglise* (Paris, 1969), pp. 138–42.

3. Cyril of Jerusalem, *Catecheses* 17, 3.

4. *Catecheses* 16, 14.

5. Cf P. Evdokimov, "L'Esprit-Saint et l'Eglise d'après la tradition liturgique," in *L'Esprit-Saint*, pp. 84–111. Western liturgy also naturally refers to the Holy Spirit, but without laying the same stress on it, and absence of an epiclesis from the rites of several sacraments has been harmful. On the Spirit in Western liturgy, see Y. Congar, *Je crois en l'Esprit Saint*, vol. 1 (Paris, 1979), pp. 147–60.

6. Cf P. Nautin, *Je crois à l'Esprit-Saint pour la résurrection de la chair* (Paris, 1947), pp. 45–53.

7. Vatican II's teaching on this point is set out in H. Cazelles, "L'Esprit-Saint dans les textes de Vatican II," in *Le Mystère de L'Esprit-Saint* (Tours, 1968), pp. 170–82.

8. See LG 6a. There is the same reserve on the idea of "soul" of the church in *Dominum et Vivificantem* 26, 1.

9. Cf H. Mühlen, "Espíritu, carisma, liberación," in Heitman and Mühlen, eds., *Experiencia y teología del Espíritu Santo* (Salamanca, 1978), pp. 186–8.

10. H. Mühlen, *El Espíritu Santo en la Iglesia* (Salamanca, 1974): Span. trans. of *Una mystica persona. Eine Person in vielen Personen* (Paderborn, 1964).

11. The patristic texts are given in S. Tromp, *De Spiritu Sancto, Anima Corporis Mystici*, 2 vols. (Rome, 1948–52).

12. III *Sent.* d. 13, q. 2, a. 1 ad 2; a. 2 q. 2; *De Ver.* q. 29, a. 4; *In Ioan.* c. 1 lect. 9 and 10; Enc. *Mystici Corporis*, nos. 54, 77.

13. Cf E. Benz, *Ecclesia Spiritualis* (Stuttgart, 1964), pp. 3–48.

14. At the time they understood the spiritualization of the church as a dissolution of all material elements. The tendency was to suppress the church as a fully human reality to make it merely an association of believing and converted individuals. Cf H. Berkhof, *The Doctrine of the Holy Spirit* (Richmond, 1964), pp. 42–65; R. Prenter, *Le Saint-Esprit et le·renouveau de l'Eglise* (Neuchâtel, 1949), pp. 15–17.

15. Cf J. Moltmann, *La Iglesia, Fuerza del Espíritu* (Salamanca, 1978): Span. trans. of *Kirche in der Kraft des Geistes* (Munich, 1975); Eng. trans., *The Church in the Power of the Spirit* (London and New York, 1979).

16. An indication of this is the virtually complete absence of indigenous peoples and blacks from the ranks of bishops, clergy and religious, as from theology, liturgy and canon law. It is true that most of them call themselves Catholics, but this is mainly for sociological reasons. Furthermore, blacks and indigenous peoples have made their own reinterpretations of Christianity, in which the aspects that touch them most are their ancestral religions, often reappearing under the guise of Catholic rites.

17. P. Evdokimov, "L'Esprit-Saint pensé par les Pères et vécu dans la liturgie," in *Le Mystère*, pp. 69–109.

18. Moltmann, *La Iglesia*, pp. 310–26.

19. Cf J. Meyendorff, *Initiation à la théologie byzantine* (Paris, 1975), pp. 232–5.

20. Meyendorff, *Initiation*, p. 232.

21. Cf J. Ratzinger, "El Espíritu Santo como *communio*. Para una relación entre pneumatología y esperitualidad en Augustín," in *Experiencia y teología*, pp. 301–20.

22. Augustine, *Serm.* 71, 12, 18. Other quotes in Congar, *Je crois*, vol. 1, p. 119.

23. Moltmann, *La Iglesia*, p. 146.

24. Ibid., pp. 147–48. Cf John 15:13–14.

25. Cf ST IIa IIae, q. 23, a. 1.

26. See Rom. 16:5; 1 Cor. 16:19; Col. 4:15; Philem. 2.

27. Cf C. Rodrigues Brandão, *Memória do sagrado* (São Paulo, 1985), pp. 13–127; P. Rodrigo de Oliveira, *Religião y dominação de classe* (Petrópolis, 1985), pp. 112–60. For the same process applied to the English situation, see A. Archer, *The Two Catholic Churches: A Study in Oppression* (London, 1986) [TRANS.].

28. See 1 Cor. 1:26.

29. Congar, *Je crois*, vol. 2, pp. 25–32.

30. Moltmann, *La Iglesia*, pp. 399–404.

31. See 1 Cor. 11:20–22; 2 Cor. 8:13–15; Philem. 15–18.

32. Christians were called "saints". Or rather, those who originally were known as "saints" were later called "Christians." Cf 1 Cor. 1:2; Phil. 1:1; Col. 3:12.

33. Congar, *Je crois*, vol. 1, pp. 83–7.

34. H. Urs von Baltasar, "Casta meretrix," in *Skizzen der Theologie* II (Einseideln, 1961).

35. It is true that Vatican II was somewhat reticent in doing so: see GS

19c; UR 4e, f; DH 12a. Puebla was more explicit: "Insofar as it is a human and earthly institution, the wayfaring Church humbly acknowledges its mistakes and sins, which obscure the visage of God in his children" (209).

36. See the Medellín "Final Document," ch. XIV; Puebla "Final Document," no. 1157.

37. Congar, *Je crois*, vol. 2, pp. 61–4.

38. Moltmann, *La Iglesia*, p. 146.

39. Cf G. Colombás, "La 'vida apostólica'," in *Historia de la espiritualidad*, vol. 1 (Barcelona, 1969), pp. 513–5.

40. Cf DV II, 1b; 12c.

41. Prenter, *Le Saint Esprit*, p. 42.

42. For the classic Protestant objections, see e.g. Berkhof, *La doctrina*, p. 57.

43. Cf 1 Cor. 2:4; 7:40; 2 Cor. 3:17–18; 6:6; Phil. 1:19; 3:3; 1 Thess. 1:5; 1 Pet. 1:12; John 14:17, 26; 16:13; Acts 1:8, etc. In Luke, John and the Pauline epistles, the Spirit is first linked to the gospel.

44. Cf DV 11.

45. Cf LG 19.

46. Cf DV 5; LG 12, 19.

47. Cf G. Bardy, *La conversion au christianisme durant les premiers siècles* (Paris, 1949), pp. 271ff.

48. *Dei Verbum* alludes to this understanding by saying that the Apostles are the authors of the NT, of the Gospels in particular: "they handed on what they had received from the lips of Christ, from living with him, and from what he did, or what they had learned through the prompting of the Holy Spirit" (DV 7a).

49. Cf H. de Lubac, *Histoire et Esprit. L'intelligence de l'Ecriture d'après Origène* (Paris, 1950).

50. Berkhof, *La doctrina*, pp. 57ff.

51. Cf P. Evdokimov, *L'orthodoxie* (Neuchâtel, 1965), pp. 262–99.

52. Moltmann, *La Iglesia*, pp. 310–26.

53. Compare AA 3d; cf G. Hasenhüttl, *Charisma, Ordnungsprinzip der Kirche* (Freiburg, 1970).

54. Cf *Dos obispos del Sur Andino: Luís Vallejo, Luís Dalle. En el corazón de su pueblo* (Lima, 1982).

55. Cf J. Brockman, *The Word Remains: A Life of Oscar Romero* (Maryknoll, N.Y., 1985); cf also *Voice of the Voiceless: The four Pastoral Letters and other statements of Oscar Romero*, with introductory essays by I. Martín-Baró and Jon Sobrino (Maryknoll, N.Y., 1985).

56. Cf *Leónidas Proaño. 25 años en Riobamba* (Lima, 1979); *Dom Helder, pastor y profeta* (São Paulo, 1984); A. Batista Fragoso, *O rosto*

de uma Igreja (São Paulo, 1982): Eng. trans., *Face of a Church* (Maryknoll, N.Y., 1987).

IV. The Holy Spirit in Persons

1. On the separation between theology and mysticism and between pneumatology and theology since the end of the Middle Ages, particularly in the great religious foundations of the sixteenth century, see L. Bouyer, *Le Consolateur. Esprit-Saint et vie de grâce* (Paris, 1980), pp. 329–32.

2. For an uncritical account of the charismatic movement, see R. Faricy, "Charismatic Movement," *New Dict. of Theology* (New York and Dublin, 1987), pp. 183–5, with bibliography [TRANS.].

3. Cf Y. Congar, *Je crois en l'Esprit Saint*, vol. 2 (Paris, 1979), pp. 187–269.

4. For recent examples of Latin American works on spirituality, see G. Gutiérrez, *Beber no próprio poço* (Petrópolis, 1984): Port. trans. of *Beber en su propio pozo* (Lima, 1982); Eng. trans., *We Drink from Our Own Wells* (Maryknoll, N.Y., 1984); S. Galilea, *The Beatitudes* and *Following Jesus* (Maryknoll, N.Y., 1984); J. Sobrino, *Spirituality of Liberation* (Maryknoll, N.Y., 1988).

5. Gutiérrez, *Beber no próprio poço*, pp. 30–35.

6. Cf P. Evdokimov, *L'orthodoxie* (Neuchâtel, 1965); V. Lossky, *Essai sur la théologie mystique de l'Eglise d'Orient* (Paris, 1944); A. Santos, "Espiritualidad ortodoxa," *Hist. de la espiritualidad*, vol. 3 (Barcelona, 1969),pp. 5–228.

7. Evdokimov, *L'orthodoxie*, p. 94.

8. Cf H. Berkhof, *The Doctrine of the Holy Spirit* (Richmond, 1964), pp. 66–93.

9. Ibid., p. 66.

10. Cf Puebla "Final Document," nos. 15–50.

11. J. Segundo, *El hombre de hoy ante Jesús de Nazaret*, (Madrid, 1985) vol II/1, pp. 481–534: Eng. trans., *Jesus of Nazareth Yesterday and Today*, vol. 3, *The Humanist Christology of Paul* (Maryknoll, N.Y. and London, 1986).

12. The concept of integral liberation is amply represented in the Puebla "Final Document": see nos. 141, 321, 475, 480, 696, 895, 1134.

13. Among works that study modernity from a theological standpoint, see J.-F. Malherbe, *La langage théologique à l'âge de la science* (Paris, 1985), pp. 21–53.

14. On religious in Latin America, see L. Boff, *A vida religiosa e a Igreja no processo da libertação*, and *A vida segundo el Espírito* (Petrópolis, 1975 and 1985). The various episcopal conferences and

200   *The Holy Spirit and Liberation*

CLAR also publish abundant literature on the subject. See also V. Codina and N. Zevallos, *Vida religiosa: historia a teología* (Petrópolis, 1987).

15. Cf M. Azevedo, *Comunidades Eclesiais de Base e inculturação da fé* (São Paulo, 1986), with abundant bibliography, esp. pp. 129–86.

16. Such was the experience of St Dominic, St Francis, St Ignatius, St Teresa and many others. The mark of the Spirit is the discovery of a new way not inherited from anyone else. See St Francis' famous *Testament*.

17. See the words spoken by Archbishop Romero in an interview with the Mexican paper *Excelsior* two weeks before his death: "I am bound, as a pastor, by a divine command to give my life for those whom I love, and that is all Salvadoreans, even those who are going to kill me. If they manage to carry out their threats, from this moment I offer my blood for the redemption and resurrection of El Salvador. Martyrdom is a gift from God which I do not believe I deserve. But if God accepts the sacrifice of my life, then may my blood be the seed of liberty, and a sign that hope may soon become a reality. May my death, if it is accepted by God, be for the liberation of my people, and as a witness of hope in what is to come. Can you tell them, if they succeed in killing me, that I pardon and bless those who do it." Quoted in *Romero, Martyr for Liberation* (London, 1982), p. 76.

18. H. Echegaray, *A prática de Jesus* (Petrópolis, 1980): Eng. trans., *The Practice of Jesus* (Maryknoll, N.Y., 1985); J. Sobrino, *Jesús en América Latina* (Santander, 1982): Eng. trans., *Jesus in Latin America* (Maryknoll, N.Y., 1986).

19. CNBB, *Comunidades Eclesiais de Base na Igreja do Brasil* (1982), n. 12.

20. Cf *A Biblia como memória dos pobres* (Petrópolis, 1984); J. Comblin, *Introdução ao comentário bíblico* (Petrópolis, 1985).

21. Segundo, *Humanist Christology*.

22. Cf E. Dussel, *El episcopado hispanoamericano. Institución misionera en defesa del indio. 1504–1620*, 7 vols. (*Sondeos* 32–8, Cuernavaca, 1969–72).

23. From the Latin translation of the *Sixth Catechesis* in PG 120, 428, quoted in J. Leclercq and others, *The Spirituality of the Middle Ages* (London and New York, 1968), p. 566.

24. On the "mystery" of God, see the outstanding article by J. Sobrino, "Disquisición sobre el misterio absoluto," *Revista Latinoamericano de teología* II (1985), pp. 209–28.

25. There is a lack of biographies of the bishops who gave the church in Latin America its character. On Archbishop Romero, see P.

Erdozaín, *Archbishop Romero, Martyr of Salvador* (Maryknoll, N.Y., 1984).

26. On *apatheia*, see Evdokimov, *L'orthodoxie*, pp. 104–7; G. Colombás, *El monacato primitivo II. La espiritualidad* (Madrid, 1975), pp. 281–7.

27. On monastic asceticism, see Colombás, *Monacato*, pp. 175–276.

28. Cf Gutiérrez, *Beber*, pp. 125–6.

29. See the investigations into the culture of the poor made by the late Oscar Lewis, *The Children of Sánchez* (New York, 1961); *La Vida* (New York and San Juan, 1966); *Five Families* (New York, 1962); etc.

30. Cf C. Mesters, *Seis dias nos porões da humanidade* (Petrópolis, 1982).

31. Cf Gutiérrez, *Beber*, pp. 43ff.

32. Cf L. Boff, "Contemplativus in liberatione. De la espiritualidad de liberación e la práctica de liberación," *Espiritualidad de la liberación*, pp. 119–34.

33. Cf J. Hernández Pico, "La oración en los procesos latinoamericanos de liberación," *Espiritualidad*, pp. 159–88.

34. Cf J. Estepa, *Espiritualidad y liberación en América Latina*, pp. 24–6.

35. Gutiérrez, *Beber*, pp. 118–20.

36. Quoted by J. Marins and others, *Martirio. Memória perigrosa na América Latina* (São Paulo, 1984), p. 59.

37. Cf G. Therrien, *Le discernement dans les écrits pauliniens* (Paris, 1973).

38. Congar recalls some of the best-known texts from St Thomas (only a few relative to theological tradition) on freedom: *In 2 Cor.* c. 3, lect. 3; *In Rom.* c. 2, lect. 3; *C. Gent.* IV, 22; ST Ia IIae, q. 108 a. 3 ad 2. Cf *Je crois*, vol. 2, p. 166. There is an aspect that was not touched on by St Thomas and emerged only recently: freedom as the creation or construction of something new. St Thomas paid little attention to history and so was reduced to producing a theology of essences.

39. Hence the wide success of *Relatos do peregrino russo*, which associated the ideas of journey and discovery of prayer.

40. Cf Congar, *Je crois*, vol. 2, pp. 147ff.

V. The Two Hands of God

1. Cf H. Mühlen, "L'événement Christ comme oeuvre de l'Esprit-Saint," in *Mysterium Salutis*, vol. 13 (Paris, 1972), pp. 177–227.

2. Cf Y. Congar, *La parole et le souffle* (Paris, 1984), pp. 139–42.

3. See Phil. 2:6–11; Rom. 1:2–4; 1 Pet. 3:18; 1 Tim. 3:16; Heb. 1:5–6.

4. Cf Congar, *La parole*, pp. 142–51.

5. Cf I. de la Potterie, "L'onction du Christ," *Nouv. Rev. Th.* 80 (1958), pp. 225–52. Pope John Paul II's encyclical *Dominum et Vivificantem* stresses the anointing of Jesus at his baptism by the Holy Spirit, but without drawing theological conclusions from this. It sets out and summarizes the gospel texts and other references in the NT on the level of textual explication, in a manner typical of European exegesis (nos. 15–21).

6. Cf *Adv. Haer.* III, II, 8.

7. See the texts given by Congar, *La parole*, pp. 35–42.

8. Ibid., pp. 38–40.

9. Cf F. Porsch, *Pneuma und Wort. Ein exegetische Beitrag zur Pneumatologie des Johannesevangeliums* (Frankfurt, 1973).

10. Compare 2 Cor. 3:3–5; Rom. 15:18–19; Gal. 3:2, 5, 14; 1 Thess. 1:6; 2 Thess. 2:16.

11. Cf Congar, *La parole*, pp. 40–41.

12. See Rev. 14:13; 22:17.

13. Cf Congar, *La parole*, p. 46.

14. Ibid., p. 48, n. 7.

15. Ibid., pp. 47–8.

16. Ibid., pp. 50–51.

17. Cf Y. Congar, *La tradition et les traditions*, vol. 1 (Paris, 1960), pp. 126 and 129, n. 20: Eng. trans., *Tradition and Traditions: An Historical and Theological Essay* (London and New York, 1966).

18. Cf Congar, *La parole*, p. 56.

19. Ibid., p. 57.

20. Cf T. Preiss, *Le témoignage intérieur du Saint-Esprit* (Neuchâtel, 1946).

21. All agree on the obedience due to the word that comes from Christ. The problem is: how to assure this obedience in practice? The Reformers held that the Bible was sufficient on its own. But how does one discern between obedience to the Bible and manipulation of the Bible? Were not certain Protestant churches accused of having replaced episcopal authority with the authority of theology professors?

22. Cf Congar, *La parole*, pp. 80–82.

23. Cf L. Ramlot, "Prophètes," *Suppl. Dict de la Bible*, vol. 3, 692–1237.

24. Cf Congar, *La parole*, pp. 113–24.

25. Cf *Estudos bíblicos* 4 (Petrópolis, 1985).

26. Cf LG 12b; AG 23a; AA 3d. Cf H. Schürmann, "Spiritual Gifts," in G. Baraúna, ed., *The Church of Vatican II* (London and New York, 1965); B. Lambert, "A Igreja como comunidade de carismas e de

mistétios," in Lambert, *A nova imagen da Igreja* (São Paulo, 1969), pp. 77–99.
27. Cf Congar, *La parole*, pp. 86–90.
28. Ibid., pp. 93–5.
29. "Antistitum et fidelium conspiratio." Cf U. Belli, "Le magistère de l'Eglise au service de la' Parole de Dieu: à propos du n. 10 de la Constitution dogmatique 'Dei Verbum'," in *Au service de la Parole de Dieu. Mélanges Mgr Charue* (Gembloux, 1969), pp. 245–51.
30. Cf John Paul II, Enc., *Slavorum Apostoli* (2 June 1985), no. 21.
31. Here is a brief bibliography on the missions question today: P. Knitter, *No Other Name? A Critical Survey of Christian Attitudes towards the World Religions* (London and Maryknoll, N.Y., 1985); C. S. Song, *Christian Mission in Reconstruction: An Asian Analysis* (Madras, 1975, and Maryknoll, N.Y., 1977); *Third-Eye Theology: Theology in Formation in Asian Settings* (Maryknoll, N.Y., 1979); *Tell Us Our Names: Story Theology from an Asian Perspective* (Maryknoll, N.Y., 1984); *The Compassionate God* (Maryknoll, N.Y., 1982); R. Schreiter, *Constructing Local Theologies* (Maryknoll, N.Y., 1985); A. Camps, *Partners in Dialogue: Christianity and Other World Religions* (Maryknoll, N.Y., 1983).

VI. The Holy Spirit and the Trinity

1. Cf St Athanasius, *Lettres à Sérapion*, SCh 15 (Paris, 1947), III, p. 164.
2. Cf V. Lossky, *Essai sur la théologie mystique de l'Eglise d'Orient* (Paris, 1944).
3. Cf N. Nissiotis, "La pneumatologie ecclésiologique au service de l'unité de l'Eglise," *Istina* (1967), pp. 323–40.
4. Cf P. Evdokimov, *L'Esprit Saint dans la tradition orthodoxe* (Paris, 1969).
5. Cf S. Boulgakov, *Le Paraclet* (Paris, 1946).
6. Cf Y. Congar, *Je crois en l'Esprit Saint*, vol. 3 (Paris, 1969), pp. 254–6.
7. The condemnation was the work of the Emperor Charlemagne at the Council of Frankfurt in 794. Later, Eastern rejection of the Council of Florence led to a corresponding Western rejection.
8. Cf Congar, *Je crois*, vol. 3, pp. 246–8.
9. Ibid., pp. 277–8.
10. Quotations in ibid., pp. 229–40.
11. Ibid., pp. 233–7.
12. Cf Evdokimov, *L'Esprit Saint*, p. 76.
13. Congar, *Je crois*, pp. 117–9.

204   *The Holy Spirit and Liberation*

14. Ibid., pp. 135–42.
15. Ibid., pp. 34–44; K. Rahner, "Dieu Trinité: Fondament transcendant de l'histoire du salut," *Mysterium Salutis*, vol. 6 (Paris, 1970), pp. 13–140.
16. Cf Congar, *Je crois*, vol. 3, pp. 107–14; L. Boff, *Trinity and Society*, in this series, esp. ch. VII, no. 3.
17. Cf Congar, *Je crois*, vol. 3, pp. 55–78.
18. Ibid., pp. 65–76.
19. Ibid., pp. 242–8.
20. Ibid., pp. 94–106.
21. Congar quotes J. Kuhlmann and G. Philips (the lynchpin of the theological commission of Vatican II). Cf *Je crois*, vol. 3, pp. 105–6.
22. Ibid., pp. 160–73.,
23. Ibid., pp. 79–86.
24. Ibid., pp. 79–84.
25. Ibid., pp. 85ff. Congar provides a translation of the main passages of the letter.
26. Ibid., vol. 1, pp. 125–30; vol. 3, pp. 160–74.
27. See the bibliography given in ibid., vol. 3, p. 160, n. 1.
28. See Luke 24:29; Acts 1:4; 2:33, 38; Gal. 3:14; Eph. 1:13.
29. See Acts 2:33; 13:23, 32; 26:6; Eph. 1:14; 1 Cor. 15:20–28, 42–50; 1 John 2:25; Heb. 4:1; 9:15; 10:36; 2 Tim. 1:1.
30. For "giving," see Acts 5:32; 8:18; 15:8; Luke 11:13; Rom. 5:5; 2 Cor. 1:22; 5:5; Eph. 1:17; 1 Thess. 4:8; 2 Tim. 1:7; John 3:34; 4:14; Rev. 21:6; 1 John 3:24; 4:13; for "receiving," see Acts 1:8; 2:33, 38; 8:15, 17, 19; 10:47; 19:2; 1 Cor. 2:12; 2 Cor. 11:4; Gal. 3:2, 14; John 7:39; 14:17; 20:22.
31. Cf Congar, *Je crois*, vol. 3, pp. 196–8.
32. Ibid., pp. 200–202. On the theme of "Gift," see the encyclical *Dominum et Vivificantem*, nos. 10–11; 22–3.
33. Cf E.-P. Siman, *L'expérience de l'Esprit par l'Eglise d'après la tradition syrienne d'Antioche* (Paris, 1971), pp. 272–7.
34. Ibid., p. 271.
35. Ibid., p. 275.
36. Cf G. Gutiérrez, *El Dios de la Vida* (Lima, 1982); F. Hinkelammert, *As armas ideológicas da morte* (São Paulo, 1983): Eng. trans., *The Ideological Weapons of Death* (Maryknoll, N.Y., 1986); J. Bonino and others, *Luta pela vida e evangelização* (São Paulo, 1985).

General Conclusion

1. Cf L. Boff, *A Ave-Maria. O feminino e o Espíritu Santo* (Petropolis, 1980), pp. 41–4.

Select Bibliography

Aldunate, C., Card, L.-J. Suenens and others. *A experiencia de Pente-costes*. São Paulo, 1975.

Berkhof, H. *The Doctrine of the Holy Spirit*. Richmond, 1964.

Boff, L. *Ecclesiogênese: as comunidades de base reinventam a Igreja*. Petrópolis, 1977. Eng. trans.: *Ecclesiogenesis: The Base Communities Reinvent the Church*. Maryknoll, N.Y.: Orbis, 1982.

————. *A vida religiosa e a Igreja no processo de libertação*. *Petrópolis, 1975*.

Boulgakov, S. *Le Paraclet*. Paris, 1946.

Comblin, J. *O Espíritu no mundo*. Petrópolis, 1978.

————. *A força da palavra*. Petrópolis, 1982.

————. "A missâo do Espíritu Santo," *Revista Eclesiástica Brasileira* 35, 138 (1975).

————. *O tempo da ação*. Petrópolis, 1982.

Congar, Y.-M. *Je crois en l'Esprit Saint*. 3 vols. Paris, 1979–80. Eng. trans.: *I Believe in the Holy Spirit*. New York: Seabury Press; London: Geoffrey Chapman, 1983.

————. *La parole et le souffle*. Paris, 1984.

Evdokimov, P. *Le Christ dans la pensée russe*. Paris, 1970.

————. *L'Esprit Saint dans la tradition orthodoxe*. Paris, 1969.

————. *L'orthodoxie*. Neuchâtel, 1965.

Gutiérrez, G. *Beber en su propio pozo*. Lima, 1982. Eng. trans.: *We Drink from Our Own Wells*. Maryknoll, N.Y.: Orbis, 1984.

Häring, B., and J. Estepa. *Espiritualidad y liberación en América Latina*. Buenos Aires, 1986.

Heitmann, C., and H. Mühlen, eds. *Erfahrung und Theologie des Heiligen Geistes*. Hamburg-Munich, 1974. Span. trans.: *Experiencia y teología del Espíritu Santo*. Salamanca, 1978.

————. *L'expérience de Dieu et le Saint Esprit*. Paris, 1985.

Lubac, H. de. *La posterité spirituelle de Joachim de Flore*, 2 vols. Paris, 1979–81.

Mollat, D. *L'expérience de l'Esprit Saint selon le Nouveau Testament.* Paris, 1975.

Moltmann, J. *Kirche in der Kraft des Geistes.* Munich, 1975. Eng. trans.: *The Church in the Power of the Spirit.* London: SCM Press; San Francisco: Harper & Row, 1979.

Mühlen, H. "L'événement Christ comme oeuvre de l'Esprit-Saint." In *Mysterium Salutis*, vol. 13. Paris, 1972.

————. "Espíritu, carisma, liberación." In Heitmann and Mühlen (see above).

————. *Una mystica persona. Eine Person in vielen Personen.* Paderborn, 1964.

Parent, R. *O Espíritu Santo e a liberdade cristã.* São Paulo, 1978.

Potterie, I. de la, and S. Lyonnet. *La vie selon l'Esprit.* Paris, 1966. Eng. trans.: *The Christian Lives by the Spirit.* New York: Alba House, 1971.

Prenter, R. *Le Saint-Esprit et le renouveau de l'Eglise.* Neuchâtel, 1949.

————. "The Holy Spirit: Conceptions throughout History." In *Concilium* 148, 1979.

Segundo, J. *El hombre de hoy ante Jesús de Nazaret*, vol. II/1. Madrid, 1985. Eng. trans.: *Jesus of Nazareth Yesterday and Today*, vol. 3, *The Humanist Christology of Paul.* Maryknoll, N.Y.: Orbis; London: Sheed & Ward, 1986.

Various *Espiritualidad de la liberación.* Lima, 1980.

————. *L'Esprit-Saint et l'Eglise.* Paris, 1969.

Index